# TWO CENTURIES
## of HISTORY
## on LONG BEACH ISLAND

# TWO CENTURIES of HISTORY on LONG BEACH ISLAND

## JOHN BAILEY LLOYD

DOWN THE SHORE PUBLISHING

Harvey Cedars, New Jersey

Down The Shore Publishing Corp.
Box 3100, Harvey Cedars, NJ 08008

**www.down-the-shore.com**

*The words "Down The Shore" and the Down The Shore Publishing logos are registered U.S. Trademarks*

*Book design by Leslee Ganss and Ray Fisk*

Manufactured in Canada
10 9 8 7 6 5 4 3 2 1
First printing, 2005

**Library of Congress Cataloging-in-Publication Data**

Lloyd, John Bailey, 1932-
    200 years of history on Long Beach Island / John
Bailey Lloyd.
      p.cm.
    Includes index.
    ISBN 0-945582-97-8
      1. Long Beach Island (N.J.)--History. 2. Long Beach Island (N.J.)--
Social life and customs. 3. Long Beach Island Region (N.J.)--Social life
and customs. I. Title: Two centuries of history on Long Beach Island.
II. Title

    F142.L65L57 2005
    974.9'48--dc22

                                                    2005041336

# Contents

# Preface

## John Bailey Lloyd – An Appreciation

For more than two decades, in newspaper columns, in public talks, in personal encounters, John Bailey Lloyd enlightened and charmed Long Beach Island. When he died suddenly in July 2003, before this book was completed, the community was deeply saddened. Not only did we lose our beloved historian, we lost a friend.

John Bailey Lloyd writes in *Eighteen Miles of History*, the companion title to this book, that "fifty years ago the euphonious expression 'Six Miles at Sea' was everywhere… although it belongs to a time and way of life that grow farther from us with each year." John resurrected that phrase, and fifty years from now both it and the name John Bailey Lloyd will continue to be an intimate part of Long Beach Island.

JBL (for that is what we all called him) and LBI are historically inseparable. John was as much a part of Long Beach Island as salt is of the sea.

*Eighteen Miles* was described by one reviewer as "this loving history," and that choice of words — *loving history* — characterized John's work and life. He loved Southern Ocean County, and he loved it with the enlightened sensibility of one who knows its past. He knew and understood this place better than almost anyone else — he felt connected to it — because he

was informed by its history. Like osmosis, the Island's past entered John's being and inspired him. It inspired others, too.

I am one who was inspired. Largely because of John and my involvement in his books, when I look at the Island from a distance today I don't see just houses and developed shoreline; I see a wild barrier beach, spotted with a few grand hotels. I see beamy catboats sailing visitors across the bay to Captain Thomas Bond's in Holgate or to the little community of Sea Haven on Tucker's Island. Or I hear the whistle of the Manahawkin and Long Beach Railroad bringing passengers from Philadelphia's summer heat to the nascent resort of Beach Haven — *Six miles at sea!* On a blustery winter night, I visualize the surfmen of the U.S. Lifesaving Service braving an Atlantic storm on the beach, watching for a wreck to come ashore. The ghosts of the Mansion of Health are present; the Barnegat Light keeper's house has not yet collapsed into the sea; and any morning on the beach I expect the pound fishermen to give hopeful children fish from their bountiful catch…. I can't help this. John has given me a sense of place. It's a gift like no other, and one that, sadly, I don't think I ever thanked him for.

I now carry this sensibility with me, even beyond the Jersey Shore.

At times I encouraged John to expand the scope of his books, perhaps broaden the focus a bit to include the rest of the Shore. After all, the history of the U.S. Lifesaving Service in Ocean City or at Long Branch (or

elsewhere in the mid-Atlantic) is not so different from here; people in Stone Harbor and Bay Head would certainly appreciate his writing as much as on this Island. But John gently resisted; he felt comfortable here — in his writing and in his living, both. He really loved this one eighteen-mile-long stretch of sand. He had a feel for it. He loved knowing who the local families were, and saying their names like a litany (Parkers, Cranmers, Spragues…); he loved seeing a place and knowing what was there before, or carrying a vignette about a particular old house (… for example, at this cottage biographer Catherine Drinker Bowen wrote memoirs that lovingly recalled her childhood and evoked the acute sensory feel of a Beach Haven house in 1900). He'd delight in telling a good story he had just picked up from an old-timer; he'd share a vicarious thrill from an old local who recalled outfoxing certain authorities years ago. And he loved telling those bar stories — "when beer was ten cents a glass."

It was the closeness of all this history that John loved. There is magic in this sort of knowledge and in the enlightenment that flows from it. The beautiful and slightly melancholy presence of the past in the face of all that is new is enchanting. I thank John Bailey Lloyd for this wonderful view revealed to us through his work, and I know that many others share in this gratitude.

John Bailey Lloyd was not a strident preservationist. He did not preach: Save this! Protect that! And when a historical structure was lost to new development, or thoughtlessly torn down by a new owner — someone without a clue or sensitivity— John was clearly saddened and disappointed. Yet he would continue to happily share tales of our past incarnations. It was his enthusiasm, affection and passion for the area's stories and its people that have inspired many others to do what is historically appropriate. Or at least try.

By evoking an appreciation of the past in others, John plainly influenced builders, developers, homeowners, and resident's historical preservation efforts more than if he had ever been a vocal advocate. If not for John Bailey Lloyd, how many more of our old homes would have been lost? Would new development have a more commercial, suburban, and less sensitive quality?

His lack of pretense and genuine interest garnered him affection and respect from all residents and visitors. Though the dichotomy between summer and year 'round, local and tourist is always present, John moved easily between those realms and had equal appeal to all. His interest in local stories and history was infectious. From yacht club to bar, from Island to mainland, he loved both the rough edges and the finer qualities of this place and its past. He recognized that it was really just one continuously shared history.

This book is the third Long Beach Island title by John Bailey Lloyd, joining *Eighteen Miles of History* and *Six Miles at Sea* in a set. It offers more personal writing from John, including a few first-person pieces. As John became comfortable in his unofficial role as Long Beach Island's historian, he began to share some personal accounts — about lifeguarding and socializing in his younger days, or his family's visits when he was a boy during the war years. John carried with him decades of summer memories — like so many others, summer on the Island was a family tradition; he'd been

*Harvesting salt hay on the bay.*

coming here every summer since he was 10. And, like so many others, he married a girl he met here and in 1977, he moved his family here permanently.

While working as a reference librarian in the Ocean County Library system, he began writing about local history. In addition to his books, three local videos based on John's work and an engaging short story called "A Strange Incident at Bond's Hotel" are in print. John was happy to see this third book nearing completion, but he was even more excited about his next project — a historical novel set in Beach Haven a century ago. I wish we all had the chance to see the novelist in the

historian.

No one else can fill this void with such credibility and charisma. And, yet, John's life continues — in his published work, in the lives and work of others he influenced, in the knowledge about Jersey Shore history he imparted, in the kindness and humor he shared, in the historical sensibility he gave all of us. His greatest legacy may be the sense of place we now share. A sense of place: It is an enormous and powerful understanding which transcends lives and time.

— *Ray Fisk, Publisher*

# Island Name Origins

For three-quarters of the 19th century Long Beach Island, controlled by several mainland townships, had no political identity and was known, because of its unusual length, simply as Long Beach. Whole tracts of land were named either for a local innkeeper or for the person who held title to them — usually they were one and the same. Changes took place every generation or so. It was this principle of ownership that also gave name to several mainland villages like Tuckerton, Parkertown and Waretown. Others, for their location on rivers and creeks already named, were called West Creek, Barnegat, Forked River and Toms River. Only one, Manahawkin, has kept its original Indian name, although, as the town continues to grow, Manahawkin has become interchangeable with Stafford Township.

In the early days on Long Beach there were locations known to all as Horner's, Bond's, Buzby's, Tommy Jones', Brown's and Double Jimmie's (for James James). Of the many possessives and proper nouns from that era, the only survivors are Holgate (originally Holgate's) and Loveladies. Harvey Cedars was not named for a person. It is derived from a mispronunciation of "Harvest Cedars." After 1871, the establishment of fully manned U.S. Lifesaving stations on the coast gave permanence to unusual place names like Loveladies, Harvey Cedars and Ship Bottom.

Beach Haven, established in 1874, was the first deliberate attempt to create a place name without any his-

*The Fortuna, wrecked in 1910 on the beach at Ship Bottom-Beach Arlington, was not the shipwreck that gave the borough its name, but did become its symbol.*

*A more spacious and undeveloped Surf City looked like this in 1940, at 19th Street and the Boulevard. Below, bathing beauties and oceanfront homes in 1919.*

torical antecedents. Its immediate success inspired the naming of a resort called Sea Haven on nearby Tucker's Island, and there would be more. Of course, in those early years, the best known seashore resort of them all was Atlantic City. Suddenly, all along the New Jersey coast it made good business sense to tack the word "city" onto any name already evocative of the sea as a means of luring investment. Barnegat City, at the Island's north end, was born at this time, and a tiny hamlet hitherto known only as "Old Mansion" acquired the lofty name of Long Beach City. After Long Beach had to change its name to Long Beach Island in 1899 (because of mail mix-ups with Long Branch, farther up the coast), Long Beach City became Surf City. There were other imitations of Atlantic City elsewhere on the coast, places like Neptune City, Sea Isle City, Ocean City and Margate City.

Barnegat is the oldest place name on the Island. The Dutch who discovered the inlet originally called it *Bar-*

*ende-gat*. It meant "gate or inlet of the breakers." English cartographers dropped some letters out of the word and created Barnegat. This unusual name was applied not only to the inlet, but to the bay, a town on the mainland, the lighthouse and, by 1880, a new resort community on the north end of the Island called Barnegat City. There were just too many Barnegats. By 1946, residents were so tired of saying and writing the slogan "Barnegat City, the home of Barnegat Lighthouse" that they changed the name of their town to Barnegat Light. It even has its own ZIP Code now to avoid more postal mix-ups.

On the bay side of the town of Barnegat Light, but not part of it, lies the community of High Bar Harbor, named for the old High Bar Harbor Gunning Club formed early in the century. The island upon which the gunning club stood had always been a part of Long Beach Township. In the 1940s, the Army Corps of Engineers built a dike to protect the inlet, inadvertently creating thousands of

acres of sand behind it. The only access road was Twentieth Street in Barnegat Light. Builder Arnold Desiderio purchased the whole tract and started the lagoon development of High Bar Harbor, which is now limited to 400 homes. It remains a part of Long Beach Township.

Loveladies acquired its name from a tiny island in the bay that no longer exists. The mysterious man who once owned it, Thomas Lovelady of Barnegat, left no descendants. The name of his island was used for the U.S.

# LONG BEACH ISLAND, NEW JERSEY
## "SIX MILES AT SEA"

*The old causeway drawbridge, approaching Long Beach Island, circa 1930, top; Ship Bottom train station in the early 1900s, above.*

Lifesaving Station, built on the beach a mile east of it in 1871, simply because there was no other suitable place name to use for this unit midway between the Barnegat Inlet and Harvey Cedars stations. It was called Lovelady's Island L.S.S., but as time passed the "island" part of the phrase was dropped. In 1915, it became Lovelady's Coast Guard Station. By the time the Long Beach Island Foundation of the Arts and Sciences was opened in 1949, the undeveloped area around it was being called Long Beach Park. As more and more houses got built there, after the completion of the Garden State Parkway in the mid-1950s, residents chose to name their growing community of homes Loveladies (with a slight spelling change) after the old Coast Guard station, then closed.

The name of the next community, Harvey Cedars, is derived not from some mythical whaler called Harvey as we've often been told, but from a once-profitable industry in New Jersey: the harvesting of salt hay. A high spot in the marshes, well shaded by cedar trees, made an excellent place to camp during the haying season in late August. The workers called it the Harvest Cedars. The only problem was that the two words together were hard to pronounce, and, in common speech, it very soon became Harvey Cedars. We still have Harvest Cove, Harvest Point and Harvest Avenue.

North Beach, the next community south of Harvey Cedars, is one of the last places on the Island to be named. For fifty years it was the Frazier Tract; before that, the Sewell Tract. As more and more homes were built on it in the 1950s, residents sought a more attractive name. They were inspired by a small real estate development on a few bayside blocks called the North Beach Estates. It had a nice ring to it, and, at a taxpayer meeting, it was adopted. North Beach, however, means something else to sailors. It is a generic term for the north side of any east-west inlet and in the case of this community the term is a misnomer. It is nowhere near an inlet.

Surf City was first incorporated as Long Beach City when the Island was known simply as Long Beach. After endless mix-ups with Long Branch in Monmouth County, in 1899, the U.S. Post Office forced a name change to Long Beach Island. At the same time Long Beach City had to change its name. Residents chose to call it Surf City. Until 1890, when Beach Haven was incorporated, the whole Island was in the control of Eagleswood, Stafford and Barnegat townships on the mainland. Harvey Cedars and Surf City (Long Beach City) were incorporated in 1894, Barnegat City in 1904 and Ship Bottom-Beach Arlington in 1925. Long Beach Township, formed in 1899, took control of all the rest of the Island. Had the first three communities not incorporated when they did, and two others withdrawn later, the whole Island might have been a single township, instead of the puzzling patchwork that is today.

Ship Bottom acquired its name from an 1817 shipwreck, when a young woman was pulled unharmed from the overturned hull of a wrecked ship. The location of this miraculous rescue was ever afterward called Ship Bottom, but the name really became fixed on maps when the spot was chosen, in 1871, as the site of one

*The new Long Beach Boulevard parallels the old railroad tracks, above, and Pennsylvania Avenue shows weeds growing in the gravel street, below, in Beach Haven Terrace.*

of the six U.S. Lifesaving stations on the Island. Then, in 1910, another ship, the steel bark *Fortuna*, ran aground in a fog and overturned, providing ample opportunity for photographs. As no picture of the early wreck in 1817 existed, the 1910 wreck became the symbol for the borough and its fire company. Ship Bottom-Beach Arlington and three smaller adjoining communities were all part of Long Beach Township until 1925, when they voted to become an independent borough with the name Ship Bottom-Beach Arlington. That was too wordy, and by 1948 the name was reduced to just Ship Bottom.

Between the boroughs of Ship Bottom and Beach

*The Barnegat City schoolhouse, circa 1930.*

PENNSYLVANIA AVE
BEACH HAVEN TERRACE NJ
A-1014

*U.S. Lifesaving Service crew from Bond's station in Holgate, left;
a new cottage in Brant Beach, above, circa 1900.*

Haven lies a five-mile stretch of township territory composed of several little communities bearing names that are mostly variations on Beach Haven. There are Beach Haven Crest, Beach Haven Terrace, Beach Haven Park, Beach Haven Gardens and even Haven Beach, all of which were born early in the century. Philadelphia-based realtors, aware that Long Beach Island was often confused in the minds of potential buyers with Long Is-

land, New York, elected to name each new development of theirs after Beach Haven, which had very high name recognition in eastern Pennsylvania.

Also in this part of the township are Peahala Park, named for an old gunning club, and Spray Beach, which up till the 1880s had been called Cranberry Hill. Then there is Brant Beach, which was first called Beach Haven North. It was getting confused with North Beach Ha-

ven until 1911, when its developer, Henry Mclaughlin, renamed it for a large cove on the bay side of the resort, whose large gravel deposit made it a gathering place for brant, a salt water goose that ingests stones to help digest food. The geese flocked there by the thousands, making Brant Beach the perfect name.

The community of Holgate, now a part of Long Beach Township, is today the only community on the Island that is still named for a former landowner. It should be noted, however, that there were times when parts of the south end were called Bond's, the Inlet Section, Venice Beach, Silver Sands and even Beach Haven Heights. It is all Holgate now.

# Summer People

## Jay Cooke, The Banker Who Financed the Civil War

In the 1890s, when Beach Haven's elegant Engleside Hotel was only 20 years old, no other hotel on the coast could match the entries to be found in its huge guest book on the lobby desk, any page of which could have been copied right out of the social registers of several eastern cities. Also among them were the names of prominent families from as far west as St. Louis, Chicago and Omaha, families who thought nothing of staying for the whole season — June 30 until Labor Day.

This regular clientele was drawn year after year to a charismatic West Jersey Quaker farmer-turned-innkeeper — Robert Barclay Engle. Engle, an energetic man, expended great effort to keep his guests busy all day long, whether it be a mid-morning concert, a sail to Tuckerton for a picnic, games on the beach or card playing and dancing every evening (except Sunday). There were activities for the children and for the ladies. Sportsmen took advantage of the nearly limitless bird and skeet shooting, and there were fishing trips for all who wished to partake. On top of this came the sumptuous three full meals a day. It was like signing aboard a great cruise ship. The only activity proscribed was the drinking of alcoholic beverages: the Engleside Hotel was a temperance house.

Among the distinguished list of guests, there was none whose request for a reservation could galvanize the entire staff to action like Jay Cooke, America's most famous banker, the man from whose Philadelphia offices the Civil War was financed and won. He and Robert Engle were the closest of friends, drawn to each other by a chemistry of personality, not a little of which had to do with their constant optimism and good cheer. The staff of the Engleside practically worshiped Mr. Cooke, whose visits to Beach Haven in the 1890s began with the arrival of his private railway car at the siding of the new Pennsylvania station, on the meadows of West Third Street. He always brought his family and as many as a score of friends with him, taking many rooms and suites. He was a very generous tipper and loved to hand out little presents to the help.

Cooke enjoyed Beach Haven, taking full advantage of the good gunning and fishing. One quaint picture of him appears from time to time in local papers, generally with the query "Who are these two?" It shows Cooke standing on the porch of the Engleside, in a hat and full beard, alongside a bow-legged, equally full-bearded and hatted Robert Engle in hip boots — two old men holding about forty freshly killed curlew they've just shot in the nearby marshes. The newspapers of the 1890s contain accounts of Cooke's frequent fishing trips on Little Egg Harbor Bay. In 1898, in just two days in August, he caught a thousand weakfish — not the record in those prodigal times, but not bad for a man in his mid-70s.

Jay Cooke was born in Sandusky, Ohio in 1821, and, with the then-standard eighth-grade education, began as

*Jay Cooke on the porch of the Engleside Hotel, 1898.*

a bank clerk in St. Louis at the age of 16. He eventually migrated eastward to join a banking house in Philadelphia, where he would make his home for the rest of his life. By 1861, he was head of his own firm, Jay Cooke & Company. Cooke's keen organizational abilities raised the initial capital for the Union armies, just after the First Battle of Bull Run in July of 1861, with a sale of $50 million worth of bonds. By war's end the firm of Jay Cooke & Company had raised nearly $600 million — an incredible feat. He played a key role in American history and fully deserved the title of "financier of the Civil War."

Until 1873, his was one of the most widely known banking houses in the country. After his remarkable success in the war, he opened branch offices in New York and London and became involved in the financing of the Northern Pacific Railroad. He was the founder of Duluth, Minnesota, the railroad's eastern terminus at the head of Lake Superior. However, before the tracks could be laid all the way to Tacoma, Washington, a fine harbor on Puget Sound, the venture was killed by poor bond sales in Europe due to the outbreak of the Franco-Prussian War.

Only a handful of photographs of Jay Cooke, all of them from family albums, have ever been published. According to one biographer, they are the only ones known to exist. In the decades after the Civil War, when it was the fashion for important personages to sit for photo portraits, Cooke shunned cameras. Entirely unknown to his biographers, two very fine photographs of Jay Cooke are still in Beach Haven. They were taken by Robert Barclay Engle's son, Robert Fry Engle, a skilled professional. He was about to make travel photography his life's work when, upon the death of his father in 1901, he took over the management of the Engleside.

Jay Cooke's Philadelphia mansion was named Ogontz, for an Indian chieftain he had known in his boyhood. He later converted it to the Ogontz School for Young Ladies, a very fashionable finishing school for daughters of the well-to-do, among them his five granddaughters. Cooke died in Philadelphia in 1905 at the age

*This photograph from an old album is titled "Spray Beach Lodge" — a scene from 1909.*

of 83. His towering mansion was torn down in 1910, five years after his death, and the Ogontz School was relocated to nearby Abington until it closed in 1950.

One of Jay Cooke's five granddaughters, Emily Barney, of the family that founded the Smith-Barney brokerage firm, was educated at Ogontz and spent all her girlhood summers in the 1880s and 1890s at the Engleside. In 1907, she married Baron Friedrich Von Hiller, a former officer in the Kaiser's army. He was the Mexico City representa-

tive for Bethlehem Steel and had large land holdings in Mexico. Emily, as a bride, lived there in regal splendor until the Madero revolution of 1910. As the Baroness Von Hiller, she traveled the world before and after the Great War, always maintaining her American citizenship. When her husband, the Baron, died suddenly of pneumonia in 1931, she returned to Beach Haven and lived in a charming little cottage on Third Street, filled with mementos of her world travels.

*Spray Beach summer cottages (1909) and dock (1910) are pictured two decades after the community was founded; the original name for the area was Cranberry Hill.*

## John Luther Long, Spray Beach, and Madame Butterfly

Spray Beach was founded in 1889 when William S. Ringgold, a Philadelphia mortgage broker, and his friends the Long and the Wallace families built temporary cottages for themselves on an empty tract called Cranberry Hill a mile north of the center of Beach Haven. The cot-tages they built on Twenty-third Street, a block in from the ocean, were meant to be torn down when newer structures could be built, but some decided to keep those first cottages. John Luther Long liked his place and Ringgold, once he had started a big new dwelling east of Atlantic Avenue on the oceanfront, chose to convert that into a hotel instead. In the summer of 1890, Ringgold's daughter, after a bracing walk on the beach in a northeaster, suggested they call the place Spray Beach. They immediately put a new signboard on the railroad-waiting shed and Ringgold applied the same name to his place, which became the Spray Beach Hotel. Cranberry Hill became one of the Island's lost names.

John Luther Long, one member of the three founding families of Spray Beach, was born in Hanover, Pennsylvania. He was admitted to the bar in Philadelphia in 1881. He became a practicing lawyer, but his passion was always for literature. He wrote many short stories, one of which, appearing in the *Century Magazine* for January 1898 and later that year in a collection, attracted much attention. It is a tragic little tale of some eighteen pages, ending in the suicide of the deserted Japanese wife of an American Naval officer, Benjamin Franklin Pinkerton, who must return to his ship and to America without his pregnant wife, Butterfly. He tells her he'll return when the robins start to nest again. Being a bit of a cad, however, he does not take Japanese marriage or their relationship seriously. She waits three years for him, and, when he finally does return, it is with his American sweetheart, now his new wife. They wish to adopt his child in Japan, and when Butterfly discovers what is happening, she goes behind a screen and stabs herself with her father's sword.

Long always claimed that he had gotten the story from his sister, Mrs. Irwin Correll, the wife of a missionary stationed at Nagasaki, and that it was based on a true incident. This incident may also have inspired French novelist Pierre Loti to use the same theme at least eleven

years earlier in a novel called *Madame Chrysantheme* about a French naval officer named Pierre who, while stationed in Japan, chooses to while away his time by marrying a geisha known as Madame Chrysanthemum. When he has to rejoin his ship, they part with no regrets. Loti's novel is short on plot but filled with exotic atmosphere for readers of that time who were just beginning to learn about the mysterious East.

These so-called "marriages" to Japanese women by business and military men stationed in Japan in the latter part of the 19th century may have been fairly commonplace, but it was John Luther Long who was able to paint the tragic elements. The rights to his story were quickly bought by David Belasco, one of the most colorful characters in the American theater of his day. All his productions are marked by astounding realism; the exotic nature of the Japanese settings undoubtedly appealed to him.

Belasco's one-act version of *Madame Butterfly* opened at the Herald Square Theater in New York on March 5, 1900, scarcely two years after its first magazine appearance. It was an immediate success. When it played in London a year later, Italian composer Giacomo Puccini saw it and chose it for the libretto of what time has proved to be his most popular opera. After a false start in Milan in 1906, the opera was lengthened into two acts, and the pathetic, wistful story of little Butterfly is now known all over the world.

Before his death in 1927 at age 66, Long was to write many more plays and prose works, now largely forgotten. He will, however, always be known as the creator of the short story that became the classic opera *Madame Butterfly* — much of it written on the porch of his cottage at 120 East Twenty-third Street in Spray Beach.

*"The Farm," on Liberty Avenue in Beach Haven, as it looked when it was purchased by Charles Beck in 1911.*

## Charles Beck, Philadelphia Printer Who Coined the Phrase "Six Miles at Sea"

One of Beach Haven's oldest and best known landmarks is a stately home at 319 West Liberty Avenue. Although it no longer functions as one, it is still called "The Farm" or "the Beck farm."

"The Farm" acquired its name in 1911, shortly after Philadelphia engraver Charles Beck bought it from the Sherborne family, who had built the sprawling three-story structure in 1875. Impressively big though it was at its purchase, it was not nearly so elegant as it was to become when Beck enlarged it by raising it several feet off its foundations and adding an additional story.

One of Beck's many hobbies was horticulture, and he soon cultivated and enriched several acres of his property located on the south edge of town, making it an Island showplace for thirty years. Much has been written about life at the Farm, but the best account is a thirteen-part piece that appeared a generation ago in the *Beach Haven Times*. It was written from personal experience by Beck's grandson, Charles Edgar Nash.

Little, however, has ever been said about the early background of Charles Beck, the man who, in his enthusiasm for Beach Haven, coined the expression "Six Miles at Sea." By this he meant, of course, the sailing distance from Tuckerton to Beach Haven at high tide when the

*The Beck farm in its glory days, circa 1926, showing Charles Beck's extensive gardens.*

*Scenes from the Beck farm, clockwise from left: Charles Beck and his wife, Julia, by one of their gardens in August 1915; a party at the farm in 1910; the boardwalk to the bay, bordered with fields of shoulder-high rye growing in sand over bay sedge, was photographed in 1916.*

broad, unspoiled meadows on both sides of the bay were under water, and when tidal creeks were deep enough to be navigable. He was stretching the distance a bit; it was closer to five miles. But to Beck the engraver, "Six Miles at Sea" had a nice typographical balance as well as a certain euphony. The phrase has survived as the official motto for both Beach Haven and the entire Island.

Charles Beck was born November 30, 1851, in Philadelphia. He had a crippling disease in childhood (probably polio), which kept him home much of the time, but from which he seems to have recovered. Fond parents saw to it that he spent several happy childhood summers in Atlantic City, giving him a lifelong interest in the shore. In the final years of the Civil War, he was physically competent enough to become a horse trainer for the

*Charles Beck with Governor Walter E. Edge (holding shotgun) at the Beck farm. The life ring on the porch, behind Beck, is from the Ship Bottom wreck, the* Fortuna.

James Baird, the son-in-law of Charles Parry of the Hotel Baldwin, Beck started coming to Beach Haven. An enthusiastic sportsman, he became a regular guest at the Baldwin and a charter member of the Corinthian Yacht and Gun Club, formed in 1907 from the old Beach Haven Gun Club. He was also very active in the promotion and development of the resort.

In 1907, he bought Baird's magnificent Nearsea Cottage on the southeast corner of Coral Street and Beach Avenue in Beach Haven. In 1911, he sold Nearsea to Frederick Ostendorff, a Philadelphia restaurateur who was building a huge automobile garage on the bay at Pearl Street. It was at this time that Beck moved to the "Farm" on Liberty Avenue, where he began to entertain his many prominent friends and pursue his hobby of gardening. He shared his abundant vegetable harvests with many local Beach Haven families.

Union Army on the home front in Philadelphia. He also served as a hospital attendant.

Beck entered the engraving business with his father and brothers. In 1876, at the Centennial celebration in Philadelphia, their firm won the contract to decorate the impressive Horticultural Hall with their engravings. They acquired many new clients, and Beck's own innovative skills and hard work in time took him to the position of leadership.

He was nearly fifty at the turn of the century, and a success in his field, when, through a friendship with

## Emily Lloyd Wilson, Beach Patrol Founder

Another Philadelphian appears in one of the more unusual photographs of early Long Beach Island. In it, two stalwart Beach Haven lifeguards in 1920s-style bathing suits stand in front of the first aid station on the boardwalk. Between them is a small woman in summer white, sporting a bowler-style linen hat and gazing intently at the camera.

This picture appears from time to time in the local papers without any explanation other than that it somehow illustrates a zany moment in the 1920s. We are left wondering about the curious juxtaposition of the lady and the lifeguards. Who was she, and why was she posing with them on that long-ago summer afternoon?

Actually, it was a formal occasion marking the open-

*Wilson organized the local Red Cross chapter, which parades on the Beach Haven boardwalk in August 1917.*

BEACHHAVEN BRANCH
AMERICAN RED CROSS
OCEAN COUNTY CHAPTER

*Emily Lloyd Wilson with two Beach Haven lifeguards at the opening of the beach emergency station at Coral Street and the boardwalk, July 1927.*

ing of a fully equipped emergency station on the boardwalk at Coral Street, in the block between the Engleside and Baldwin hotels. The date is July 1927, and the two lifeguards in the picture are actually beholden to the woman for their jobs. She is Emily Lloyd Wilson, and no individual fought longer and harder than she to establish a borough-managed beach patrol. Since the 1890s, beach patrol had always been handled by the town's

two major hotels, the Engleside and the Baldwin. Back then their lifeguards were called "beach masters."

Miss Wilson, as early as 1916, was appointed to the Board of Health, becoming the first woman ever to hold political office in Beach Haven. A year later, when America entered the war, she established a Red Cross chapter in town that grew to a membership of 337. For more than a decade after the war, she conducted swimming

and lifesaving lessons for every child in Beach Haven at the Little Egg Harbor Yacht Club. The new first aid station on the boardwalk was another result of her public-spirited efforts.

Emily was the youngest daughter of the distinguished Philadelphia architect John Allston Wilson, the man who, in 1883, designed the magnificent Hotel Baldwin and several fine summer cottages that grace Beach Haven's historic district to this day.

Wilson had four daughters — Elizabeth, Helen, Jane and Emily. Jane and Emily, who never married, lived in two of the three celebrated Shakespeare cottages on Amber Street — "Rosalind," "Sylvia" and "Audrey" were designed and named by their father. His own twin-chimneyed "Portia," a Beach Haven landmark, stands behind them on Coral Street, and was bequeathed to his daughter Helen.

The two lifeguards in the photograph on the left are holding diamond-shaped buoys of cork, part of their standard equipment. The vehicle between them is a gurney, or rolling stretcher, its narrow wheels more suitable, it would seem, for a hospital corridor than a beach. In those years, however, the town had more than a mile of smooth, oceanfront boardwalk extending from Seventh Street on the north all the way south to Holyoke Avenue. In the event of an emergency, someone could race down the boards with the gurney in a matter of minutes.

Emily Lloyd Wilson sold Rosalind on Amber Street and moved to 114 East Second Street, across the street from her sister Elizabeth Wilson Pharo, who summered at the stately "Louella Cottage." Built in 1874, Louella Cottage is the oldest residence still standing in Beach Haven. Emily Wilson always left for St. Augustine, Florida shortly after Election Day and returned around Easter. She remained active in Beach Haven civic affairs all her life.

Beach Haven lifeguards, July 1930.

## Warren Webster Jr., Pilot of the Miss Beach Haven Autogiro

Organized sandlot ball hasn't been played in Beach Haven since the late 1930s, but, in the 75 years of its existence, Walsh Field has been put to uses other than pure athletics. In the early 1930s it was a private landing field for a glamorous summer resident named Warren Webster Jr., after whom the Webster tract in Beach Haven is named. His father was the president and founder of the Webster Iron and Furnace Works in Camden. Young Webster commuted regularly from the airfield in that city to his summer home in Beach Haven in his autogiro, a form of aircraft now as nonexistent as the zeppelin.

The autogiro was a vertical lift-off airplane with four whirling overhead blades that were actually its wings. A young Spanish aristocrat and engineer, Juan de la Cierva, invented it in Madrid in 1920. Unlike the helicopter, then

Warren Webster Jr. and his autogiro.

electrical wires, struck a utility pole and fell forty feet onto Ocean Street. His $8,000 *Miss Beach Haven* was badly crippled but Webster suffered only a broken nose. He was treated at the site by Dr. William Dodd, who had been in town only a year, and whose office and home were on Second Street.

The dashing 29-year-old Webster did not give up flying. His next purchase was a seaplane, which he kept moored in the Liberty Thorofare behind Mordecai Island. He also had a small hangar built on the edge of the bay near the Little Egg Harbor Yacht Club where he kept a powerful speedboat. He used the plane only in the summer months. Any time he landed in front of the club, a dozen or more young skippers were ready to plunge into the water to grab the lines and pull him to his wooden ramp.

## Charles Durborow and Surf City

in its infancy in Europe, the overhead blades of the autogiro were not motor driven. They spun by themselves in the wind or when the craft was dropping or moving forward — hence the name autogiro (auto-spin). All that was needed was a lightweight engine and propeller to provide forward thrust. Perfected in 1923, the "flying windmill" had become, by 1930, a practical aircraft, although fewer than a thousand were ever built around the world. In 1936, Cierva, at the age of 41, was killed in the crash of a Dutch airliner. All his sophisticated discoveries were applied to the further development of the helicopter, and the autogiro was forgotten.

Webster's plane, the *Miss Beach Haven*, was one of twenty-two manufactured by the Kellett Company in Camden. In 1931, the borough council of Beach Haven

voted to give Webster the privilege of using the ball field for his nearly vertical landings and takeoffs. His summer residence was next to the Little Egg Harbor Yacht Club, and his autogiro was sheltered in a garage on West Ocean Street, across from the ball field.

On the afternoon of July 30, 1932, a crowd of a hundred or so were watching a baseball game when they heard the nasal drone of young Webster's machine whizzing across the bay toward them at 60 miles per hour. He slowed to circle the field and waved from the cockpit. The teams retreated to the edges as Webster began his gradual descent onto the diamond. He was only several feet off the ground when a sudden gust of wind from the north drifted the plane toward the grandstand. Webster attempted to rise but got caught in the telephone and

Of the many fresh-water bogs on Long Beach Island in the 19th century, the Great Swamp was by far the largest. Its great natural beauty and abundant game attracted not only the early shore whaling families who built their dwellings along its southern edge, but scores of vacationing Burlington County farmers who cooperated to build the Mansion of Health in 1821. It was the very year that the most powerful hurricane ever to strike New Jersey washed over the dunes and utterly destroyed the delicate fresh-water ecology of the Great Swamp by inundating it with salt water. The trees all died, but the hotel was spared and continued to operate successfully until the 1850s. It is uncertain whether the eastward extension of the swamp was lost in 1821, or at an earlier time.

For more than a century, the community of Surf City,

renamed in 1899 from Long Beach City, managed to get along without the swamp. Its former presence, however, was still with them in a tangled, nearly impassable growth of stunted red cedar and bayberry in a great triple ring of sand hills north of Twelfth Street. Once there was an automobile road on the north end of the Island, something had to be done to improve the marketability of this potentially valuable territory. It was at this point, in the middle 1920s, that Charles B. Durborow, one of the most energetic and colorful real estate promoters in Long Beach Island history, entered the scene.

Durborow, a former Philadelphia stockbroker and bank officer, came to Long Beach Island in 1925 at the age of forty-three. Within the year, he had teamed up with William J. Noonan Sr., who arrived at the same time and was the same age. Noonan was a former vice president with the American Tobacco Company. Together they formed a partnership with an established Island realtor, Robert Osborn, and began to develop the northern half of Brant Beach from Fifty-fifth Street to the Ship Bottom line at Thirty-second Street. It was an ambitious project. They built the Ockonickon Hotel, later to become Wida's, an automobile garage on Forty-third Street, and the Brant Beach Movie Theater. They also had plans for a boardwalk and two more hotels.

Long Beach Island was booming in the 1920s. The talented Durborow soon became president of the Long Beach Island Board of Trade and set his sights on the development of Surf City. He hired John Robbins Inman to clean out all the brush and old stumps of the former Great Swamp. In those days, fire was the only way to do a job like that. For the next several weeks, towering columns of smoke rose from several locations until the bigger dunes could be leveled to fill in all the low spots. Within one season, the whole area was as flat and

SURF VILLA INN, SURF CITY, N. J.

*The Surf Villa, at 16th Street and the Boulevard, was built in 1928.*

treeless as a prairie. Durborow announced plans to bulkhead a section of the bay side of Surf City, dredge the bay and fill the meadows with mud and sand for building lots and a bathing beach. From his offices on South Broad Street in Philadelphia, he sent out regular newsletters praising every aspect of the Island. One of them extols the virtues of a proposed $500,000 bridge across Barnegat Inlet. It was to have been started with private funds in the autumn of 1929, just as the stock market crashed.

One of the few side streets in Surf City in those years that actually ran to the bay was Ninth Street, the location of a public dock. On the evening of August 11, 1928 at a dinner for the Surf City Improvement Association (of which he was president) held at the brand new Surf

Villa Hotel (which he had built and of which he was the proprietor), Durborow made a gift of $1,000 to start a Surf City Yacht Club on the site of the old dock at Ninth Street.

Durborow, like many others then, was heavily invested in the stock market and was hard hit by the Depression. He died in 1938 at the age of 56. If anyone can be said to have flashed across the sky like a meteor, it would be Charles Durborow. One of the great long-distance swimmers of all time, Durborow swam across the Delaware Bay from Cape May to Cape Henlopen in 14½ hours on July 1, 1912. On June 15, 1916 he swam across the Chesapeake Bay from Cape Charles to Cape Henry in eight hours and six minutes, the first person ever to do it. These are considered two of the most difficult swims in America. He also swam from the Battery to Sandy Hook, and from Boston Harbor to the Boston Light. He held nearly every record for swimming up, down and across the Delaware and was the organizer of the "Polar Bear Club," whose membership vowed to take a dip in the Delaware every day of the year regardless of the weather.

Durborow had a beautiful summer cottage on Atlantic Avenue in Beach Haven, and when there, made the ocean a substitute for the Delaware. He died on May 12, 1938 at his other home in Edgewater Park, New Jersey on the banks of the Delaware, where he had so often chopped holes in the ice to take a plunge. He is buried in Bryn Mawr, Pennsylvania. His only regret, he often said, was that the Great War of 1914-18 frustrated his plans to swim the English Channel in the very years he was in peak condition.

## Fredrick P. Small, American Express, and the Small Estate

If Long Beach Island has been the vacation retreat of some fascinating characters over the years, none is remembered with greater fondness and admiration than Frederick P. Small of Harvey Cedars. The sprawling Small Estate, reaching from ocean to bay on both sides of the main highway, ran three full blocks from Seventieth Street to Seventy-third Street. In the decades of the 1930s, '40s and '50s, the incredible profusion and variety of his vast flower beds caught the eye of every passing motorist.

In the summer months Small had as many as twenty men in his employ to tend to his spectacular gardens and greenhouse. Not even Charles Beck's celebrated "Beck Farm" in Beach Haven was more carefully manicured than the Small Estate in Harvey Cedars. Today the estate is the site of Maris Stella (Star of the Sea), the summer retreat of the Sisters of Charity of Convent Station, New Jersey.

Today the gardens have been covered over with grass. In Small's day, there was considerably more oceanfront property as well. The stately main house on the ocean and the three-car garage washed away in The Great Atlantic Storm of 1962. That storm wreaked havoc on Harvey Cedars, actually cutting the Island in two at Seventy-sixth Street, scarcely a dozen blocks north of Small's.

Although everyone called it the Small Estate, Small himself liked to think of it as "the Cobblestones," which was the name he chose for it. The foundation, chimney and long wall of the main house on the oceanfront were made of cobblestones, all of which came from the Delaware River. Small employed stonemason Ed Lange to build all the walls and walkways and oversee the care of the flowerbeds. Ed's older brother Bill was Mr. Small's chauffeur, but he was far more than that. He actually ran the whole estate, ordering all the supplies and hiring the help. He drove Small back and forth to his residence in Ridgewood, New Jersey, and into New York several times a week. Bill had his own home on the bay at the Harvey Cedars estate and another at Ridgewood.

Small trusted him with all the details. "Talk with William," he would say to tradesmen and contractors. He never used nicknames. It was always "Joseph or Edmund or Robert, please cut a bouquet for these people." People were always wandering in off the highway to look at the flowers; if Small was there, they always got something to take home.

Frederick Percival Small was an impressive figure striding about his beautifully manicured gardens. He always wore tweed or flannel knickers, which he bought in Scotland on his frequent trips abroad. His shirts and neckties were of silk. He wore diamond cuff links and favored the high, stiff "Herbert Hoover" collar. He would occasionally remove the necktie to pitch in with the workmen, whose company he enjoyed. He smoked expensive cigars in a little holder and was seldom seen without a pocket full of them to give away to friends. These were 25-cent cigars in a day when cigarettes were 15 cents a pack. Although he preferred beer, Small would occasionally drink scotch. He insisted that whoever was tending bar pour the scotch no higher than the line of the boom of the sailboat imprinted on the glass.

Small loved good cigars and had them rolled especially for him by a retired manufacturer in Havana. They were seven inches long, unusually thick, and came in boxes with his personal seal. He never laid one down until it was finished, nor did he ever hold one in his mouth or chew the ends. It was always in his hand, and when he lifted it to his lips for a gentle draw, at least three diamonds glinted on his fingers.

Every Saturday morning at 11:00 was bar time. The entire workforce, off until Monday morning, was invited into the "Play House" on the edge of the bay for several rounds of beer before heading home. Small's Play House was on the northwest corner of the bay property. The bay was dredged here to a depth of fifteen feet, and Small erected an Olympic diving board. He generously opened his bay beach to the public, but there were seldom more than a few cars with mothers and children. He was a great benefactor to the community of Harvey Cedars. In the 1930s, he sponsored sailboat races for all the Island children. After the races, he would have them and their parents over for a big lobster dinner.

He built a large, well-equipped boathouse on his prop-

*The estate of Frederick P. Small ran from ocean to bay, from 70th Street to 73rd Street, in Harvey Cedars. It is now Maris Stella, the Sisters of Charity retreat.*

erty and bought a boat, but neither Bill nor Ed Lange knew anything about boats and their lack of enthusiasm was passed on to Small. He lost interest, sold the boat and converted the boathouse into a machine shop.

The Play House, despite its name, was not for children. Inside were a bowling alley, a pistol range, two pool tables and a small bar with a first-rate tap system. This was where men played. Every Friday night when Small

was in Harvey Cedars he invited his cronies in for an evening of cards, pool or bowling. He liked their company and they were delighted to be there. They were all men like him — successful in business. Charles Butler of

Barnegat City had a trucking company, and Lloyd Behmke, also of that town, later became its mayor. Firman Cranmer of Beach Haven, the sole supplier of lumber for the estate, and bar owner Tommy Lind of Ship Bottom were regular guests. Dick Myers of the Barnegat City Fishery and one-time owner of the Sunset Hotel, Ollie Cox of Cox & Cox Gravel and Joe Bozarth, the painting contractor, were always there, along with a half dozen others who were not as prominent but made good company. None could ever come close to being as successful as their host.

Small was born in Augusta, Maine, in 1874, where he had his early schooling. He graduated from Boston Shorthand School in 1892 and served as official stenographer for the Maine House of Representatives. He went to Cornell Law School for a term and then the Eastman Business School. In 1896, he joined the American Express Company. Within one year, at the age of 22, he was head cashier of the eastern division and by 1912, he had risen to assistant to the first vice president. Three years later, he was made first vice president himself. By 1923, he had become president of American Express. He had risen from stenographer to president and chairman of the board in 52 years. It was during his regime that American Express travelers' checks became recognized as the international medium of exchange. The company prospered even during the Depression.

Small, as president of American Express, the only truly solvent large financial institution during the Depression years, could afford to hire more than twenty men to cultivate his gardens, day in and day out, from early spring until late fall. He raised 150 varieties of orchids in his hothouse at Harvey Cedars and exchanged bulbs and slips with growers all over the world. Every Saturday morning at 11:00 he paid each man the sum of $25 for the week's work — money that was always in crisp notes fresh from the bank and never before used. Small had a fetish about always using new money. If he acquired any used bank notes in change, or in the conduct of business at his summer home in Harvey Cedars, he would never re-circulate them or even carry them around. Instead, he put this "dirty money," as he called it, into an old brass spittoon he had in his big house on the oceanfront. When it was filled up, he would have his foreman take it to the bank and exchange it for new money.

He had similarly eccentric notions about accepting coins in change for any purchases he made. He would slide them all back across the counter, even if it was as much as ninety cents, and clerks were always glad to wait on him. His coin collection was another matter. It was composed almost entirely of newly minted or uncirculated pieces from all over the world, kept in trays in a huge safe nearly six feet high. It had thick walls of steel and concrete and was so heavy that, when his house was partially undermined by Hurricane Carol in 1954, the safe fell through to the sand.

It was retrieved, but the incident has spawned a legend. According to history, in 1962 the Great Atlantic Storm destroyed the whole house but the safe may still be there, just off shore, filled with a great treasure of rare coins, waiting to be found with the right metal detector.

Small retired from American Express in 1944, but he continued to attend board meetings in New York. Although he had a chauffeur and several big cars, he chose to ride the 6:00 morning bus from Harvey Cedars up Route 9, arriving at his *pied-a-terre* on Park Avenue, where he would take a nap and freshen up before the

*Small employed 20 men to tend to the extensive gardens and greenhouses at the Small Estate from the 1930s through the 1950s.*

*Small's stately main house on the oceanfront washed away in The Great Atlantic Storm of 1962.*

noon meeting. In the 1920s, each board member would find a newly minted $10 gold piece on his plate. With the end of the gold standard in the 1930s, it became a crisp new hundred-dollar bill. Small was a man who believed that tastefully chosen things in life made a lasting impression.

He died in 1958, at the age of 83, leaving a son, Frederick A., a daughter, Katherine Conkling, and eight grandchildren. The Harvey Cedars property was to have been split three ways among the son, daughter and Bill Lange.

However, Katherine died shortly after her father. In 1959, Frederick A. (always known as Ted) and Bill jointly sold the property on both sides of the road to the Sisters of Charity. The nuns sold a portion of the ocean side of the estate to builders after the March storm in 1962. The beach has cut in so much that the remains of Small's old bulkhead are now out in the ocean where the waves break. Today, pieces of his pilings can be seen at very low tides.

# Long Beach Islanders

## Charlie Cramer
## Milkman, Grocer, Mayor

There are nearly as many Cramers in the Ocean County telephone directory as there are Cranmers. The two names, when both are pronounced with a short "a," sound very much alike. In earlier generations, there were undoubtedly enough crossovers in spelling to reinforce the belief that they are one and the same surname.

Cramer, without the "n," sometimes spelled Kramer or Krehmer, is of German origin and is an occupational term meaning tradesman or shopkeeper, specifically of the kind who traveled the countryside buying up eggs, butter and hens to be resold on market day for a profit. The "cramer" carried these items in a large backpack called a "cram."

Cranmer, with the "n," is English and is a place name derived from Cranmore or Cranmere, a lake in Somerset. The most famous member of this family was Thomas Cranmer (1489-1556), the first Protestant Archbishop of Canterbury, who, as the author of the celebrated *Book of Common Prayer*, became the intellectual head of the English Reformation. Catholic Queen Mary, who was herself soon to be deposed by her half-sister, Protestant Queen Elizabeth had him executed for his heresy.

Thomas Cranmer, a celibate, unmarried clergyman, had no children, so no Cranmers in this country are descended directly from him. However, they are descendants of the same family of Cranmers who lived in England in the 16th and 17th centuries and later emigrated to America. Whatever their roots, the Cramer and Cranmer families are well established in southern Ocean County.

Best known of the Cramers is Roger "Doc" Cramer, who played major league baseball in the 1930s and '40s and is a candidate for the Baseball Hall of Fame. Doc Cramer was born in Beach Haven and moved with his family to Manahawkin when he was one year old.

Another Cramer remembered with great fondness in Beach Haven was Doc's cousin Charles M. Cramer — grocer, milkman, Beach Haven commissioner and, at the time of his death in 1963, the mayor of the town. To everyone who knew him, he was always "Charlie." When his little grocery store across from the library on Beach Avenue, between Second and Third streets, closed that same year, it was the end of an era. His was the last shop to operate on what was once the town's main business thoroughfare.

Charlie Cramer's Grocery on Beach Avenue, now a private dwelling, was built by his father in 1910. Charlie's parents, Darius and Minnie Cramer, came as newlyweds to Beach Haven from New Gretna in 1889. For the next twenty years, Darius was employed in the meat market of his brother-in-law, Thomas Cale. Cale's store, located at Amber Street and Beach, was the first year-round butch-

*Charlie Cramer in his store in the 1940s.*

er shop on the Island. It, too, is now a private dwelling. Darius was paid $25 a month. To supplement his income, he served with the U. S. Lifesaving Service each winter. When he retired in 1910, he erected a small building at the rear of his home on Third Street and opened a milk depot to which he added a line of bakery goods, including cakes and cookies, shipped in daily by train from Ivin's Bakery in Philadelphia.

Darius and Minnie's only son, Charles M. Cramer, was born in August 1889, in the family home at 207 Third Street, and he lived within a stone's throw of that spot all his life. He and his three sisters went to Beach Haven's one-room schoolhouse across the street. Those were the good years, Charlie always said, when he could tumble out of bed and be at his desk in two minutes.

He did well in school, especially in mathematics. When he finished eighth grade, he became the first boy in Beach Haven to go on to high school. It was not easy to do in those days. He had to take the 7 o'clock train every morning. As the only boy on the train, he had the privilege of riding in the cab of the engine with the engineer, as the train chugged slowly up the Island, making stops only at those sheds where someone was waiting. It crossed the bay over the narrow trestle to the meadows of Manahawkin. Although Charlie's high school was two miles north at Barnegat, he had to stay aboard while the train ran south to Tuckerton. After a turnaround and a brief wait to take on passengers, it headed north to Whiting. It passed Barnegat within a block of the school.

Trains were always on schedule, so Charlie walked in the doors of his school every morning at 9:00. Each afternoon at 5:00, he boarded the train to make the same roundabout run to Tuckerton and then back across the bay, arriving at Beach Haven at 7:00 PM. He did his homework on the train. Barnegat had only a three-year program then, so Charlie switched to Tuckerton High School for his senior year, boarding with his aunt.

Charlie next attended Rider College in Trenton, known in those years as The Rider, Moore and Stuart College. He was an honor student, but he had to drop out after a year and a half when his father died in 1913. He came home to help his mother manage the store and run the milk business. He was only 20, but he was up to the task, and worked hard to build up his route.

Starting with a horse-drawn wagon, in a territory that ran from Holgate to Spray Beach, he was, within a dozen years, delivering a minimum of 1,000 quarts a day in summer. In time, he had a truck, and by the 1930s, his day began at 3:00 AM with a drive to Atlantic City to pick up the milk, butter and cheese. He did all the bookkeeping and he was generous to a fault, keeping many families on credit all winter. He ran the store with the aid of his wife and mother, and eventually his daughters. Somehow, he still found the time to play third base with the old championship Beach Haven baseball team in the years after World War I, when the field was still located at Eighth Street, east of the Beach Haven School.

Charlie met his future wife, Eugenie Breton, on a blind date on the boardwalk in 1912. Eugenie, always known as Jennie, would come from Boston every summer to work as waitress at the Engleside Hotel. They were married the following year. Together, they ran the store for more than fifty years. They had two daughters, Louise and Eleanor.

A life-long Democrat, Charlie loved politics. He became a natural vote-getter and served in the 1920s as one of the six councilmen in the old form of Beach Haven municipal government. In the election of November 1929 he defeated Mayor Herbert Willis by a vote of 281 to 193, sweeping the old Republican Party from the throne.

He served two years. Defeated by Firman Cranmer in 1932, he continued as one of the council. When the commission form of government was adopted in 1946, he was still in office. He eventually became mayor again in 1960, a post he held until his death in 1963. Charlie Cramer was given a full military funeral; the whole town turned out to mourn a man whose kindness and generosity were legendary.

## "Citizen" Bill Kane and the Mason-Dixon Line

The popular notion that the Mason-Dixon Line crossed New Jersey is a modern one. It started in March

*Kane offers to make a souvenir photograph of fishermen's prize catches.*

of 1952 with a front-page cartoon in the *Beach Haven Times* drawn by William Kane of Beach Haven Terrace. Kane first came to Beach Haven Terrace in 1907, at two months old, when the place was all marsh and meadowland, with a wall of gigantic dunes on the oceanfront and an imposing new Coast Guard station on what was soon to become New Jersey Avenue. Bill's father was J. J. Kane, the sales manager for the Fidelity Land Company of Philadelphia, the founders of Beach Haven Terrace that same year.

*The Beach Haven Terrace post office and store in 1913, above, and a counter inside the Nor'easter when Bill Kane ran the store.*

Bill Kane saw all the early history of the town and in time became, with his wife, Edna, the proprietor of the Nor'easter convenience store, post office and newsstand on the Boulevard in Beach Haven Terrace. During World War II, he commuted every day in a car pool with others on the Island to a defense job at the Philadelphia Navy Yard, which he chronicled in a delightful book of narrative and cartoons. If ever a man grew into the role of delightful old codger, it was Bill Kane. Until they got to know him, strangers waiting to make purchases in his store waited nervously as he sat behind the counter on his stool, talking in grunts and monosyllables while jotting down sums for the sale of groceries and newspapers on the backs of paper bags. He refused to use a cash register. Often outspoken in his opinions, he was known to many as "Citizen Kane" — but there was not a soul who didn't love him for his gruff sense of humor.

Although he also painted and sketched, he was primarily a cartoonist whose work is now scattered far and wide. Fifty of his drawings depicting scenes of local history, along with some of his photographs, appeared in a little booklet published in 1957 to mark the fiftieth

*Bill Kane was an avid photographer and, in addition to documenting events and places on the Island, captured this evocative period scene of his Nor'easter store and post office in Beach Haven Terrace.*

anniversary of Beach Haven Terrace. He was also a re-markably fine photographer who managed to be on the scene at every major event or incident in Island history — from hurricanes to plane crashes and hotel fires. His work was published all around the state.

Bill Kane loved to create attention, and the car-toon in the *Beach Haven Times* in 1952 was a perfect example of his occasional playfulness. He knew that the Mason-Dixon Line never crossed New Jersey, but he decided to extend it with a ruler and see where it would come out. The resulting imaginary line runs right through Manahawkin and exits into the ocean at North First Street in Surf City just above the Ship Bottom line.

Kane enjoyed every bit of this scenario. He published and sold posters, and put up signs outside his store wel-coming "y'all" to Beach Haven Terrace — "geographically located on LBI, six miles at sea, and six and a half miles below the famous Mason-Dixon Line." There was, for a time, a small monument placed at North First Street in Surf City, everything north of which was, of course, Yan-kee land. Kane urged everyone south of the line to start drinking mint juleps. In those carefree summers of the 1950s, many acquiesced.

Now for the facts about the Mason-Dixon Line. The original line was the east-west boundary between Maryland and Pennsylvania, first surveyed between 1763 and 1767 by two British astronomers, Charles Mason and Jeremiah Dixon. The job was undertaken to settle a dispute between the Calvert and Penn families, the landholders of the two states in question. The line of the survey does not extend eastward beyond the northeast corner of Maryland. In fact, at that point, it makes a right angle abruptly south to become the border between Delaware and Maryland on the Delmarva Peninsula. There was never any need for it to cross the Delaware River, as the land then known as the East and West Jerseys was never in disputed ownership. Nor did the line extend westward any farther than thirty miles short of the Pennsylvania-Ohio border.

While the Mason-Dixon Line was never meant to be such, it did eventually become a rallying cry, dividing the free states from the slave-holding states simply because it ran between Pennsylvania and Maryland. There was never any reason to think that New Jersey was anything but a free state by the early 19th century. It is somewhat ironic that, in Colonial times, had there been any such dividing line between what we call North Jersey and South Jersey, nearly all the slaves in the colony would have been in the more populous north.

## Doctor Dodd

Doctor William E. Dodd practiced medicine in Beach Haven for thirty-three years, until his retirement in 1964 at the age of 70. Dodd's place still stands at the southeast corner of Ocean Street and Bay Avenue across from

### DR. WM. E. DODD

# Dr. Wm. E. Dodd Honored By Cape May Doctors

*Biography of Beach Haven Physician to Appear in Cape May County Medical Journal*

The Journal of the Cape May County Medical Society will feature a cover biography with photograph of Dr. Wm. Earle Dodd, Beach Haven Doctor and

Walsh Field. Built in 1937, it was more than just a doctor's office. It was actually a small hospital where appendectomies and all sorts of routine operations could be performed.

Dr. Dodd modestly referred to himself as "just a country doctor," but he impressed all who knew him as far more than that. He was a tall, erect and courtly man with a waxed moustache. He became chief of staff at Paul Kimball Hospital in Lakewood in 1945 and was the most respected physician who ever operated there. The nurses and younger doctors were in such awe of him that they would stand at attention when he entered to begin surgery. The American College of Surgeons described William E. Dodd, M.D. as "not only a household word in Beach Haven but along the whole length of the Jersey shore."

Dodd was born on a farm in Berkeley County in eastern West Virginia near Harper's Ferry on July 28, 1893. Both his mother and father were schoolteachers. His father taught for fifty years and became a county superintendent of schools. Young William attended a one-room school until he was 12 and his family moved to Martinsburg, West Virginia, where he then completed high school and went on to take his pre-medical training at Gettysburg College. He entered the School of Medicine at the University of Pennsylvania in 1914. After serving with the Medical Corps in France in the last months of 1918, he returned as a volunteer worker in the influenza epidemic in Philadelphia. He graduated in 1920.

He married in 1923 and entered practice as a "mine surgeon" in Rossiter in the coalfields of western Pennsylvania. It was the practice of the coal companies to hire physicians to treat victims of mine accidents and to care for the families of miners. In his four years in Rossiter he delivered 1,500 babies. He returned briefly to Martinsburg for general practice but overwork had brought on ill health. After he underwent an operation in Philadelphia, his doctors urged a more restful environment for him and suggested Beach Haven, where the Long Beach Board of Trade was advertising for a doctor. The only year-round doctor on the eighteen-mile island was Dr. Herbert Willis.

Here, in Dodd's own words given at a testimonial dinner in his honor in 1954, are his first impressions of the Island he was to make his home:

"Thanks to some of your very responsible citizens I had heard that Long Beach Island was a good place for a young doctor to settle. It was back in 1930 that I first set foot on these shores. I was looking for a place to begin practice, a place to call home. I boarded the Pennsylvania Railroad running out of Camden taking one of their one-dollar excursions to the seashore. As I went through the Jersey pines I saw nothing but an occasional hunting lodge here and there and I wondered where I was going. In the course of time I came to Whitings. There I had to change trains and I got on what was known as the Tuckerton Railroad, which after many starts and stops brought me to Long Beach Island.

"The first stop was at Ship Bottom. Then as I passed southward along the Island I saw many modest homes sitting up on stilts with sea gulls feeding beneath them and again I wondered where I was going. The further south I went, the more numerous the sand dunes became and the more numerous the sea gulls seemed to be.

"But, in due course of time, I arrived at Beach Haven. I got off the train and looked about me. The sky was blue, the sun was bright and the air was pure and invigorating. I went to the Real Estate Office and inquired where I could find the Secretary of the Board of Trade. After being directed, I was put in touch with a man by the name of Flannery. He took me around and introduced me to a number of leading citizens of the community.

"I remember 'Firm' Cranmer, Charlie Conrad and a number of others including the local druggist, Mr. Paxson, and somewhere along the line I got some sand in my shoes. Well that settled it. After the day was over, I went back over the same halting railroad trip to Camden and on to Martinsburg, West Virginia and told my wife that we had found the place where we were going."

She said, "Do you think it's wise?" She told him a telegram had come and the mining company wanted him back and would increase his salary. Then he showed her a dozen post cards he had bought at the drugstore. She asked to hear more about the sea gulls. He said he would not go back to the mines. "No. I want to live where the skies are blue and the air is pure. We are going to Beach Haven."

So about a month later they arrived, renting a house on Second Street near Dr. Willis' home, where Dodd practiced from 1930 until 1937, when he built a new home and moved his practice to South Bay Avenue at Ocean Street.

Dr. Dodd was very fond of westerns. Any time one was playing at the Colony Theater in Beach Haven, he was sure to be there, although he was often so tired he fell asleep. No one disturbed him between the shows, and he would have to sit through two shows just to see the whole picture. In his office he had dozens of fish hooks displayed in frames. All of them had been removed from victims of fishing accidents, most of which had occurred at the nearby Berkeley Avenue fishing pier, where fishermen were always conking each other with sinkers and snagging ears.

He had a fabulous collection of seashells from all over the world. In his later years, he traveled the world collecting specimens for the Academy of Natural Sciences in Philadelphia. Some of the bigger ones, weighing many hundreds of pounds, were displayed on his front lawn. After his death, his entire collection went to the Delaware Museum of Natural History in Greenville, Delaware.

## Bird and Betty Clutter, The Acme Hotel, and Local Color

Ever since 1904, the Acme Hotel, on the bay at Dock Road, had been a fishermen's bar. This was true in the Tueckmantel years from 1925 through the early '50s, but things began to change when Ernie Tueckmantel's two brothers, Gus and Whitey, built a bar and restaurant of their own only two blocks away. They called it "Gus and Whitey's," and it attracted most of the old Acme clientele. Ernie held on until the end of the decade, then, nearing 60, he decided to retire and sold the place to Bird and Betty Clutter of Little Washington in western Pennsylvania. Bird's sister was married to Pete Morrison of Morrison's restaurant at the end of Second Street near the Acme. The Morrison family was from Pittsburgh, and their establishment, built in 1946, stood on the site that had been occupied by the Beach Haven Yacht Club from 1883 until it was moved in 1930.

When Bird and Betty bought the Acme in 1959, they chose to concentrate on the bar business. However, they were new and had no clientele to inherit. The fishing crowd had gone to Gus and Whitey's. The college crowd was packing Dracula's Castle in the Baldwin every summer night to jump to the fabulous Morizzo Brothers of Wyckoff, New Jersey. For quiet conversation and true social drinking, there were Britz's and Buckalew's in the heart of town. An older crowd in Beach Haven frequented the new motel bars or went to the Bay View or to Herb Feiler's musical bar, right next door to the Acme in what

*Bird and Betty Clutter at the old Acme Hotel.*

had once been the Antlers Grill.

Then, in the last week of September 1960, on a windy night, the huge, old Hotel Baldwin, empty at the time, caught fire and burned to the ground in a spectacular blaze that could be seen all over the mainland. In the summer of 1961, with Dracula's Castle gone, the younger crowd, those in their twenties and thirties, discovered the Acme and made it their own gathering place. These were the years when everyone still went barefoot to the bars at night. Broken glass and lit cigarette butts on the floors plus backed-up plumbing in the men's and ladies' rooms seemed to trouble no one. Being barefoot meant you were a part of the shore crowd — here for the whole summer. Only "shoobies" wore shoes.

Beer was 25 cents a 10-ounce draft then, up a nickel or two from the previous decade, and the Acme was standing room only on hot summer nights. Music came from the jukebox, all the current hits right out of Cousin Brucie's top ten on "W-A-Beatle-C" in New York. A favorite at the Acme in 1966 was Sam the Sham and the Pharoahs singing "Little Red Riding Hood... you sure are lookin' good... how's about walkin' in the woods with me?" And then a great wolf's howl would echo through the place. Bird and Betty, behind the bar, concentrating intensely, could not draw the beers fast enough on those weekend nights. Four beers; $1. Eight beers; 2$. On and on and on until 3:00 in the morning. And then they had to clean up and be back again to open at 9:00 the same morning. They hardly ever slept.

The tempo slowed in the winter months. Within a year or two, it seemed that Bird and Betty had begun to attract characters that, were this Monterey and not Beach Haven, could have stepped out of the pages of John Steinbeck's *Cannery Row* or *Sweet Thursday*. Where else could you find people like John Crosta, Chester Coole, Bill Pinnix, Bill Leonard and Joe Lieberman?

Joe Lieberman had been around for many years. A brilliant student who joined the U.S. Navy in World War II to become a radioman, he developed into a lightning-fast telegrapher in the days when Morse code was essential. Unfortunately, while in the service, he had a nervous breakdown from which he never fully recovered. Settling with his blind mother in a tiny, former garage near Flo's Diner in Spray Beach, he walked the Boulevard nearly every day, all through the 1950s and '60s, into Beach Haven, usually to Britz's Bar, where he would order — always from the top shelf and at half-hour intervals — a bourbon followed by a rye, and then a scotch, then perhaps an expensive gin. Then he would walk home. He wouldn't allow anyone to buy him a drink. He paid for everything with his own money and would talk only if he thought he had an audience who cared to listen. If you turned away from him, he would stop talking.

Always presentably dressed, summer and winter, in coat and tie, Joe also wore a black fedora with about fifteen little magnets inside the hatband. He was completely bald, and he had invented this device to grow new hair. It was also important to consume a lot of iron tablets, which he downed with every drink. There was a patent pending on this device, he would tell strangers, at the same time informing them he had written every one of the songs on the juke box, and the scraps of handwritten notes he carried in his pockets, all of them copied from poetry anthologies, were being looked at by publishers. He sold stock certificates in outer space and gave several of them to Betty Clutter to help her with the mortgage.

Paying his own way for everything out of his Navy disability pension, Joe Lieberman was never a burden to anyone and had the respect of all who knew him for the care he gave his mother. His eccentric behavior amused the regulars at the Acme, many of whom were eccentrics themselves. None could match the sardonic wit and repartee of Bill Pinnix, whose Esso tow truck bore the legend "Bill Pinnix, the Widow's Home Companion" until enough angry letters got through to Standard Oil to force him to remove it. And then there was the delightful Bill Leonard, who liked to play the role of a shy, former concert pianist down on his luck. After much urging and a free beer or two, he would sit down at the keyboard in a dark corner and startle strangers with a rendition of Mozart or Rachmaninoff that, unbeknownst to them, Bird had piped into the piano from his stereo behind the bar.

It was all a setup for people who were new to the bar, and behind all this great fun were the gentle good humor of Bird and the nearly infinite patience of the hard-working Betty. It lasted sixteen years, during which Bird and Betty finally got to build their dream house and horse farm on an 80-acre tract in Barnegat, between the Garden State Parkway and Route 9. They sold the Acme in 1976.

Being a tavern owner was only a small part of Bird's very active life and varied interests, which included a first-rate art collection. He was widely recognized for his outstanding accomplishments in animal breeding and stock raising. His circle of friends and his reputation grew wider and wider. Finally, to cap it all off, the governor of Kentucky, on May 14, 1979, made Bird Garrett Clutter a full-fledged Kentucky colonel, a signal honor for a man who had worked so hard all his life. Bird, in ill health, died the following year. Betty moved to Florida to another dream house they had planned and built together on a lagoon in Fort Myers. Sadly, Bird had never had a chance to spend even one night there. Betty died fifteen years later in 1995 at the age of 79.

## "Hammy" the Game Warden, and Coast Guard Rumrunners

J. Hamilton Evernham was his lofty-sounding name. He was not a bank president, a railroad magnate, a philanthropist, or anything of the sort. In the 1920s, he was the most hated and feared man in southern Ocean County. So notorious was he in Beach Haven that the gatekeeper of the drawbridge would telephone the

Acme Hotel the moment his car was spotted crossing the causeway onto Long Beach Island. Restaurant and hotel owners shuddered every time he asked to see a menu. Everyone at the docks knew him on sight, and everyone avoided him. His nickname was "Hammy" as in the oft-repeated phrase "Watch out! Hammy's in town." J. Hamilton Evernham was the game warden.

Since 1918, Hammy Evernham had been using every trick and stratagem in the book to catch local gunners who were shooting ducks and geese out of season. He also tried to catch anyone who exceeded, in season, what now seems a rather generous bag limit of 30 a day per man. By 1926, he had caught just about everyone at least once. The fine was pretty stiff for the times — $20 a bird out of season, and the same for each one over the bag limit in season. That is also the fine that a hotel owner had to pay if he tried to cook and serve a game bird at any time of the year. The passage of the Federal Migratory Bird Act of 1918 had made all these acts illegal.

For generations on both sides of Little Egg Harbor Bay, ducks and geese (just like clams, oysters and fish) were a regular source of income for the local population. For most of the 19th century, market gunners shot birds from dawn till dusk all around the seasons and shipped them to the New York markets by boat and by train. Even the old gunning clubs, whose members shot hundreds of ducks at a single outing, sent their birds to the New York market. Nothing really went to waste, even though it was obvious to many that this prodigality might soon reduce the waterfowl population to near-extinction. After 1934, the eelgrass blight and two years of drought in the northern prairies made everyone notice what was happening — the once unbelievably abundant brant, and several other species, had all but disappeared from the Jersey marshlands.

In the mid-1920s, however, there was still plenty of ducks and geese. Residents and visitors firmly believed that it was everyone's right — especially if you were a native of the region — to kill as many as you wished. Not only was it great sport, but there was also a ready market for everything shot. It may have been illegal to exceed the limits or shoot out of season, but everyone winked

*A hunting party displays their kill on the porch of the Beck farm in Beach Haven. Many locals considered it their right to hunt as many ducks and geese as they wanted and considered game laws as ridiculous as Prohibition.*

*Dock Road, the Beach Haven public dock, and the Acme Hotel (to the right of the catboat mast) was a familiar setting for duck hunters, rumrunners, and enforcement officers. The Beach Haven Yacht Club building is at the center of this 1910 photograph.*

at the new game laws in the same way they disregarded the recently passed Eighteenth Amendment, which, since 1920, had forbidden the selling or transporting of alcoholic beverages. The only crime was getting caught. Watch out for the game warden. Watch out for the sheriff and the revenue agents. As for the Coast Guard — they were all family. There wasn't a young man in Beach Ha-ven who didn't have some connection with the Coast Guard — be it father, brother, cousin or good friend — at any of the several stations on Long Beach Island.

On a Wednesday morning, January 26, 1926, a very nicely dressed, handsome woman in an expensive car showed up at the Beach Haven Public Dock on Dock Road, seeking to purchase some freshly shot game. She said she had motored down from the city, and needed all she could get for a dinner party. She explained that it was a very unusual dinner party. Her husband was in a small, private hospital and she wanted to surprise him with a duck or goose dinner. The people who ran the hospital would not permit it unless she provided enough to serve all the other patients. It wasn't a very big place, but she would need all the game birds the men could find.

She certainly was the center of attention. A number of young men scurried to their boats and, although it was against the law to sell game birds, they had soon provided her with two dozen ducks and Canada geese at their asking price of $4 a bird. She did not quibble. She paid them in cash. They could scarcely believe their good fortune as she got them to write down their names and addresses for future sales. Giving them all a warm smile she waved goodbye as she drove off down Dock Road, with a trunk full of birds, shot out of season.

Later that very afternoon, Warden Evernham was in town. He made several arrests and took the men before Justice Edward F. Potter at West Creek. At a hearing in Potter's office Wednesday evening, fines were imposed on the four Beach Haven men involved in the transaction that morning, at the rate of $20 per bird for each one illegally sold to Mrs. Arnold. She was there to present all the evidence from the trunk of her car. Lauren Beer was fined $60, Elmer King, $220, Harvey Allen, $160 and William Meyers, $60. The total amount for the four men came to $500.

Today, it is difficult to imagine how angry the whole town of Beach Haven was over this matter. The local people felt that the game laws were absurd. A large number of them followed the game warden over to West Creek to register their protests at what they considered a cheap, underhanded trick. It was at this point, just after the fines were imposed, that Sheriff Grant appeared on the scene. He had received a telephone call at his office in Toms River telling him to hurry down to West Creek, where he would find "a little secret" in Warden Evernham's car. Tom Beer, keeper of the Loveladies Coast Guard Station, said that he had made the discovery himself.

The sheriff looked in the back seat of the car and found a pint bottle of whiskey. During Prohibition, it was illegal to transport whiskey. Beer, of the Loveladies station, was the father of Lauren Beer, one of the men arrested. The sheriff said that it looked a lot like a frame-up, but if the men who found it would swear out a warrant, he would arrest the warden. He said he would not, however, take him in. The talk was hot and bitter. The sheriff wound up taking Evernham back to Toms River in his car, leaving one of his deputies to drive the warden's car.

The woman who had bought the ducks, and thus laid the foundation for the arrests, was Mary C. Arnold of Point Pleasant Beach. She was one of Warden Evern-

*The causeway drawbridge gatekeeper in Manahawkin would telephone the Acme Hotel in Beach Haven when game warden J. Hamilton Evernham crossed the bridge.*

# Gunning on Ice

Joseph K. Ridgway, who was born in Barnegat, began his hotel career at Loveladies in the spring of 1875, when he took over proprietorship of the Long Beach Club House from Charles Cox. Ridgway remained in charge of the Club House until 1888, when he moved from Loveladies to Long Beach City (Surf City), to take charge of the Mansion House. The Mansion House acquired its name from having been built on the foundations of the old Mansion of Health on West Seventh Street. With the advent of the railroad in 1886, its location proved unsuitable, and it was moved to East Eighth Street just before Ridgway was made manager.

The following piece appeared in the *Ocean County Courier* in March of 1919.

## Why I Quit Gunning on Ice
### by Joseph K. Ridgway

To begin with, this will be a simple statement of facts. I was at the time keeping a hotel on Long Beach and my family lived at Barnegat during each winter. This particular winter had been very severe, but late in February we had a few warmer days and the wildfowl began to return from the South. The ice broke away from the flats and left an open lead about a half-mile wide and two miles long in a northwesterly direction from my house. In this lead were a thousand or more geese and black ducks. It

was past noon but I decided to go for 'em. With the help of a hired man, I pulled the boat over a half mile of ice between the beach and open water, then the man returned and I rowed to the northwest driving the fowl out as I went.

The iceberg that I wanted to shoot from was near the end of the open water, but I was not long in getting there and putting out the decoys. Putting on a white canvas shirt over my other clothes and white cover over my cap, I was soon ready for business. Lots of geese and ducks were in sight, and in less than five minutes a dozen geese were over the decoys and when the smoke cleared there were four dead ones drifting away from the decoys. For the next two hours I was fairly busy and fourteen geese and more than that many ducks were lying dead to the east of me. I had gathered none as I thought I could pick them all up on the way home.

The short afternoon was near gone, but I waited for just one more shot. Suddenly the ice began to move and looking to the northwest, I saw that a black squall of wind and snow was coming. Shoving the broken ice from the deck of my boat, I began pulling up the decoys but the squall struck. It was almost of hurricane force and I was glad to get into the lee of the iceberg to keep out of the way of the heavy ice that was now running. The roar of the gale and crushing ice was fearful and the temperature had dropped to near zero. All I could do was to wait for the squall to pass. It was dark before the ice stopped running. My decoys were either crushed or buried in the ice and I had

gathered but three of the geese and no ducks.

As soon as the ice stopped running, I headed for the beach, but dragging that boat over that rough ice was very hard work and I made slow progress. It was nine o'clock when I reached the Island a half mile west of the beach. Being very tired, I decided to leave the boat and take the chance of getting home without hitting open water, the ice having been perfectly solid from that point when I started out. I could see the light from my house and I headed straight for it carrying nothing but my gun. For the first hundred yards all was well,

then I walked into an air hole and the water was just deep enough to fill my hip boots. Gee, but that water was cold! It was but a few yards to solid ice and I soon scrambled out and again headed for the beach. A yard ahead of me the water and the ice looked the same. Fifty yards further on I broke in again. This time the water was a little deeper and I had to break the ice for several yards with my gunstock before it was solid enough to crawl out on. Next, I tried crawling over the ice, thinking it might bear my weight better, but had gone only a short distance before I went into open water head first. When I again got onto the ice, there wasn't a dry thread on me. My legs were numb and I could not get on my feet and I said to myself, "Joe, the game is up and you might as well quit now as later."

For a minute or two I lay still, then decided for one more try at it and began rolling over and over on the ice. This again started circulation, and presently, by using my gun as a brace, I got on my feet. My clothes were freezing on me, but fortunately I hit no more open water and soon reached the beach. Now I no

longer felt cold. I just wanted to lie down and rest, but I knew that if I lay down in that grass, I would never get up again. For a few yards I would hurry on and again the desire to lie down would seize me, but I kept going and at last reached the kitchen door and hit it with my gun. The housekeeper opened it and with the help of her sister they got me in the house. Later they said that I told them to give me hot whiskey, but I do not remember doing that.

Four o'clock next morning I woke up alongside the kitchen range, rolled up in blankets and sweating something fierce. The hired man had gone to the lifeguard station and those girls were alone with what they thought a dying man. Most of my clothes they had cut off — I know that I had none on when I awoke — and when morning came, I looked out over the ice and felt no desire whatsoever to go to an iceberg to shoot geese. And I don't to this day.

\* \* \*

Ridgway's story of why he quit gunning on ice was probably one he had told many times before being asked to write it. He does not say when it took place. It must have been in the 1890s, which was in the decade that he was in charge of Mansion House. The fact that the hired man left in the morning to go to the "Lifeguard station" meant he had a long walk to either Ship Bottom or Harvey Cedars and this would explain the length of his absence.

Ridgway uses the word "beach" several times in the course of this short narrative; he means Long Beach Island itself. Old time inhabitants of the region always refer to a barrier island as a "beach."

ham's regular decoys. The incident involving the whiskey in the warden's car was to confirm some suspicions that the sheriff had had for some time about the connections between the Coast Guard and the rumrunners. It would lead to an investigation and a bigger scandal than anyone could then possibly imagine.

The warden's sting operation in January 1926 at Beach Haven to catch a few game poachers would set in motion forces leading to the arrest, conviction and jailing of eleven Coast Guardsmen from the Ship Bottom station, and a scandal that involved all the other stations on the Island as well.

This incident at West Creek and the obviously phony charge made by Chief Beer convinced Sheriff Grant that the Coast Guard was actively involved in much of the local rum-running. He proceeded with a quiet investigation that soon centered on the Ship Bottom Coast Guard Station. The sheriff had first had his suspicions aroused the previous Thanksgiving weekend when, in hot pursuit of a suspicious car leaving Ship Bottom, he was stopped for speeding at the entrance to the causeway by two armed Coast Guardsmen. They, of course, apologized profusely when they "discovered" it was the sheriff. Still, they had held him just long enough, in the search for proof of his identity, to let the car he was chasing make a clean getaway onto the mainland.

Becoming more suspicious, the sheriff started planting his spies everywhere to gather evidence. The superintendent of all Coast Guard activities on the New Jersey coast came to Long Beach Island from Washington, D.C., in June, at the request of Sheriff Grant. He interrogated all of the men at each of the stations on Long Beach Island separately. The result was a breakdown, which exposed the whole story of the rum-running — what the men had been receiving and how the stuff was being landed.

The number one man, Tom Beer, had been bribed by the rum-running syndicate with the sum of $30,000. He was told to dole the money out among the men in his charge as an incentive for them simply to look the other way when they saw a suspicious boat lying off the beach at night. "Just don't interfere," they were told. Most of the stuff that wasn't coming through the inlets was being landed at night along the miles of empty beach between Loveladies and Beach Haven Terrace. He and the other keepers of the three stations responsible for the territory were getting $2 each for every case landed. A "case," during Prohibition, was usually six quart bottles in a padded and tightly wrapped burlap bag. Each case was worth $60 when delivered.

Within twenty-four hours, confessions had been obtained from eleven men besides the chief. There was a court martial in September, and all of them were sentenced to a year in Portsmouth Naval Prison. At the intervention of New Jersey State Senator Thomas Mathis, their sentences were reduced to four months. With time off for good behavior, they were all home in time for Christmas.

Rum-running, along the East Coast and elsewhere, continued unabated for another six years until the Eighteenth Amendment — admitted by nearly everyone to have been a mistake — was repealed in March of 1933. In that time from 1920 until 1933, it was never illegal to buy or drink alcohol. It was only illegal to sell, manufacture or transport it — and therein lay the contradiction. It was a law especially unenforceable in coastal areas. The long and proud tradition of the Coast Guard, whose strength came from its closeness to the local population, was tarnished by the scandal. But it should never be forgotten that these were the same men who often risked their lives in the pursuit of fast contact boats, operated by organized criminals, who did not hesitate to use guns.

# Good Times on the Island

## Ladies' Baseball

At Beach Haven in the 1890s, hotel guests sat in rocking chairs along the shaded piazzas of the Baldwin or the Engleside every other Sunday in July and August to watch a team sport called Ladies' Baseball. The two hotels played each other, and the participants on each team were drawn from the guest registers, although neighboring cottagers were always welcome to play on one side or the other. One week, the playing field would be Engleside Avenue and the next week Pearl Street.

Ladies' baseball was really not just for ladies. Old photographs show that nearly half of each hotel team was composed of clean-shaven young men in spotless Arrow shirts and neckties. They were also clad in ankle-length, women's skirts. These skirts were meant to handicap their running ability and make the games more fun for players and spectators alike. At 3:00, an hour or so after the big noon meal, an umpire called out "Play ball!" The game progressed with lots of cheering and applause from both sides up on the porches. To the male spectators, it was amusing to watch a woman try to throw a ball from the outfield all the way to first without a bounce. It was just as funny, however, to see a man, hobbled in a long skirt, try to snag a line drive in the infield or steal a base.

Both men and women players took the games seri-

*Male and female guests of the Baldwin and Engleside played Sunday afternoon baseball until about the first World War.*

ously and did their best to win. The college girls, certainly those who went to Vassar and Smith, where there were several organized intramural teams as early as the 1870s, knew all about being on a baseball team. At college, however, they were used to playing in the secluded atmosphere of a private campus, far from the eyes of men. And in those benighted times, men had a tendency to ridicule the efforts made by women to play team sports, no matter how good they were.

Sunday afternoon street games, with men in women's clothing playing right alongside the women, were not invented in Beach Haven. The contests were probably inspired by the very popular "Bloomer Girls" teams of the 1890s, who were then going about the nation challenging established sandlot, semi-professional or minor league teams for exhibition games. The Bloomer Girls were made up of both male and female players. Both sexes dressed in bloomers, those Turkish-style pantaloons made popular in the 1850s by the women's rights crusader Amelia Bloomer, and adopted by women nearly everywhere for sports. The men wore them to attract attention and to draw crowds.

The Bloomer Girls did not belong to a league and did not play each other. There were many of them around the country and, like the bearded and zany "House of David" teams out of Benton Harbor, Michigan and the many Negro teams as well, they relied on side-show antics to draw paying crowds. They loved the sport, but money was their ultimate goal. They were also quite good and rarely lost a game. Some of the women were outstanding athletes, but being on the Bloomer Girls was about as far as they could go in the world of professional baseball. Aspiring young men, on the other hand, had a chance to catch the attention of major league scouts. Being constantly on the move gave them better exposure. When the farm teams started up in the late 1920s and early '30s, it was the beginning of the end for the Bloomer Girls. The last of the Bloomer Girl teams disbanded in 1934, after forty years on the American scene.

Ladies' baseball at Beach Haven ceased somewhere around the eve of World War I, just about the time skirts were getting shorter, the causeway was built and the first automobile appeared on the side streets of town.

*America's pastime was certainly Beach Haven's pastime in the decades before World War I.*

# A Day in Old Beach Haven

From a handwritten, unsigned note.

Pound fishermen and horses bring ashore a morning's catch.

When I was very young (many, many, many years ago) this was our town:

In the early morning I would wake up and hear motors. The sound came from the pound boats (fish boats) out in the ocean. This meant the fishermen were up before dawn. They had big, powerful, open cockpit, heavy, strong boats that had to be pushed out over the breakers before the men could jump in, start the motor and steer out to the pound and their nets. The pounds were poles driven into the sea floor around which were nets strung to catch the fish as they swam by.

It was a thrill to me to see the boats come over the breakers. They were heavily laden with the catch and the men, usually four to a boat, were standing and ready to jump off and grab the rope that was waiting to be fastened to the bow to drag the boat up onto the beach.

Two big, powerful, black Percheron horses were hitched to the rope and then the men would put large logs under the keel. The foreman yelled and the horses would strain and strain and pull and pull and finally the boats were up on the beach — a safe distance from the high tides. As a treat — each horse was given a fish — a big one. Each horse ate it like a piece of cake — head, tail, bones and all.

Aunt Mary and I always walked up the beach to see the boats come in and we took our peach basket with us. You could buy fish right from the boat. You gave your basket to one of the big Norwegians in the boat and he would fill it and charge twenty-five cents! These men always looked extra big and powerful in their yellow oilskin overalls and jackets, of course. We walked home along the beach with our heavy basket and had to scale and clean the fish, but to me it was fun.

On days when we did not get up to meet the pound boats before 8:00 AM, we had to walk up Bay Avenue (the main drag) to Twelfth Street to the loading platform by the railroad tracks. There, the men were packing the fresh fish into the barrels with ice, nailing on the lids and lining them up on the edge of the platform ready to put on the baggage car to go to the big city.

When we walked along Bay Avenue from the loading station at Twelfth Street there were no houses or stores. Just wildlife — fields of tall grass, cattails, goldenrod, etc. It was a pretty sight. Along the path were tiny, tiny turtles and weeny hop toads, lots and lots of them. The female turtles would come up from the bay, cross over the main street, lay their eggs in the field and go back to the bay again. There were not many cars in the "good old days." As for the tiny hop toads — they were to grow to be big helpful friends and eat the bugs, flies and mosquitoes that are so bothersome to humans.

Our grocery stores were not like today's. One that I loved was Charlie Cramer's — opposite the present library on Beach Avenue just before Third Street. He had everything — almost — to sell. There were lots of cookies, cheese, vegetables, ham, etc. For milk, I always had to go with my nickel to the back of the Engleside Hotel for my bottle of milk. In those days, milk came in a glass bottle and was only five cents!

When it was "crabbing day" I would go south on Beach Avenue to the corner of Amber Street to Mr. Cale's meat shop to get bait. It was rotten smelling stuff but it did the trick. For ten cents Mr. Cale would fill my bag and off I would go. Happy, I would take a net, basket, line, sinker and bait down to the end of Dock Road and crab.

Another store was Penrod's just across the street from Cale's. Penrod sold everything too. I always had to take the oilcan to get coal oil for the lamps. In those days there was no electricity or gas. We did not have electric refrigerators, just an icebox. It was something like a large blanket chest with a lid and several shelves inside. The shelves were slate

and there was a large space on the bottom for a piece of ice. The ice man would come every day to the back door carrying your order — twenty-five pounds or more — in a heavy iron ice tong resting on his hip.

Around early afternoon people would gather to sit and chat on the beach. The children played and jumped on the sand dunes, which were very big then. We would climb up and slide down. Great fun! In the evening we always walked on the boardwalk before turning in. Many times we would see the phosphorescence when the waves broke and wonder at the magic.

Evening and bedtime were different, too. When the wind was west, the odors from the fish factory that was over on the bay towards Tuckerton were horrible. In a west wind, we could also hear the motors thumping in the icehouse on the corner of Engleside and Beach Avenue. Sometimes, if it were not too late, I would go with my mother to see the moon rise over the ocean.

Today, it is a far cry from our small, pleasant country town of long ago. It was friendly. Everyone knew everyone else and where he or she lived. We didn't bother to learn the names of the streets either. It was a very pleasant, healthy place to live.

## The Circus and Other Nightlife

Early in the 20th century, any small town on the route of a railroad was likely to be visited by a traveling tent circus. All that such a show needed was enough land near the tracks to set up tents and equipment. Beach Haven, in the 1920s, still had plenty of open land in the meadows near the station. The circuses that did come were not large. Usually they were of the one ring variety: several horses and riders, a trapeze, an elephant or two, and perhaps a tiger and a bear. There was always a sideshow with the standard fat lady and thin man, a few monsters, usually fake, and enough fortune-tellers and hucksters to snare the unwary. There was a band concert and often a popular tent show reserved for men, age twenty and over, who paid to watch sequined and feathered hootchie-kootchie dancers perform in various stages of undress.

The lights and the calliope music came from electric generators in the nearby railroad cars belonging to the circus. The site usually chosen for the one-day and one-night event in Beach Haven was a big, empty lot on the west side of Bay Avenue, between Third and Fifth Streets. During the day, the elephants were paraded through town to advertise the circus. Citizens were warned quite frankly by the *Ocean County Courier* to keep their doors locked at night, because there were always certain "low types" who worked with the circus as roustabouts. There was, however, seldom any serious crime beyond the raiding of clotheslines at night. Some circus hands, it seemed, could never get enough towels and damp woolen bathing suits.

Beach Haven (and the whole Island) prided itself on being a family resort, devoted to ocean bathing and

*Elephants parade in front of the Engleside Hotel to advertise that evening's circus.*

games and sports, such as sailing, gunning and fishing. Other than the very infrequent visits by the circus, there were no honky tonk amusements of the sort to be found in Atlantic City. The Beach Haven boardwalk, built in 1898, was doubled in size to a mile and a quarter in 1917, but it didn't have an amusement arcade until the late 1920s. The boardwalk had fewer than six businesses on it when it was destroyed during the 1944 hurricane.

Nightlife on the Island was quite limited, unless one was staying at one of the big hotels. There were no movie theaters to go to until 1914, and there were only about six bars on the whole Island — nearly all of them in Beach Haven. There were dances at the big hotels, but

they were dressy affairs limited to guests and cottagers. Going outside after dark was not much fun because of the mosquitoes. Most people stayed home and played cards in screened porches, or headed for the beach to build fires out of a seemingly unlimited supply of driftwood. The earliest accounts of Brant Beach and Ship Bottom always mention the well-attended community clambakes and marshmallow roasts.

Beach fires, absolutely forbidden today, were first interrupted by the coastal blackouts of the two world wars. What ultimately put an end to them was the building of oceanfront houses right on the dunes. These structures were potentially endangered by wind-driven sparks, so ordinances were passed in every community. By the late 1950s, the oldest and perhaps best Long Beach Island tradition was gone forever. Two whole generations have never shared the experience of a beach party or clambake on the sand. Those fortunate enough to remember the 1950s agree that there has never been anything at the shore as much fun as a beach party with a nice fire, a blanket, a good date, plenty of cold beer and someone in the crowd with a ukulele to accompany the singing.

## Ocean County Day, 1922

Ocean County Day, July 15, 1922, one of the best planned events ever held on Long Beach Island, had little to do with the county itself and almost everything to do with Beach Haven. The Ocean County Society of Philadelphia, the sponsor of the event, had been formed only the previous fall, especially for that purpose. The society was led by Robert Engle of the Engleside, Beach Haven's staunchest promoter, and Island realtor Lafayette Taylor. Enthusiasm for the forthcoming event began to mount with a February dinner at the Hotel Adelphia, followed by a big theater party in May.

Saturday, July 15 was chosen for the date, and headquarters would be at the Engleside Hotel in Beach Haven. The Ocean County Society invited track and field athletes from Haverford College and the University of Pennsylvania to participate in the full day of competitive sports. The Pennsylvania Railroad scheduled a special excursion train from Philadelphia to Beach Haven and back. It was to leave the city at 6:44 AM and depart Beach Haven that evening at 8:00 PM. In the morning there would be brief stops at Barnegat and Manahawkin for the band to get out on the platform and play and for a brief address; then it was on to Beach Haven.

*A pie-eating contest was part of the fun during 1922's Ocean County Day.*

About three hundred persons took the excursion train, many more came by other trains, and hundreds motored across the causeway bridge from various parts of the county. In the morning hours, a crowd of a thousand or more gathered on the boardwalk to watch sports like tug-of-war and wheelbarrow and three-legged races on the beach, followed by various dashes held on the graveled street in front of the Engleside Hotel. College champions fresh from the Penn Relays left local athletes in the dust.

Joe Sprague of Beach Haven recalled one of those moments vividly. He was using his foot as a starting block for his older brother Edward in the 50-yard dash. "The gun went off and Eddie might as well have been standing still. The college boys were already at the finish line." Edward was much better at ocean swimming, though. Later in the day, he took the free-style event, which began with a dive from a wooden float anchored out beyond the breakers off the Amber Street beach and finished at the same place, after a turn around a buoy off Centre Street two blocks to the north. His prize was an Ingersol watch.

Swimming and fancy diving exhibitions, given by a squad of professional women athletes (in white bath-

ing caps and blue woolen suits) at the dock of the Little Egg Harbor Yacht Club, drew crowds to the bay side of the Island. Spectators filled the upper decks of the club-house to watch flawless performances of every popular swimming stroke. It was not a perfect summer day. There was intermittent rain, but everyone enjoyed the events, especially a late-afternoon game of baseball on the old field at Seventh Street, across from the school. Beach Haven beat Tuckerton by a close score of 3 to 2 in twelve innings.

It had been a long day of fun and picnics and even — for some of the winners of events — a seaplane ride. Nearly everyone, including most of the children, got a chance to participate in a sport. At 8:00 PM, just as the train was pulling out of the Third Street Station, the Ocean County Society of Philadelphia sat down in the Engleside dining room for a long dinner and congratu-latory speeches. Most of its membership had a financial stake in the future development of Long Beach Island and, to them, it had been a job well done. So well done, in fact, that they later decided it would be impossible to whip up that degree of enthusiasm ever again. It had served its purpose. Ocean County Day 1922 was to be the one and only event of its kind.

*Track and field athletes from Haverford and the University of Pennsylvania competed with locals in front of the Engleside Hotel on the one and only Ocean County Day. Three-legged races and tug-of-war contests on the beach were all part of the fun.*

*In this photograph of Beach Haven from the 1930s, Walsh Field is a landmark, along with the Engleside and Baldwin hotels on the oceanfront, and the Little Egg Harbor Yacht Club on the bay.*

## Walsh Field, Boxing, and Baseball

In the summer of 1926, Beach Haven got a new baseball field. Walsh Field was dedicated on July 31. Three weeks after the baseball season had ended, on an unseasonably cold, overcast September evening, a crowd of men in overcoats filed into Beach Haven's big, new double-decker grandstand. It was chilly enough for football, but that was not to be the sport played that evening. It was boxing. This was Beach Haven's first, and only, fight night.

The fans paid 25 cents to watch eight bouts. The events were staged at three rounds apiece and held in a ring erected in front of the grandstand so that every customer had a clear view of the participants, who had all been matched by weight. They were nearly all local men in their 20s and the only one who had ever had even a modicum of boxing training was local baseball hero "Iron Man" Joe Sprague. He had no trouble out-pointing Mickey Matherson, "The Fighting Mail Carrier," who actually outweighed him by forty pounds.

Sprague, in an interview just before his death at the age of 99, recalled that evening vividly. He remembered Bert Stratton, in a long overcoat, bellowing out, "In this corner Vic Hayes, the South Carolina boy, weighing in at 140... In this corner Johnnie Crosta of North Beach Haven... In this corner Watson (Kinky) Pharo of Beach Haven." According to the reporters, Watson and his opponent from Beach Arlington danced around each other for three rounds and put the crowd to sleep. Most of the fights were equally lackluster. There were no knockouts and nobody got hurt, but a decision had to be made in each case to declare a winner. There was a lot of cheering and betting, and a lot of fun. One of the best bouts of the evening was between Maurice Hart, another "Fighting Mail Carrier," and Lawrence "Whiskey" Beer, both weighing in at 156. The ropes around the ring were so loose competitors were more worried about going off

*Walsh Field, shortly after it was built in 1926, hosted baseball, boxing and soldiers during World War II. Today it is the location of Beach Haven's public tennis courts.*

the edge than their opponent's punches.

Everyone watched the sky anxiously. Thick clouds obscured the setting sun, but a big moon was rising over the ocean. The fighters shivered when they took their robes off, but the reporters covering the matches declared them all to be such "whirling, waltzing windmills" that they never really felt the cold. To keep themselves warm, some of the well-wrapped spectators carried flasks of bootleg booze, not hard to obtain in Beach Haven during Prohibition. There were a couple of profes-

sionals from Philadelphia who put on a good show, and the evening ended before it got too dark to see the ring.

It was to be another five years before Walsh Field had lighting for night baseball. The first game played under the newly installed arc lights was between Beach Haven and the strange, braided and bewhiskered — but highly competitive — House of David team out of Benton Harbor, Michigan. The House of David teams roamed the country for decades from about 1900 until the mid-1930s, playing and defeating semi-professional teams

everywhere. There was more than one House of David team on tour in those years. They proved to be a great attraction to the baseball-minded public, who probably knew little of the despotic religious cult to which they belonged back in Michigan. Devotees of its rigid Old Testament style faith were brainwashed into total submission and poverty by perverted King Ben and Queen Mary, to whom they gave up all their property in exchange for salvation. They were worked like slaves in various highly profitable enterprises while the shrewd

*A 1920s Beach Haven team that won 40 out of 49 games. Left to right, first row: Lud Wray, Clarence (Tuck) Parker, Chris Sprague, "Weary" Walker, Edward Sprague; second row: Charles Cramer, Yeomon Penrod, George "Tip" Barclay, A. Paul King, Alec Wray.*

It was badly in need of painting and there were complaints from nearby residents that it had become an eyesore. Many boards were loose and it was actually dangerous on the upper levels. Eventually, the stand and the high fence around the field were torn down.

When World War II, with its blackouts and beach patrols, came to Beach Haven, a company of the Army and the New Jersey State Guard used Walsh Field for an encampment. Prior to the invasion of Normandy, they would all be transferred to England, but during the winter of 1942-43, they lived in neat rows of four-man pyramidal tents heated by kerosene stoves. The mess hall, latrines and showers were located in long, wooden buildings at the edge of Ocean Street, on the very site of the former grandstand. Once the war was over, baseball at Beach Haven was not resumed. It was the end of a tradition that had lasted more than fifty years. In 1936, Walsh Field became the site of the public tennis courts.

## The Lucy Evelyn At Christmas

One memory of the *Lucy Evelyn*, cargo schooner turned gift shop, evokes the holiday season. A single decorated spruce atop the tallest of her three masts always signaled the Christmas shopping season, luring visitors from far and wide to marvel at the fine quality and infinite variety of her merchandise. It scarcely seems possible that decades have come and gone since the terrible fire, on a windy February night in 1972, took her from Beach Haven forever.

Let the "Ghost of Christmas Past" transport us back across the decades to West Ninth Street, to that familiar thick door, cut into the starboard side hull, near the waterline of the huge, black ship. It opens and we enter

King and Queen made millions for themselves. It was not the first such cult in American history, nor was it the last. Grover Cleveland Alexander, known as Alexander the Great, the former Philadelphia Phillies pitching star and Hall of Famer, managed the House of David teams. They played many times at Beach Haven.

"Donkey baseball" was another attraction at Walsh Field in the 1930s. It was always advertised well in advance to assure a crowd. It was not so much a sporting event as it was good for laughs. As with any baseball game, there was a pitcher, a catcher and a couple of fielders. The batter, once he had swung and hit the ball, had to jump on a donkey and ride to the bases. But donkeys have wills of their own, and it might take forever to get such a stubborn beast to walk, much less go in the direction of first base. The rider could not touch the ground until he had got his donkey to the right bag, and then he had to remount to get to the next one, if he could, while another batter tried to get to first. There were penalties for taking too long or for leaving the infield. The real fun began when the bases were loaded, and the players were all hollering at each other and at their mounts, while the crowd laughed and cheered.

In the late 1930s, the popularity of hometown baseball began to wane with the formation of county and regional teams. No longer were teams made up exclusively of local boys. Attendance dropped. By 1941, the big, wooden grandstand, once painted bright green to match the fence around the field, had begun to decay. Fifteen years of exposure to sun, wind and rain had taken its toll.

*For two decades, the* Lucy Evelyn *was as much a Long Beach Island landmark as Barnegat Lighthouse and, during the holidays, it was a special focal point and a requisite shopping visit.*

a magical world. Outside, chill winds howl in off the Atlantic, but inside, in the glint of copper, brass and crystal, with the buzz of happy conversation, muted carols and the chinging of cash registers, the first of our senses to be aroused is smell. We are overwhelmed by the pleasant fragrance of bayberry candles, scented soaps, potpourri and oiled hardwood, mingled with ancient timber and tar, dried rope, metal polish, oakum and pitch. There has never been anything like it. Today, were one

to chance upon even a trace of those mingled scents, it would open the floodgates of memory.

Our eyes adjust to winter light filtering through a huge skylight, panes ticking with sleet, that had once been a cargo hatch. Beneath the skylight hangs a massive ship's wheel of mahogany and brass, now converted into a chandelier. At night and on dim days, the chandelier illuminates a round table, ten feet below it, made from a matching ship's wheel. The table is cov-

ered in glass and artfully decorated with place settings of china, glass, pewter and crockery from all over the world. Betty Ewer (who, with her husband, Nat, bought the ship in New Bedford, Massachusetts in 1948 and had it towed to Beach Haven) changes the arrangement on the table every other day. The table display is seldom the same. The theme right now is Christmas, but in a week, it will be filled with porcelain angels, crystal champagne glasses, little brass horns, silver bells and clocks, to symbolize the coming New Year.

The cavernous interior of the ship reaches half the length of a football field, obstructed only by the butt ends of the three masts, which at this level are ten feet around. The hardwood floor slopes upward toward the narrow bow where there is a figurehead of a mermaid whimsically placed on the inside. Here are leather goods of exquisite softness, made to last a lifetime — gloves, wallets, handbags and the incomparable Etienne Aigner shoes. There are silk scarves and little girl's dresses, hand stitched and smocked.

Overhead, the massive ceiling beams, fifteen feet up amidships, are hung with long, highly polished oars used to hold and hook mugs and steins of every shape and size. Shelves full of Hummels, figurines of pirates and sailors, encircle each of the masts. On every horizontal surface there are sets of Royal Copenhagen, Royal Doulton and Irish Belleek. Among thick salad bowls of teakwood and walnut, heavy brass ship's lamps glow through green and red glass.

In the roomy stern of the ship we find everything for the home bar: myriad sets of glasses, silver corkscrews, tall sangria pitchers and cocktail shakers of the finest quality. For the sailor — real and would-be — there are brass telescopes, barometers, thermometers, sextants, signal flags, rain gear and framed prints of sea battles. In every corner are deep wicker baskets filled with nautical charts rolled up and tied with ribbon, like ancient scrolls.

Most of the south, or starboard, side of the ship's interior is taken up with the long checkout counter, cluttered with impulse purchase items. There are glass cases of exquisite jewelry, managed by Peg Taylor, who has been with Nat and Betty Ewer since the shop opened on Memorial Day, 1949. Near each cash register are open jars filled with stick candy in a variety of striped colors and flavors, like beach plum, root beer and pineapple. Nearly everyone buys one on the way out.

This was the *Lucy Evelyn*. Nostalgia for it only grows; to this day, in many households on Long Beach Island, older occupants — if they lived here in the 1950s and '60s — will point with pride to some object, however small, and say, "This came from the *Lucy Evelyn*."

## Long Beach Township Lifeguards

In 1952, there were fewer than sixteen guards on the Long Beach Township Beach Patrol. It was Captain Art Jocher's first year. All of the guards were really impressed with Art, and no one ever questioned his authority. He was a born leader. In those early years, the patrol covered only about five miles out of the township's total eleven miles of territory. Guarded beaches extended from Fifteenth Street in North Beach Haven to Thirty-seventh Street in Brant Beach, five blocks short of the Ship Bottom line. There was also a guard, usually the only girl on the patrol, at the bay-bathing beach. North of Surf City, the township territory was not covered at all, because the beaches there were all privately owned, and only a handful of people used them. Loveladies, with only a few scattered houses, was a desolate stretch of mountainous sand dunes. As for Holgate, there would probably not have been a guard there, either, if the owner of the trailer park had not asked for one. Art visited all of his lifeguards at least once a day in his jeep, which he drove only on the streets, never on the beach. There was little traffic on the roads back then.

The lifeguards cherished their regular beaches, where they got to know the people who returned year after year. The regulars usually watched their own children and they knew and respected the ocean. They took turns making lunches for the guards, and always bought tickets for the lifeguards' dances, which were held twice every summer, at the end of July and at the end of August. These dances were an important source of additional revenue, and lifeguards sold tickets in the evenings, house to house, in their territories. Cocktail hour was the best time to sell tickets. Neighbors would be gathered together on porches and in living rooms, thinking about how best to spend the remaining weeks of summer.

With only sixteen guards then, the dances were easily managed affairs. Members of the beach patrol were expected to wear white dinner jackets, which they either owned or rented, and their dates wore long gowns with corsages. The dance was held in the assembly room of the municipal building. An orchestra was hired and the whole room was decorated with fishnet and balloons. The front lawn, which was much wider then when the highway had only two lanes, was set up with tables and chairs. There was ice, and all of the set-ups were contributed by local merchants.

There was never more than one guard to each beach. It was pleasant work being outside all day, near the water, getting a nice tan and talking to the girls. Lifeguards were paid from $45 to $60 a week. Although that doesn't sound like very much now, in those years you could rent a decent room, almost anywhere on the Island, for $15 a week. Most of the guards lived with their parents. They worked six days a week, from 10:00 AM until 5:00 PM. They were lucky indeed if it rained, because they didn't have to go to the beach at all and still got paid. They didn't even have to report to the captain, but if the sun came out, the guards were expected to show up — and

Long Beach Township Beach Patrol, 1953: Front, left to right: Nicholas Bradshaw, James Draper, John Lloyd, Robert Flanigan; second row: Nicholas Coles, Vincent Abbattiello, John Brudon, Mary Ann Deiniger, Daniel Gothie, Richard Grob; third row: Dennis Griffin, James Griffith, Ronald Weidler, Arthur Jocher (Captain), Harris Ward, George Mulqueen, John Labash. (Missing: Albert Stevens, Howard Rosell)

and that is the white sun helmet. They went out of style in the early 1970s. Art Jocher said the guards wouldn't wear them anymore, and just sailed them around like Frisbees, preferring, instead, a simple tennis visor.

Those red jackets were great for hitchhiking. No one would pass up a lifeguard. And in the 1950s guards could still wear their red lifeguard jackets in a bar. Later some people complained that it wasn't right for them to advertise their presence in a bar at 3:00 AM. and still be going on the beach the next day. After 1954, guards couldn't wear them at night anymore.

## Fun With DDT

Back in the 1950s and '60s on quiet summer evenings at the shore, there was never a sound that excited children more than the hiss of the approaching DDT, or as it was called, the "Drop Dead Twice" truck. Not even the tinkling bell of the Good Humor man could stir an equal frenzy, as kids on every block dashed out into the street to run alongside the slow-moving vehicle, usually a jeep, as it spewed out the long, gray gas cloud that killed all the gnats and mosquitoes.

The idea was to run just ahead of the trailing cloud, to play tag with it, but if you got shoved into it or ran through the mist on a dare, it didn't really matter because no mosquito would bite you for the rest of the evening. You could breathe it and even rub it into your hair. DDT was good for you and bad for bugs.

Even the adults half believed this, sitting on their screened porches at cocktail hour. When the thick mist from the jeep enveloped them, they simply put a hand over their gin and tonics, and someone might put a napkin over the dip, until the air was clear again.

If the jeep passed upwind when dinner was actual-

they did.

Everyone on the Long Beach Township Beach Patrol got new equipment at the beginning of each season, which was theirs to keep. They got a cork ring-buoy, a sun helmet, a blue canvas bathing suit and an Acme Thunderer whistle, but their most prized piece of equipment was a thick, woolen lifeguard jacket. They were beauti-

fully made, red with dark blue and white trim, and the letters LBTBP (Long Beach Township Beach Patrol) in white across the front. They had raglan shoulders, snaps instead of buttons, and being 100 percent wool, were comfortable in all kinds of weather.

Lifeguards look pretty much the same today as they did forty-five years ago. But one item of wear is definitely gone,

ly on the table, there might be a rush to shut the windows, but otherwise people did not care whether they breathed the stuff or not. And they were probably right, because DDT, one of the most effective killers of flying insects ever invented, has never been proven to harm human beings.

Evidence began mounting, though, that DDT was upsetting the food chain and killing off the bird population. We first heard about it in 1962, when Rachel Carson's book *Silent Spring* was serialized in the *New Yorker*. Nothing much was done, however, to stop the spraying until a full decade had passed.

The last year for the mosquito trucks was 1972, but by then there were fewer mosquitoes anyway. The bayside meadows, the best breeding areas for mosquitoes on Long Beach Island, had been filled with sand and gravel and were rapidly being built upon.

The first serious attempts to eradicate the salt water mosquito began as early as 1900. Ditches were dug in the meadows on both sides of the bay to drain the many stagnant pools, allowing the tide to wash in the small fish called "killies," or "killifish," which ate the mosquito larvae, or "wrigglers," just before they were ready to grow wings. It was a good start. By 1924, nearly a thousand miles of ditches had been uniformly dug, 25 inches deep and 10 inches wide, in the marshlands of New Jersey. That was also the year of the introduction of a massive device called the ditching machine.

All of the early ditches had been dug by hand at considerable expense. By the 1930s, with the invention of the huge ditching machine, the cost had been reduced to a

*Spraying a Long Beach Island salt marsh pond with insecticide in the 1930s, top. Bottom, DDT is sprayed on a street in the Dunes section of Long Beach Township in the 1950s.*

penny a foot. Ten thousand miles of ditches were soon to criss-cross the salt water meadows of southern New Jersey. Then operated by the Federal Works Progress Administration these monster vehicles, eighteen feet high with extra-wide caterpillar treads, advanced over the grassy areas at low tide, straddling new paths as they rapidly and precisely scooped down into the thick mud, with an endless chain of sharpened steel buckets. Robert F. Engle, president of the Ocean County Mosquito Extermination Commission and proprietor and owner of the Engleside Hotel in Beach Haven, advocated the spreading of fuel oil in the marshes, despite the harm it might do to aquatic birds. Little of that was ever done on the Island. Fuel oil was used mainly to combat the fresh water mosquito, which bred in stagnant, non-tidal waters. Engle did not live to see the widespread use of DDT.

The filling in of the many ponds that once dotted the Island has nearly eliminated the freshwater mosquito. These ponds or bogs, often well hidden in dense thickets of bayberry, were low areas midway between the bay and the ocean. They were fed by springs, and proved to be perfect breeding grounds for the kind of mosquito that also bred in rain barrels and buckets.

Few people realize how bad the mosquito problem once was on the Island. We see old photographs of people at the shore wearing far too many clothes than would seem comfortable on a summer afternoon. It wasn't only fashion; it was the constant presence of gnats, flies and greenheads, which we now get only a small taste of when there is a moist west wind for a few days.

# "Shoobie"

"Shoobie" is a distinctively South Jersey expression, meaning a person who visits the seashore for a single day, primarily to use the beach. (The term was never applied to the fishermen who were also making day trips.)

*It has been said that "shoobie" is a slang formation of "shoebox" or "shoe-boxer," meaning someone who carries his lunch to the beach in such a container. However, the question arises as to why anyone would ever want to use a shoebox for anything other than a card file. They are certainly not airtight. The lids won't stay on. And how many pairs of shoes would a significant percentage of day visitors have to buy in order to*

*get enough boxes for them to become symbolic?*

*I was a lifeguard for six years in the late 1940s and early 1950s, first at Surf City and then at Long Beach Township. In six years, I never once saw anyone eat lunch out of a shoebox. Admittedly, our regular neighborhood beaches were not generally frequented by day-trippers, but, I did, from time to time, have to take my turn on the south end of the Island. We guards all hated the Holgate beach and referred to it as "Siberia." It was far from the other lifeguards, and our ordinary customers, and was made up almost entirely of day-trippers. They didn't understand the surf and took unnecessary risks. Otherwise, they were nice people who had come to the shore for the day to have fun, get badly sunburned and eat as many hot dogs as they* could. Why would they bring shoeboxes to carry food? The answer is that they never did carry shoeboxes. They were the food vendor's best customers. Still, we called them "shoobies."

In the post World War II years, when prosperity and the automobile were bringing more and more day-trippers to the shore during the summer, I first became aware of "shoobies." In 1948, my parents summered in North Beach, then known as the Frazier Tract, while all of my friends were in Surf City. In those years, there were fewer than twenty teenaged boys in the whole town. As for girls, they were all our younger or older sisters, and so we, 15- and 16-year-old boys, all hung out together in front of Ken Smith's store at Eighth Street and the Boulevard near the Surf City Hotel.

The one thing we all had in common, besides a love of jokes and the latest information on new automobiles, was that we never wore shoes and neither, for that matter, did anyone else on the Island in those years. Being at work was different, but going barefoot all the rest of the time was part of being at the shore. The soles of our feet were as tough as leather and we could spot a "shoobie" from a mile away.

We used to see strangers get out of their cars in their bathing suits — where they had changed we never knew — but they would be wearing street shoes to walk the graveled side streets up to the beach. "Here come the 'shoobies'" we would say. Their feet were too tender for the gravel and there were no sidewalks to use. At the end of the street, where the sand started, they would often remove their shoes and leave them all parked in a row under the benches. Canvas tennis shoes were unknown to "shoobies." Women wore sandals and their kids wore ankle-high, black basketball shoes. Flip-flops were a whole generation away. Once in a while you would actually see someone on the sand, well above the water line of course, wearing a bathing suit and strolling along in brown or black leather oxfords with socks. He would be your quintessential "shoobie."

It all has to do with wearing shoes while the inside crowd did not, by custom, wear them. Though a "b" has been added to word, it has a purpose. You can't say "shooey" with ease and "shoosey" would be baby talk and a little too cute. "Shoobie" is the perfect formation. It also has a slight rhyme with "rube," meaning hayseed, and even summons up that connotation. Never for a moment did it have an ethnic or class connotation. Most "shoobies" did not even know they were "shoobies," because they were never taunted. They were simply observed, and perhaps commented upon by summer residents and natives alike, all of whom felt a measure of superiority for having tough feet. "Shoobies" are not so easy to spot anymore, because we are living in an era when all of us wear shoes everywhere but on the beach itself.

# Out of the Past

## Gas Lighting

In 1901, at the dawn of the 20th century, when the world seemed full of marvelous new inventions like the telephone, railroad, telegraph, the electric light and the gasoline engine, Long Beach Island had them all, save one — municipal electric lighting.

When the sun went down over the bay, people did what they had fifty years earlier; they got out candles or kerosene lanterns and struck a wooden match. Beach Haven had some forty street lamps set atop wooden posts around town and on the boardwalk. They were all filled with just the right amount of kerosene during the day, so that when the town lamplighter lit them at dusk, they would all burn out just after dawn.

The first building in Beach Haven to install any form of lighting other than kerosene was the Engleside Hotel. The hotel was gas-lit in 1895 with more than a hundred lights throughout the three-story structure, a far cry from the days when guests had to light their way to bed with small lamps set up for them in the lobby by porters. The Hotel Baldwin followed soon after, and, within the decade, several summer cottages and the Corinthian Yacht and Gun Club on the southwest corner of Marine Street and Beach Avenue all had their own private acetylene gas plants. These systems were expensive, but proved so effective that the town was inspired to build a gas house on the site of today's borough hall for street lighting and for public buildings. It cost the taxpayers $10,000.

Acetylene gas is generated when calcium carbide pellets are poured through a funnel into water enclosed in a heavy upright tank. The opening at the top is immediately sealed shut so that the gas that is generated has no place to escape except through a small-gauge, copper pipeline connected to remote gas fixtures. When any one of these fixtures is opened with a valve, the gas, which can be lit with a spark or match, will burn with a bright, clear, odorless flame. Unlike natural gas, which comes from deep within the earth, artificially produced acetylene gas is not very suitable for cooking and was used only for light.

Beach Haven's acetylene plant was ready in June of 1908, when sixty-five lamps on every street and the boardwalk were turned on, illuminating the resort as never before. The new lampposts, more stylish than the old wooden kerosene lampposts, were tall, gracefully curved and made of iron. The gas was turned on at the gashouse by the twisting of a single valve. Once the gas was on and flowing, the lamps all had to be individually lit by the town's official lamplighter, Thomas H. Crane. Using a battery pack and wire on a long pole, he went swiftly from lamp to lamp, striking sparks until each lamp flared into bright light. The lamps were extinguished all at the same time every morning with a simple turn of the gas valve at the plant.

The Baldwin and the Engleside eventually installed coal-burning generators for electric lighting, and there

*The first lights in Beach Haven, like this one on the boardwalk, burned kereosene and were lit by hand.*

were several houses around town with similar expensive systems. The most ambitious of those was the massive Lord family cottage, built on the corner of Chatsworth and Atlantic avenues in 1920. When all the electric lights were turned on, the glow from the great dining and living room windows of the house was a marvel to behold from the boardwalk. Other communities on Long Beach Island continued to make do with kerosene lanterns until the spring of 1927. There was one exception, however, and that was Brant Beach. As early as 1911 it had the very first public electric lighting on the Island.

*Electricity was brought to Beach Haven in 1921 and the boardwalk, seen in these 1930s photographs, was wired for electric lamps.*

Henry McLaughlin, the founder of Brant Beach, had drilled an artesian well and built a water tank on a tall tower to supply pressure. He used a gasoline engine to pump water into the tank, and, each evening, he switched the belt from the pump to an electric generator so that about twenty houses in the area were provided with low-wattage lighting each summer evening from 8:00 until about 11:30 — a delightful novelty at the shore in those years.

As good as it was for lighting, Beach Haven's municipal acetylene system, when introduced to private houses, was found to be impractical for cooking. This evoked a demand for natural gas. Beach Haven, however, elected to build an electric generating plant fueled by coal.

This plant was finally ready in 1921, and once more, all the existing lights around town were modified. This transition also prompted the town to erect more lampposts. The new abundance of light caused some complaints among the younger folk. "Centre Street," said one, "with its beautiful, shadowy trees, was now too bright to be the delightful lovers' lane it always was."

Public electric lighting did not come to the rest of the Island until February 1927, when Atlantic City Electric ran cables across the bay, and utility poles were erected along the entire 18-mile length of the Boulevard. The first years of electricity were filled with mishaps. Transformers, not constructed to withstand the Island's dampness and salt air, often exploded, throwing several blocks of streets at a time into darkness. It sometimes took days to get these transformers replaced.

Atlantic City Electric eventually purchased the Beach Haven electric generating plant for $90,000 and built a storage facility for spare parts. In May of 1929, the State Highway Commission installed lights on the causeway bridge, and the Island fully entered the modern era.

*Acetylene gas plants like the Baldwin's, above, provided the first lights on the Island. Beach Haven built an acetylene gas plant for street lighting in 1908.*

## Water Towers

There has always been fresh surface water of varying quality on New Jersey's barrier islands. This water may not have been as potable all the year 'round as water on the mainland, but it was certainly good enough for the cattle and horses sent there to roam and breed in Colonial times.

One of the largest areas of fresh water on Long Beach Island during this time was the Great Swamp, which once covered all of the northern half of Surf City. White cedars grew to an impressive size there, until a violent 1821 hurricane swept the ocean through the dunes and

into the swamp, killing the trees. There were several other low areas, some fed by natural springs, which formed ponds that attracted wildfowl by the thousands. Wild cranberries grew in a Spray Beach pond. Purkey's Pond, in Holgate, was pure enough, at least in winter, that the ice cut from it was used by guests of the Engleside Hotel in July and August.

Drinkable as the water in these ponds might have been in winter and spring, in the heat of summer the water turned brackish, as the ponds shrank in size and stagnated, under great clouds of mosquitoes. To compensate, all Island cottages had some means of gathering rainwater. But that was never an adequate resource for the big hotels in the early days, and water had to be brought over in barrels from the mainland.

Another source of fresh water lay in great abundance only about fifteen feet underground atop an impermeable layer of peat moss. It was trapped rainwater

*Beach Haven's first water tower was a cedar tank 75 feet high on a wooden frame, built in 1893 on Engleside Avenue.*

*Two Centuries of History* **65**

*Ship Bottom-Beach Arlington's new standpipe and water works were featured in this postcard, above. At left, Beach Haven's old cedar tank had begun to leak badly, and a distinctive new water tower replaced it in 1911; it was a quaint Island landmark until 1960.*

that had filtered through the sand and could easily be pumped up through a hollow pipe stuck into the dunes. One bucket of water poured down the tube was all that was needed to get the pump primed. In the 1880s, many houses on the Island had windmills that perpetually pumped this surface water into cisterns.

A few private individuals who could afford the cost drilled the first artesian wells on the Island around a hundred years ago. As early as 1892, there was an artesian well near the train depot at Passaic Avenue in Harvey Cedars. All visitors remarked upon the handsome statue of a small boy holding one boot upside down in his hand. Water ran from the boot constantly. The first hotel to have its own artesian well was the Oceanic in Barnegat City. Steam pumps forced the water up into

tanks in the twin cupolas atop the roof.

Once tapped, the water from an artesian well runs continually, seemingly forever. Hydrostatic pressure forces the water to the surface, but not much farther. From there a pump is required to lift the water into a tank or a standpipe in order to create the additional pressure to move it any distance. The first big water tank on the Island was built at Beach Haven in 1893, after a well had been drilled, at a cost of $20,000.

It was a cedar tank on a complex wooden frame. Its height of seventy-five feet provided enough pressure to send water to the second and third floors of every house in town. It also inspired the creation of many beautiful

gardens and lawns. However, by 1911 the wooden tank had begun to leak badly, and the town soon erected a new steel tank tower that was a hundred feet from its base to the bottom of the tank and another forty-five feet to the flagstaff atop its peculiar lid, a lid that resembled nothing so much as a big Chinese coolie hat. A quaint old landmark by 1960, the tower was replaced by a more modern structure.

Other tanks and standpipes were built around the Island in the next few decades. Until then, residents had no choice but to bring a couple of buckets to the nearest artesian well, usually located at a Coast Guard station. This was a way of life at Holgate until 1939, when they finally got their tank. There are no longer any bogs or fresh water ponds on the Island. Once the scene of happy winter skating parties, most of the ponds became trash dumps more than seventy years ago. They have long since been covered over and planted with houses.

## The Blizzard of 1920

When writers use the well-worn phrase "storm of the century" in regard to Long Beach Island and the central coast of New Jersey, they mean either the Great Atlantic Hurricane of 1944 or the Great Atlantic Storm of 1962. Both were terribly destructive. One was, of course, a hurricane, which was all over within a few hours. It was the first hurricane to score a direct hit on the Island since 1821. The March storm of '62 was a northeaster of the sort that plagues us every winter, but much larger. This one came in conjunction with a new moon and the highest tides of the year, along with a freezing, 60-knot wind, directly out of the east, that struck the oceanfront with unimaginable fury. It lasted three days and each successive tide rose higher.

Both the hurricane in '44 and the March storm in '62 qualify, without question, for storm of the century. Picking the more damaging of the two would be moot. There was, however, a third storm that came a little earlier in the century and is usually overlooked when journalists compile lists of this type. It was a massive storm, quite comparable to the other two, but the Island was a lot less developed then. If it were to occur now, there would be unimaginable property damage. I refer, of course, to the great northeast blizzard of February 4, 1920.

It was a three-day snowstorm with high easterly winds, coupled with a full moon, causing abnormally high tides and gigantic surf. The depth of the snow was

*The blizzard of February 1920 destroyed the Barnegat Lighthouse keeper's house, and threatened East Fourth Street, above, including the Oceanic Hotel and the Haddock House. At the south end of the Island, the storm created a new inlet — Beach Haven Inlet — which eventually migrated south to topple the Little Egg Harbor Lighthouse on Tucker's Island.*

short of the record-breaking blizzard of 1888, but even so there were many five-foot drifts. There was one mitigating feature that prevented disaster. During the blizzard of February 1920, the mercury stood just below the freezing point, about 28 or 30 degrees Fahrenheit. In the big blizzard of 1888, it was near zero, and there was great suffering, and even death.

Barnegat City, on the north end of the Island, bore the brunt of the high tides and pounding surf. The citizens of that tiny community were actually cut off from the world for a full week; everyone on the rest of the Island and the mainland feared the worst.

The telephone wires were down and parts of the railroad track in Loveladies were washed away. The steady east wind drove enough water into the bay to cover the one-mile-long rail trestle from the Manahawkin meadows to the Bonnet islands; wind-driven waves lifted a whole section of it off the pilings. A train was stranded on Long Beach Island until the trestle was repaired. The automobile causeway was intact, but there was as yet no road north of Ship Bottom.

Word soon filtered down the beach that Barnegat City had borne up rather well. People had plenty of food, and school had been closed only for one day. High though the water might have been, no home was flooded. The most destruction in the resort was at East Fourth Street. There, the east end of the Oceanic Hotel, as far as the first cupola, had fallen in. The building had been in danger for more than a year due to the eroding shoreline and was scheduled for demolition.

The three-family keepers' house at the base of the Barnegat Lighthouse was badly undermined and had to be abandoned. It was sold and torn down later that spring. East Fourth Street, where the proud old Oceanic had stood since 1882, was so badly cut in, it could never survive another storm. The Haddock House, the Oceanic's across-the-street neighbor, lost its front porch to the high surf, as well as several out buildings and the ornate housing for its artesian well. Within a few weeks, owner Captain A. R. Myers moved it south several blocks on Central Avenue to Eighth Street. There is no longer an East Fourth Street.

There were washouts the whole length of the Island, but most houses then were built well back from the beachfront. The incident for which the February blizzard of 1920 ought to be remembered occurred on the south end of the Island. It was the creation of a new inlet several hundred yards below the last street, today in Holgate. There had been an inlet there that had closed up in the 1880s. Within a year that new, storm-born inlet had a name — the Beach Haven Inlet. It began to widen and drift southward; within seven years, it toppled the Little Egg Harbor Lighthouse on Tucker's Island.

## 1932 Seaplane Crash

In the 1920s and '30s, aviation was still very new. It was a perfect sunny day in June of 1929 when the crash of a seaplane in the bay took the lives of several local men, as their families and friends looked on in horror. It was this experience that led to the immediate purchase of an ambulance for the town and, within a decade, to the formation of the Beach Haven First Aid Squad.

Three men were killed that dreadful Thursday afternoon of June 27, 1929. They were: Beach Haven Police Chief Frank B. Conklin, 32; plumber Harold Potts, 36; and charter-boat captain Leslie Broome, 28. All had been born in Beach Haven and had been residents of the town for their entire lives. The crash occurred just west of Mordecai Island in the Liberty Thoroughfare, while friends and family watched from the public dock at Centre Street a half mile away. The pilot, Paul Micelli, of Brooklyn, New York, and 20-year old Ellison Price, of Beach Haven, survived the crash with bruises, cuts and broken bones.

The plane involved in the accident was a Curtiss seaplane that had been brought to Beach Haven at the request of the Board of Trade, with the idea of making the town a scheduled stop on the regular New York to Atlantic City route. Politicians and businessmen involved in the enterprise had been aloft earlier in the afternoon, and, with the day drawing to a close, Micelli decided to make just one more flight to satisfy the eager demand of at least three men willing to pay for the thrill of seeing Beach Haven from the air. Young Ellison Price, who didn't have the necessary $10 for a ticket, was picked at random by Micelli out of the crowd at the dock just to fill an empty fourth seat. His friends on the dock envied his good luck.

The plane taxied out into the channel between Parker Island and the Beach Haven Yacht Club. Many of the crowd stood on the upper deck of the clubhouse. The big, rear-mounted engine got louder as the graceful craft skimmed down the bay faster than any speedboat. It was soon aloft and climbing skyward. It leveled off to make several passes out over the ocean and the town, dipping wings to the waving crowd at the dock. Pilot Micelli then banked and, passing the dock in the glowing red of a setting sun, began a slow descent toward the broad, marshy area south of town.

When the craft, now partially hidden from the crowd by the bushes of Mordecai Island, was only a dozen feet off the water, its engine cut off prematurely. Seconds later, it roared back into life, followed by a great splash that tossed debris high into the air.

There was a sudden silence, and then shouts and cries arose from onlookers. Every available boat was untied and started up. Youngsters darted across the broad sand flats of the recently filled-in cove, south of Centre Street, in the direction of the Little Egg Harbor Yacht Club. People piled into automobiles and raced south to West Avenue to a point opposite the crash where they could only stand on the edge of the bay. The first boats to get to the site were those out fishing or watching the flights from the water.

It was a horrifying scene. Apparently when the engine cut out, the nose dipped. When the pilot got it started up again, its full thrust drove the plane nose first into the water, causing it to flip. Potts and Conklin were found horribly mangled in the wreckage, crushed by the weight of the engine. Micelli and Price were gathered out of the shallow water in shock but relatively unhurt. Broome had also apparently been thrown out, but, since he could not be found in the gathering darkness, it was presumed that he had drowned. His body was discovered ten days later, nearly two miles up the bay off Beach Haven Terrace.

At the inquest, the triple death was declared "an unavoidable accident" caused, not by pilot error, but by a defect in the gas line. Micelli, a veteran World War I flier ,fell into a deep depression and, unable to recover from his minor injuries, died within the year. Ellison Price and his mother brought a $30,000 lawsuit against Curtiss Flying Service Inc. and settled out of court for an undisclosed sum. Conklin left a widow and a three-year-old daughter. Both Potts and Broome had been unmarried. Contributions began pouring in for the purchase of an ambulance, which had not been available at the time. The town was able to buy a 1929 Buick — still in service when the Beach Haven First Aid Squad drew up its official charter in May of 1939 — as a memorial to three of the town's fine, young men and the accident that took them in the prime of their lives.

## Hindenburg Over Beach Haven

From 1929 until 1937, the great trans-Atlantic zeppelins passed over Long Beach Island on their way to and from the Naval Air Station at Lakehurst. Their departure times from Germany, as well as their arrival at or lift-offs from Ocean County, were widely publicized in the newspapers and on the early radio stations. American military airship flights were not on a schedule, but they were often seen as well.

With foreknowledge of the comings and goings of the German airships so readily available, it is disappointing that amateur Long Beach Island photographers did little more than point their cameras straight up into the sky. As a result, one picture of a zeppelin today looks just like any other, and there is rarely any way to indicate the location of the viewer. Why didn't more of them use, let's say, the Engleside Hotel tower in Beach Haven, or some other recognizable object, like Barnegat Lighthouse, in the foreground?

There are, of course, striking photographs, taken from airplanes, of zeppelins passing over Boston and New York City or hovering over huge ocean liners almost their equal in length. Of the nearly dozen or so times a summer that they cruised over Long Beach Island, at a stately 50 miles per hour, only one shot reveals any sort of landmark. This photograph, on the following page, is of the *Hindenburg* heading south over Gifford's Garage in Beach Haven, in

*On May 6, 1937, the* Hindenburg *sails over a house in Beach Haven.*

*The* Hindenburg *sails over Beach Haven in August 1936.*

August of 1936. The *Hindenburg* had just left Lakehurst, and would make its turn out into the Atlantic from Atlantic City, in a tradition established by the *Graf Zeppelin* in 1929.

A lot of nonsense has been written about this photograph. It was not the zeppelin's last flight before burning, nor did the *Hindenburg*, like the *Titanic*, perish on its maiden voyage. It made a total of ten trips to the United States in 1936, and seven to South America from its air-field in Frankfurt, Germany. The flight of the *Hindenburg* over Gifford's Garage, captured on film in August of 1936, took place exactly nine months before its disastrous end on May 6, 1937. Observe the sign "Donkey Baseball Tonight." Those games were played on the Beach Haven ball field in August, and so it had to be 1936.

Commercial Atlantic crossings began with the *Graf Zeppelin* in 1929. The *Graf Zeppelin* was to make, in its illustrious career, a total of 578 successful flights, mostly between Germany and Rio de Janeiro and one around-the-world trip. Not until 1939 were there any commercial airplanes in service designed to carry passengers across the Atlantic, and they had to refuel in Newfoundland or Bermuda. The *Hindenburg,* which dwarfed the *Graf,* was introduced in 1936. It had been built for the stormy North Atlantic and the profitable New York route. It made seventeen flights in its first year, and in 1937, its second year, it was scheduled to make eighteen more.

But disaster struck on its very first voyage of 1937, on May 6, which seems to have given rise to the maiden voyage myth.

There are those who will tell you that the *Hindenburg's* flight over Gifford's Garage, or New York, or Boston, or wherever, was the only time a swastika flew over U.S. soil and then the airship caught fire and burned at Lakehurst. This is more arrant nonsense tied to the maiden voyage myth. The swastika, later to become a deservedly evil symbol, was nonetheless the flag of Germany in the years of the great airships, which were then the very best in the world. The emblem was also painted on the tail fins of the *Graf Zeppelin*, which made flights for seven years over the U.S. Some historical revisionists will airbrush the swastika out when it appears in local publications, as if a whole era never happened.

# Camping on Long Beach Island

In the decade after the building of the automobile causeway, Long Beach Island presented a vastly different prospect from today's vista of a house on every available lot, and traffic that barely crawls at the height of the summer. Back in the mid-1920s along the new eighteen-mile "Inlet to Inlet" automobile boulevard, the lonely motorist passed miles of bayberry-filled lots with no more than a scattering of dwellings and only an occasional store. On the whole north end there were only a few paved side roads, and the bay, indented in many places by broad coves ending in little sandy beaches, came to the very edge of the highway.

Camping was still a popular outdoor activity on the Island in those years, just as it had been in the generations when the train was the sole means of transporta-

tion. All one needed now was to park a car on the side of the road, pitch a tent in the dunes, gather driftwood and dig a hole in the sand to catch rain water in a rubber blanket. That was really roughing it, because it was always possible to obtain fresh water from any of the six Coast Guard stations on the Island if one wished.

A retired surgeon loved to tell about the days when he was still in medical school at the University of Pennsylvania, in the years before the "Great War," as he called it. When he and his wife were first married they would take the train from Camden to Long Beach Island, board a smaller train at Ship Bottom and, while it was chugging northward through the vast emptiness between the tiny hamlets of Surf City and Harvey Cedars, toss their cumbersome camping equipment and supplies off the only passenger car and then jump into the sand while the train was still moving.

There was driftwood everywhere for a fire. The doctor and his wife lived on bacon, baked beans, canned fruit and all the fish they could catch on their ten-day vacation. At night, sheltered in their tent, they listened to the howling of the tailless Manx cats in the dunes. So deserted was that stretch of beach that never in the whole ten days did they wear bathing suits when they went swimming. In the 1930s he was to build his huge, summer home on the very spot, when lots in the Frazier Tract (now North Beach), 200 feet wide and extending from ocean to bay, sold for a mere $1,200.

The greatest influx of campers came after the opening of the Beach Haven Inlet in 1920, when the incredible abundance of big weakfish, called "tide runners," attracted fishermen from all over the east. Their tents dotted the then-very- wide beaches of Holgate, and their cars lined the edge of the road. They were to enjoy this unfettered life-style for only about another decade. In

1935, Long Beach Township ordinances — passed for reasons of sanitation and the inability to collect taxes — forbade all camping on the beach.

By then there were several kinds of more-formal camps on the Island, well managed and not at all subject to proscription. In North Beach Haven, one of these camps was run by the privileged Hill School of Pottstown, Pennsylvania, for underprivileged boys from Philadelphia orphanages. Two others, Camp Dune by-the-Sea at Ship Bottom (for girls) and Camp Miquon at Brant Beach (for boys), both established in the 1920s, were very expensive and very exclusive. The campers lived in comfortable quarters on the beachfront. They had indoor plumbing, well-planned meals, and a daily round of activities ranging from crafts and games to sailing and horseback riding. The two camps were only a few miles apart, but the very young campers almost never shared any recreational activities with each other.

# World War II

## Coast Guard on Patrol

The buildup of the military on Long Beach Island got started in early 1942. Within several months of Pearl Harbor there were nearly 700 men in uniform on the Island in three branches of the service: the Army, the Coast Guard and the New Jersey State Guard. The Army units were here in a coordinated effort with the Coast Guard to stand watch over the drawbridge, causeway and waterways, and to assist in patrolling the beaches. The soldiers lived in tents in two camps. One was set up in a vacant oceanfront block in Ship Bottom where the causeway entered the Island; the other was on the baseball field between Pearl and Marine streets in Beach Haven.

By the early spring of 1943, the Army units were cut back while the Coast Guard built up its forces with new recruits pouring out of boot camp. Every station was soon filled, and the extra complement of men needed to

*Soldiers in front of the boarded-up and closed Engleside Hotel in 1942.*
*At right, Bob Earnhart, in front of the St. Rita Hotel, and patrolling with dog on the beach.*

# Coast Guard Christmas, 1943

**B**y December of 1943, Long Beach Island was closer to the action of World War II than any other part of the mainland United States. German submarines spotted off the coast and rumors of spy landings had put the local Coast Guard at full strength. But the tide of the war was turning, and a morale-boosting Christmas greeting card with a holiday dinner menu was given out to all personnel at each of the eight stations on the Island, from Bond's to Barnegat Light.

The front depicts a jolly Santa Claus standing on the roof of a Coast Guard tower. He is out of the sight of several anxious men on watch in the cabin. They scan the horizon with binoculars looking for him, while far below on the beach, men on foot and horseback are also engaged in the search, as are the ships at sea. Comic book aficionados who grew up in the Golden Age will recognize the signature of cartoonist Joe Simon, the creator of Blue Bolt, Captain America and the Young Allies. Simon served in the Coast Guard during the war.

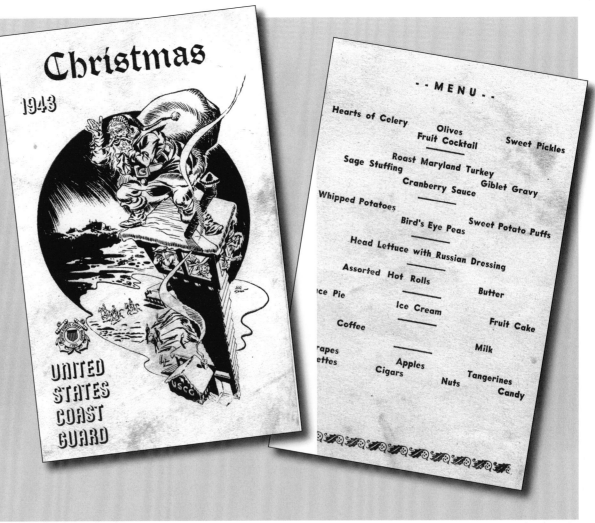

protect the Island was housed for the duration in two hotels — the St. Rita on Engleside Avenue in Beach Haven and Wida's on Forty-fourth Street in Brant Beach. Mounted patrols were used for the first time on the beaches. The horses were stabled at Beach Haven Terrace and at Ship Bottom and transported by van where needed to other parts of the Island. Foot patrols had been using dogs on the beach for a year. The dog-training centers were at Bond's in Holgate and at Ship Bottom. The Har-

vey Cedars and Loveladies Coast Guard stations, decommissioned in the 1930s, were put back into service.

Bob Earnhart was from Indiana and had never been east until he went to Coast Guard boot camp at Manhattan Beach, New York in the fall of 1942. Just after Thanksgiving, and with a mere four weeks of training, he and his mates packed their sea bags, got orders to take a train to Philadelphia and from there were to take a bus to a destination unknown. It was wartime and every movement

was kept secret until the very last minute, so there could be no phone calls.

The bus crossed over the bridge to New Jersey. Not until they were rolling through the flat farm country just east of Camden did their civilian driver relax and inform them that they were going to an island. An island! To them, islands were where all the fighting was in this war. Never mind that they were headed toward the Atlantic, not the Pacific. They were not much reassured when, an

*Coast Guard beach patrol on horseback, above, and the Ship Bottom Coast Guard Station, with watchtower at the street end, below. At right, Bob Earnhart poses with rifle while on beach patrol.*

hour or so later, they crossed the rumbling bridges of the old causeway, smelled the salt air and saw the soldiers and machine gun emplacements at the drawbridge and an Army camp at the entrance to the Island in Ship Bottom.

The bus made a right turn toward Beach Haven where Bob and the others were assigned to the St. Rita Hotel Coast Guard barracks across from the boarded-up Engleside Hotel. The Engleside had been closed since the 1940 season and was about to be torn down. While it was standing, the military occasionally used its broad porches for calisthenics on rainy days. Nothing in Beach Haven was open in the winter, except the movies on weekends and the U.S.O. at the Anchor Inn at Second Street and Bay Avenue.

There was little free time, however, due to all the endless watches and patrols, most of them at night. The men constantly checked the watch station and quarter bill for their assignments. They had to be taken by trucks to get the dogs to patrol the more remote parts of the Island. Many of the men staying at the St. Rita were on the horse patrol and were presented with more-complicated lo-

gistics. Reveille for all hands was at 7:00 AM. Only those who had been on the midnight to 4:00 AM watches could sleep in until 10:00 in the morning. At the St. Rita, all the upstairs rooms, including the present lobby, were filled with double-decker bunk beds. Daytime hours were spent in training and drills.

Tower duty was preferred on the cold winter nights, but few could swing that. The beach patrol, clad in fleece-lined brown parkas, worked in pairs. Both were armed. The man with the leashed dog had a holstered .45 automatic pistol so both his hands were free to hold the dog. He preceded the rifleman by some ten feet. Patrols were continued throughout the day if the visibility was poor.

# Wartime Summers

Looking at old 8mm movies my parents took in the summer of 1942, I am struck by the vast emptiness of the bay side of the Island; there was scarcely a single structure in all of Brant Beach. The bay often came to the very edge of the Boulevard and every quarter mile or so there was a little cove with a sandy beach. Occasional rowboats were anchored in these coves or pulled up onto the meadows, and no one ever disturbed them.

We rented a house on Fifty-fifth Street for the months of July and August that first summer of the war when I was 10. My sister, who was 8, was entered in Camp Dune by-the-Sea, located on the beachfront in Ship Bottom. The girl campers used the old Camp Miquon dock at Fifty-sixth Street in Brant Beach. I have lots of photographs of swimming and diving exhibitions put on by the older girls, including shots of camp director Marguerite Sibley's big, mahogany Chris-Craft speedboat towing aquaplaners. For those occasions, every piling on the long dock was decorated with the bayberry that grew everywhere on the Island.

In wartime, the ocean beaches were thick with tar from torpedoed oil tankers and freighters. We only went there on days of a west wind when the mosquitoes and greenheads were too thick on the bay. We had to dig out a clean spot in the sand for beach towels. There is only occasional movie footage since cameras and binoculars were forbidden by order of the Coast Guard and could be confiscated. In one scene of crashing waves, with foam as brown as Coca Cola, my father has put a towel over his head to hide the camera and the edge of it is flapping in the wind.

At the end of the summer of 1942, we bought a newly-built Cape Cod fully furnished with detached garage on Thirty-fourth Street in the block behind the Colonial Movie Theater. We kept that house until after the war when my parents built a bigger one on the ocean in North Beach, then called the Frazier Tract.

The trips to the shore in the war years from far out in western Pennsylvania were not lightly undertaken. We lived in Johnstown and it took ten hours on the old Lincoln Highway. In June of 1943, we kids, my mother and a teenaged babysitter piled into our 1941 Ford station wagon with — believe it or not — a drum in the back filled with forty gallons of gasoline. It sloshed around while we tried to sleep next to it. We left at 10:00 in the evening and drove all night to avoid agents of the Office of Price Administration. Gasoline was rationed and certainly not to be wasted on long vacation trips. We stopped occasionally at darkened gas stations to siphon gas from our drum into the tank and breathed a sigh of relief when we got to the Chester-Bridgeport ferry at dawn. My father took the train to Philadelphia and the bus to the shore whenever he could.

Those were great summers. We had the movie theater within a block; it was only 17cents for kids, and we played baseball on their parking lot. We played commandos in the sand dunes, but mostly we practically lived in the bay. Only eight blocks away was a great bathing beach at Twenty-sixth Street in Ship Bottom and a long dock that could be used for crabbing and diving.

There is scarcely a person from the middle of the Island who does not remember with great fondness that wonderful bathing beach. The sand came right to the edge of the street where there was a small set of wooden steps. I do not remember a lifeguard ever being there in the early years, but there were so many parents around that it was considered quite safe. We were always permitted to take our bikes and go there alone for a swim. It was shallow for a long way out and the water was crystal clear over the sand. It was always pleasantly warm on cold days.

The dogs, which were penned at Ship Bottom and at Beach Haven Terrace, were unpredictable and always kept leashed. Some were friendly and others very dangerous. It was the custom for every guardsman approaching another with a dog in the darkness of the night to ask which dog he had before getting too close. The Coast Guard employed 2,000 dogs throughout the nation. They were gathered through an organization called "Dogs for Defense" and trained at two places: the 300-acre Widener Estate in Elkins Park, Pennsylvania, and on Hilton Head Island, South Carolina. Of the 18 acceptable breeds, Dobermans, German shepherds and airedales were preferred.

The beaches were thick with tar from oil tankers sunk by enemy submarines. Any unusual debris washed in with the tide had to be reported lest it be explosive or reveal a clue to an enemy landing. It was not unusual to find the life-jacketed and tar-covered bodies of drowned sailors. The men on patrol wore knee-high canvas leggings and rubber overshoes, which had to be cleaned with kerosene at the end of each watch. The dogs were returned to their pens, and Bob Earnhart was not certain how they were kept clean of the sticky, black tar. He admitted it must have been very difficult.

## Blimps Over Barnegat Inlet

Another memory of wartime comes with a strikingly clear, sixty-year-old photograph of three U.S. Navy blimps high aloft over Barnegat Inlet. Enlarged and framed, it now hangs in the meeting room of the Barnegat Light Borough Hall, and is seen at right. It was an official U. S. Navy photograph and the unknown cameraman who took this remarkable picture from a fourth blimp was

aiming his lens southward in the direction of the upper end of Long Beach Island. From his vantage point and altitude, the lighthouse, barely noticeable in the picture, is dwarfed by a great steel tower in the foreground on the southern tip of Island Beach. The time was 1943, during the construction of the north jetty. All the material for its construction had to be hauled by truck to what was then known as Barnegat City.

In the photograph, a second tower is visible across Barnegat Inlet on Long Beach Island. Cables strung between these two, huge towers carried massive granite boulders, one by one, on slings across the inlet where they were lowered onto a flat car, to be taken by a small steam engine out to the north jetty for placement by a crane. It took several years, but once the jetty was finished, the flat car, steam engine and tracks were re-

*Two towers erected on either side of Barnegat Inlet supported a cable and sling for delivering huge boulders used in the construction of the north jetty in 1943.*

wrecks, two convoys and three other blimps but no submarines. He was a year too late for the Nazi wolf packs that had turned the Atlantic seaboard into a veritable shooting gallery.

Hitler declared war on the U.S. on December 11, 1941, less than a week after Pearl Harbor, suddenly lifting all restrictions against attacking ships along the Atlantic coast. America was unprepared for the destruction. In 1942, between January and August, 360 merchant ships were sunk and only eight U-boats were destroyed. Masts and smokestacks were visible above the waves off Barnegat Light and all beaches along the coast of New Jersey were thick with oil and tar. Residents could hear the dull thud of explosions at sea. Blackouts were enforced, and the military patrolled the beaches around the clock.

In the spring of 1943, *National Geographic* sent its correspondent Mason Sutherland to Lakehurst. After a few paragraphs about the Navy base, the huge hangars, and the role of lighter-than-air craft thus far in the war, Sutherland introduces the reader to the blimp.

He described the cabin as "longer than a Greyhound bus" with lounge seats along one side, and, on the rear half of the other side, a long settee facing the interior. There was an instrument panel, radio equipment, a mess table, a pantry and a navigator's chart table. All along both sides, forward and aft, there were deep windows. The pilot and co-pilot sat up forward in a semi-enclosed compartment. Counting himself and the photographer, Sutherland noted, there were twelve men aboard.

The ground crew released the ropes. "9:30 AM: We roar into the air at a 40-degree angle and I, lacking a side rest on the couch, sway and clutch for support. I was told that a favorite trick of peacetime lighter-than-air men is to take airplane pilots up at a steep angle and, 100 feet above the ground, kill the motors. Heavier-than-air guests turn pale;

moved and the towers torn down. All that remains today, rising above the sand, are the concrete anchors once used to hold the guy wires attached to the towers.

The photograph was one of fifteen pictures used in the July 1943 issue of the *National Geographic* to illus-

trate an article titled *Aboard a Blimp Hunting U-Boats*. The author, Mason Sutherland, spent a day aboard a training blimp out of Lakehurst looking for enemy submarines. Allowing eight weeks for production time, his day aloft was probably in April or May. He saw several such a stall in a plane may mean death. But a blimp continues its climb. Leveling off at 500 feet, we could see our shadow, a fat, black cigar, zipping across the scrub oaks. As our motors are throttled down, toy automobiles pace the shadow at their 35-mile-an-hour limit."

Two 500-horsepower engines gave her the forward thrust, but the blimp had only two basic controls: a steering wheel with wires leading to a rudder to turn it to port or starboard and foot controls running to the elevator to drive the ship up or down. In calm weather, the airship responded as smoothly as an automobile, but winds drove it incessantly off course. A gadget like a carpenter's level kept a fog-bound pilot on an even keel.

Navigation had to be done by dead reckoning aided by a radio direction finder. Because of the huge gasbag right over their heads, it was impossible for the men to see the sun or the stars. Air speed was determined by how long it took their 250-foot shadow to pass over a whitecap far below.

In thick fog, the blimp pilot would shut off the engines and drift just above the water. There is a story that, once, off Barnegat Light, while on one of these silent patrols over the ocean, the crew of an airship distinctly heard voices speaking in German below them, but they could see nothing. Upon their return to the hangar they learned that what they had more than likely heard were local pound fishermen at work on their nets, speaking Norwegian, not German.

A blimp had no firepower to speak of, and while there were never any enemy planes to fear along American shores, they were extremely vulnerable to the deck guns of a surfaced submarine. Two blimps were lost during the war in this fashion. Only rarely did a blimp have occasion to drop a depth charge, and even then without any perceptible results. In fact, depth charges suitable for

Barnegat Lighthouse is framed by towers erected on either side of the inlet in 1943. The two towers were used in the construction of the north jetty.

an airship platform were not in production until 1944, when the submarine threat was all but gone.

Early in the war, the blimps were equipped with Magnetic Airborne Detectors, or MAD gear. In order for the device to be effective, the airship cabin had to be no more than 200 feet over the water. This was extremely fatiguing for a pilot and co-pilot on an eight-hour shift, and all too often the metallic mass located was not a submarine, but one of many sunken ships not yet marked on the charts.

MAD was a failure. It was radar, perfected after 1943, that finally gave blimps the ability to spot submarines when they surfaced at night to charge their batteries. In the long run, however, the primary purpose of the ZNP

(Zeppelin Non-Rigid Patrol) was observation by day, and in this they were quite effective. Once a submarine was spotted from the air near a convoy, a radio message sent one of the swift, fully armed escort vessels over to get it.

For a time the Navy officially called all their lighter-than-air craft with engines "zeppelins" after their German inventor, but the true generic term was "dirigible." There are rigid and non-rigid dirigibles, and no two words in juxtaposition are more confusing. Dirigible is derived from the Latin *dirigere*, which means to direct. The very first lighter-than-air craft invented were gas- or hot air–filled balloons which, once untethered, were at the mercy of the winds. They could not be directed or turned.

*This Navy blimp was employed in the search for a body in 1960.*

By the late 19th century, the balloon was elongated and a small motor and propeller gave it forward thrust. With the addition of a rudder, it could be turned or directed, and it became a dirigible.

In Germany, Count Zeppelin made many improvements. Dirigibles soon got bigger and longer, and a rigid, metallic framework was needed to keep the enormous gasbag from collapsing. This was a rigid dirigible.

Certain dirigibles did not have an interior framework of metal and were called "non-rigids." The English preferred the term "limp" for such craft to describe the way they looked when they lost gas or air and the envelope began to sag. Experimenting with a B-type limp, as they called all non-rigids, they ran the letter and the word together and came up with "blimp." This was just about the time, in the 1930s, that British cartoonist David Low invented the character Colonel Blimp, a fat, mustachioed buffoon. A new word had come into the language.

# Fishing

## The Fishing Pier

Three ancient cedar pilings, each about fifteen feet tall, stand in a row in the surf at Berkeley Avenue in Beach Haven. They are all that is left of the town's ocean fishing pier, a municipal project completed in 1924 and destroyed just twenty years later by the Great Atlantic Hurricane of 1944, which also took away the boardwalk. There are always people who, knowing little of the town's history, think that those three withered, gray posts may once have been supports for the town's famous boardwalk and that the beach has greatly receded since then.

But such is not the case. Actually, the Beach Haven boardwalk, completed in 1917 to replace an earlier one on the same route, was positioned two hundred feet west of those three pilings. It ran along the edge of today's dune line, down the beach from Seventh Street, on the north, to Holyoke Avenue, on the south, for a distance of a mile and a quarter. It was twenty feet wide and was equipped with benches and lamps for lighting, but it never had any railings. It was seldom more than a foot or two off the sand, but in beach washouts, the drop-off could be six feet or more. Timid souls avoided walking too close to the edge. Beach conditions worsened, and the southernmost seven blocks of the boardwalk, below Belvoir Avenue, washed away in a storm in 1928.

Earl King, contractor and owner of the icehouse on Engleside Avenue, built the municipal fishing pier in 1924. The all-wooden pier ran out two hundred feet, at right angles to the boardwalk, ending in a lofty, T-shaped platform where the waves broke at low tide. Here, one stood to cast a line out into deeper water or to fish right off the bottom when the tide was high. This platform was supported by many sturdy pilings, only three of which have survived to this day.

Until the March storm of 1962, there were still at least

*The fishing pier stood in the surf at Berkeley Avenue in Beach Haven from 1924 until 1944. Fishermen were more likely to find big fish, like the channel bass at right, near the inlet.*

fifteen of the posts, all criss-crossed with huge, bolted beams, towering out of the surf in some strange, purposeless assemblage. Seen in silhouette from the beach in the red light of dawn, they were, for a time, Beach Haven's very own wooden Stonehenge.

In its first years, the ocean fishing pier was free to all users, but, by 1927, the borough put up a gate and decided to charge 50 cents a day in the summer months. There were never any really big fish caught from the pier, but there was always something biting, whether it was flounder, sea bass, stripers or — best of all — bluefish, when they were running. It was easiest, when the tide was high, simply to bottom-fish for flounder, but there were many who preferred to cast from the pier, to improve their chances.

On crowded days, this could be a hazardous pursuit. An occasional angler got conked with a sinker or hooked in the ear or scalp. Dr. Dodd, whose offices were three blocks west at Ocean Street and the Boulevard, always said, half in jest, that he made more money out of the fishing pier than the borough ever did. He kept a macabre display of errant fishhooks — not all from the pier, of course — on framed boards around his waiting room walls.

It was not just fishermen and strollers who used the pier. In the winter months, when the bay was frozen over and the broadbill ducks had no water to land on, they would light on the ocean to rest. Local gunners, knowing this, took advantage of the pier's length to toss stools, on anchored lines, out as far as possible past the breaking surf and then lie in wait behind the railing until the birds spotted the floating decoys. Upon their approach, the waiting gunners opened fire on them from the end of the pier. The dead or disabled broadbills were gathered later on the beach when they washed in. Local men in

*The Beach Haven fishing pier, left, was one of two on Long Beach Island. The other was at 20th Street in Ship Bottom (Beach Arlington), above. Both were destroyed by the hurricane of September 1944.*

# Fishing Trip, 1892

Mary Mapes Dodge (1831-1905), best known for her popular children's classic *Hans Brinker, or the Silver Skates* (1865), was the first editor, in 1873, of *St. Nicholas*, easily the finest American children's magazine of all time. In the September 1892 issue, John Whitehead authored a short piece titled *A Fishing Trip to Barnegat*. It is of interest to us today because of its matter-of-fact account of everyday life a hundred years ago and because it is about fishing on Barnegat Bay, something most of us are acquainted with in one way or another. The fish caught then — with the exception of the sheepshead, which is gone forever from these waters — are exactly the same, except that they may have been a little bigger, and certainly there were a lot more of them.

Jack turned to his uncle with an inquiry on his open lips; but just then his uncle felt a tug at his line, and up he pulled, deftly and quickly, a beautiful shining fish radiant with almost all the colors of the rainbow. "What a monster!" thought Jack; and, forgetting his toad-fish, he rushed forward to his uncle to examine this beautiful prize. There it lay, beating the hard board with head and tail, gasping for air, its life fast ebbing away.

"Come," said Uncle John, "and look at my fish; and, Captain, you take Jack's fish off his hook and bring it here, and we'll examine the two side by side."

Detaching his fish from the hook, Uncle John laid it upon the deck. The captain brought Jack's line down from the sail, took the fish from the hook, and laid it beside the beautiful one that Uncle John had just caught.

"Now, this fish of yours, Jack," said the uncle, "is not only called the toad-fish and the oyster-fish but, sometimes, the grunting toad-fish. There are species of it found all over the world but this is the regular American toad-fish.

"This fish of mine is called the weakfish. Notice its beautiful colors, brownish blue on its back, with irregular brown spots, the sides silvery, and the belly white. It grows from one to three feet long, and is a very sharp biter. When one takes the hook, there is no difficulty in knowing when to pull in. Why it is called the weakfish I do not know, unless because when it has been out of the water its flesh softens and soon becomes unfit for food. When eaten soon after it is caught, it is very good."

Just as Uncle John finished his little lecture, an exclamation from Will, who had baited with a piece of the crab, and dropped his line into the water, attracted their attention. Not quite so impetuous as Jack, he landed his prize more carefully, and stood looking at it with wonder, hardly knowing what to say. At last he called out:

"Well, what have I caught?"

It was a beautiful fish, though entirely different from Uncle John's. It had a small head and the funniest little tail that ever was seen. Its back was of a bright brown color, but its belly was almost pure white; it was quite round and flat, with a rough skin.

"Turn him over on his back, and rub him gently," said the captain. "Do it softly, and watch him."

Will complied, and gently rubbed him. Immediately the fish began swelling, and as Will continued the rubbing it grew larger and larger until Will feared that the fish would burst its little body.

"Well," he said, "I never saw anything like that, Captain! Do tell me what this is."

"This we call, here in Barnegat, the balloon-fish. It is elsewhere called the puffer, swell-fish and globe-fish. One kind is called the sea-porcupine, because of its being covered with short, sharp spines. It is of no value for food."

Jack thought his time had come to catch another prodigy; and when his hook had been rebaited by the skipper, he dropped his line into the water, and was soon rewarded by another bite. Using more caution this time, he landed his fish securely on deck instead of over the sail, and exclaimed:

"Wonders will never cease! I don't know what I've got now, but I suppose that Captain John can tell."

those days seldom used dogs to retrieve shot birds.

Beach Haven was not the only community on the Island with an ocean pier. Another built at Twentieth Street in Ship Bottom during the 1930s was privately owned by Emilio Guida of the Gateway Bar. He listed it for sale during the war, and made settlement the very day before the 1944 hurricane struck, destroying the pier. The proud new owner never even got a chance to catch so much as a sea robin off it. Nor will anyone else on Long Beach Island ever enjoy the use of an ocean fishing pier. They've been considered a risky investment since 1944.

## Call of the Surf

Surf fishing, with rudimentary types of the modern rod and reel, had been practiced for nearly a generation on the beaches of New Jersey before the first book ever written on the subject, *Call of the Surf,* appeared in 1920. It was the work of two very young authors, Van Campen Heilner and Frank Stick.

*Call of the Surf,* illustrated with Stick's paintings and many photographs by both authors, is now among the rarest of items in that genre. It describes a way of life: boating in the waters around Beach Haven, camping on Tucker's Beach and shooting birds for supper in the meadows off Little Sheepshead Creek. It was published by the distinguished firm of Doubleday, Page & Company in 1920, and has long been out of print.

Van Campen Heilner was only 21 when the book first appeared. Some of his six chapters, out of the total of twelve in the book, had been written while he was still a student at the Phillips Academy in Andover, Massachusetts. After college, he would become a world-famous editor, author and explorer, writing many more books on duck shooting and salt water fishing. He hunted brown bear in Alaska and tigers in India. He was a frequent fish-

*A captain and friend, with a typical catch at the Beach Haven Yacht Club dock in the late 1800s.*

While he was saying this the fish began to utter some sounds that, by a stretch of the imagination, might be called musical. They were almost as harmonious as the croak of a frog.

It was of a dark brown color, with a head larger than the rest of its body, but not disproportioned. Like the toad-fish, its body tapered toward the tail, but not so sharply; its head was shovel-shaped, and just below its gills there were two large projecting fins and some feelers.

"Give him a pinch just below the gills, and see what he will do," said the captain.

Will was rather afraid to risk the experiment, but being assured that there was no danger, he at once grasped the fish with thumb and finger, and was rewarded by a repetition of the musical sounds.

"That is what we call a sea-robin. Perhaps your uncle can tell you something about it," said the captain. So they carried the musical fish to Uncle John, who was at the bow.

"That is sometimes called a gurnard," said he; "and there are several species of it. Its flesh is white and, when properly cooked, it is said to be very good."

ing companion of Ernest Hemingway, in the Bahamas, and was decorated by the Cuban government for his exploration of that country. He was the editor of *Field and Stream* until his retirement in 1960, after which he continued to lecture and travel, until his death in 1970. He died at his home in Hampton Bays, Long Island.

Frank Stick, who wrote the other half of the twelve chapters of *Call of the Surf*, was not quite as young as his co-author. He was born in 1884, and would have been in his mid-30s in 1920, when the book was written. He continued to paint seascapes while living most of his life in Interlaken, New Jersey, where he was mayor during the 1920s. He later moved to North Carolina, where he established the Wright Brothers Memorial at Kitty Hawk. He died in 1966 at the age of 82.

Heilner was born in Philadelphia and spent his childhood summers in Beach Haven. At Long Key, Florida, when he was 16 and still a student at Andover, he met western novelist and outdoorsman Zane Grey. Grey showed him how he could make a career out of exploration, adventure and writing.

He wrote a number of pieces published in the *American Angler*, centering around his fishing trips on Barnegat Bay. He called the forty-foot cabin cruiser his father had bought him the *Nepenthe,* after a magic potion used by the ancient Egyptians to make them forget their misfortunes. He would later take the *Nepenthe*, with three companions, from Atlantic City to Venezuela, a four-thousand-mile trip. It was the first time an ocean voyage of such a length had ever been made by a gasoline-powered boat of that size.

Two of the best chapters having to do with Long Beach Island were written by Heilner. They are "Down Barnegat Way" and "With the Tide Runners of the Inlet." In the six chapters by his co-author, Stick, are two long ones on sharks and another on beach camping. The *Call of the Surf* also describes the years just after the Great War. At that time there were warehouses full of Army equipment, useful for camping, which could be gotten at unbelievably cheap prices. Fishing equipment was another story. Getting good reels and even good line was expensive. Only the privileged few could even own a boat like Heilner's *Nepenthe*.

When Heilner was writing about cruising on Little Egg Harbor Bay, and camping and surf casting on the nearby beaches, there was really only one inlet, some six miles south of Beach Haven. Unless one lived on Tucker's Island, the inlet was reachable only by boat. This was Little Egg Harbor Inlet, but in Heilner's time, and actually for more than a hundred years prior to that, it was known only as "New Inlet." After the February Blizzard of 1920, another newer "New Inlet" appeared only two miles south of Beach Haven. It was soon being called Beach Haven Inlet. Easily accessible by automobile from Beach Haven in the 1920s, it became one of the best-known spots for weakfishing in New Jersey.

*"Eureka."*

*Surf fishing at the inlet in Holgate.*

Hundreds of anglers camped at Holgate and fished every tide there.

Beach camping has been outlawed since the 1930s, and now we can only read about it. Here is an evocative passage of Heilner's from Chapter Six of *Call of the Surf*:

"Many the night I have lain in my tent on the north point o' Barnegat, listening to the whistle and moan of the wind across the dreary sand and to the breakers roaring in fury like great beasts who would kill and destroy. And suddenly, out of the darkness, would come, like the cry of a tortured soul, a long, unearthly scream. It was the Manx cats, remnants of their tailless ancestors who were shipwrecked on the shoals more than three score and ten years ago. Along that desert shore for nearly a century these felines, now as wild and savage as their fiercest jungle relations, have subsisted and bred until their numbers are uncountable. Upon wakening in the mornings we would often find that ham, sausages, or various other articles of camp diet had vanished — carried off to some hellish lair."

# Barnegat Light & Barnegat City

## Fever at the Oceanic Hotel

The new Barnegat Lighthouse, completed in 1859, was such a remarkable feat of engineering that it quickly became a drawing card for summer visitors Most had to return to the mainland the same day for there were very few family accommodations on the north end of the Island at mid-century. What few hotels there were catered primarily to sportsmen interested in hunting and fishing. The term sportsmen does not exclude women for, as wives, they were most certainly on hand in the summer months for the bird shooting and bluefishing and their tallies appear in the old hotel registers. Gunning in the fall and spring migrations, however, was still a strictly male-oriented activity.

Nearly a generation had passed before a true family resort was established near the lighthouse when, in 1878, Benjamin Franklin Archer of Camden saw possibilities in the area and formed the Barnegat City Beach Association. He bought six hundred acres of land to be laid out in streets and building lots in the style of the already very successful resort at Beach Haven, established four years earlier.

Labeling his enterprise a "city" in imitation of Atlantic

*The Oceanic Hotel on East Fourth Street was built in 1881.*

*East Fourth St. in Barnegat City. The cupolas on top of the Oceanic hid the hotel's water tanks.*

City was done to stimulate investment. In the spring of 1881, when the surveys for Barnegat City had been completed, he began to build a resort hotel that he named the Oceanic. Archer boldly leveled all the oceanfront dunes and laid his foundation along the north side of East Fourth Street, defiantly close to the ocean.

The hotel was completed the following year. It was an imposing four stories high, encircled by balconies and designed to accommodate 150 guests. There was a grand ballroom for dancing and a magnificent dining room with an unobstructed view of the ocean. The most distinguishing characteristic of the Oceanic, however, was the two great cupolas on the roof. Their purpose was not to serve as observation rooms but rather to disguise commodious water tanks kept filled by a steam pump from an artesian well, the first ever drilled on the Island. These tanks were used to provide pressure for water taps throughout the hotel and would, ironically, become the grand hotel's undoing. The wood and coal-fired steam pump was used to run an elevator carrying guests to all four floors.

The role of the tanks in the hotel's demise came to light when a collector unearthed a picture postcard.

Most of the messages found on these old cards are — from the viewpoint of several decades later — quaint and funny. Unlike letters, the postcard, with its picture on the reverse side, seems to have had an intrinsic value to

POST CARD - CARTE POSTALE

*Dear Friend,*
*I have been waiting*
*for a letter for a*
*long while and*
*I thought maybe you*
*where sick. I saw*
*in the paper that*
*they had sickness in*
*the hotel from the*
*water. We all send*
*Love from E.D.*

Miss Minnie Kroeger,

Barnegat City.

Ocean Co.

N. J.

water. We all send love. E.D."

The postmark is September 10, 1909. The correspondent, "E.D.", is referring to something more than mere "sickness from the water." It was the dreaded typhoid fever. A young woman had died in late August at the Oceanic, almost certainly from drinking the water there. Several others got sick but managed to survive. There were attempts by management to blame it on contaminated shellfish and even on digging in Indian graves in the Forked River "mountains," once a popular excursion for vacationers staying at the Oceanic.

There is not a word about "sickness from water" in the *New Jersey Courier* in the months of August and September 1909. The *Courier*, published weekly in Toms River at the time, was Ocean County's principal journal of record. Earlier, in the last week of July 1909, it carried an article about the pleasures of Barnegat City and how all three hotels, the Oceanic, the Sunset and the Social, were filled to capacity. A whole year was to pass be-

the receiver and was put away in a drawer, eventually to find its way into the hands of a collector. Occasionally one of these cards contains a priceless nugget of information and the collector will call a museum or a local historian and share that information.

This particular postcard is not a Long Beach Island card, but a view of Toms River that happened to be addressed to Barnegat City to Miss Minnie Kroeger, whose family owned the Social Hotel near the lighthouse. The Social, on West Fifth Street, was not as big as the statelier Sunset and Oceanic hotels, but it was open all winter and had a loyal clientele. What is important about the card is the message, which reads as follows:

"Dear Friend, I have been waiting for a letter for a long while and I thought maybe you were sick. I saw in the paper that they had a sickness in the hotel from the

*The Oceanic Hotel was abandoned for a decade until a northeast storm undermined it in 1920 and it was torn down. The postcard refers to "sickness in the hotel from the water."*

On the image: *Fourth St West Barnegat City N.J.*

*Fourth Street, West, Barnegat City, N.J.* 5764-C.

1915

*The Oceanic Hotel, at right, remained closed for a decade until a northeast storm in 1920 claimed it and much of the rest of the street. East Fourth Street in Barnegat Light no longer exists.*

Although the regular Barnegat City reporter, clearly part of a cover-up, never wrote a word about it, a story has been circulated for years that dead rats were found floating in the ornamental roof-top cisterns when the lids were removed. This contamination could easily have been the cause of the young woman's illness and death, and also the reason the hotel failed to draw enough reservations to open the following season.

The incident was a public relations disaster for the grand old hotel, which for nearly thirty years had been a landmark on the Island's north end. There was a failed attempt to reopen the next year, but its reputation had been destroyed. The Oceanic remained closed for a decade until February of 1920, when it was so badly undermined by a raging northeast storm that it had to be torn down. The street upon which it stood no longer exists.

## *Barnegat Lighthouse, 1882*

The earliest images of Barnegat Lighthouse, after its completion in 1859, were line drawings that did not start to appear in the popular magazines of the day until after the Civil War when the desolate marshes and barrier beaches of New Jersey were attracting sportsmen for the marvelous fishing and gunning. Especially popular was the new sport of trolling for bluefish in the inlets from big sailing catboats. Artists liked to portray this exciting activity by sketching swiftly moving craft under full sail in choppy seas with clouds of gulls in the wake. Six or seven spray-soaked anglers worked the lines and a lighthouse was always in the background, usually

fore Barnegat City would be written about in that paper again.

When it was, there were only a few scant words in August 1910 that read: "One of the largest hotels remained open all last winter and did not seem to hurt business in the smaller one that has always stayed open." By this, the reporter meant the Sunset on the bay side of the resort and, of course, the much smaller Social that never closed. There is no mention at all of the Oceanic, almost

as though it would be better not to talk about it. To do so might even have hurt the economy of the whole resort.

Until the discovery of the Toms River post card from the person known only as "E.D.," it has never been clear just when the typhoid incident took place. Now we know that it had to have been sometime in August of 1909 because of the date of the early September postmark on this newly discovered card. But it is still not certain in which paper elsewhere in the state "E.D." read about it.

*This 1882 photograph may be the earliest picture of Barnegat Lighthouse. It was dated by the large flags flying on the cupolas of the Oceanic Hotel at left during its opening season. It also shows a smaller, simpler lighthouse keeper's house that would be greatly expanded in 1889.*

Barnegat Lighthouse.

The first photographs of the lighthouse came later, mostly after 1900, and they are easily dated by the appearance in them of the sprawling, three-family keepers' house at the base of the tower, as much a landmark as the light itself. The keepers' house, built for the three-man crew who maintained the operation of the light, was ready in 1889. There had to have been an earlier lodging for the crew, but only an earlier photograph would show it and prove its existence.

In 1972, a collector of early lantern slides acquired one quite by accident that may be the earliest known photograph of Barnegat Lighthouse. It came in a mahogany box of glass slides of the 1898 Cuban campaign. The original owner, when asked about it, had no idea how the view of the lighthouse got in among them. There was no date etched anywhere on the glass or its frame.

The collector contacted Mrs. Catherine Zeiber, a lifelong summer resident of Barnegat Light. At that time, in 1972, she was in her early 80s and, as the granddaughter of Benjamin Archer, founder of Barnegat City and the builder of the Oceanic Hotel, she knew a lot of local history and quickly found a solid clue to work with. She observed that the Oceanic Hotel, which appears in this photograph to the left of the lighthouse, is flying two huge flags from its twin cupolas. She said these flags were flown only once, and that was during the opening season of the Oceanic, and, as best as she could recollect from stories her parents told her, that would have been in 1880.

They were flown day and night and were probably specially made with the name of the new hotel for people on passing ships to read. Strong winds, however, had begun to weaken the structure of the cupolas. So at season's end the flags were taken down and no others of such great size were ever flown again. This, according to Mrs. Zeiber, fixed the date of the photograph.

But Mrs. Zeiber, right though she was about the flag story, got the date wrong for the opening season of the Oceanic. Her grandfather did not begin to build the Oceanic until the early spring of 1881 and it was not ready for its grand opening until July of 1882. All of this is well documented in the *Ocean County Courier* and so, 1882 must have been the year that the flags flew from the twin cupolas. It still predates, however, all other photographs of Barnegat Lighthouse in existence. One other aspect affirms this early date: the simple style of the keepers' house at the base of the light. It is one-third the size of, and bears only a partial resemblance to, the impressive, three-family structure that would be built around and over it on the same site in 1889.

## Signal House, 1898

A landmark that has survived for generations is the Signal House. An unusually tall, wood-framed dwelling, it has stood on the northwest corner of Seventh Street and Central Avenue in Barnegat Light without any clear explanation as to why and when it was built. It has a story to tell that begins far away from Long Beach Island on another island, Cuba.

In 1898, Cuban patriots, demanding independence from Spain, had taken over one half of that island, then the richest of the mother country's several colonies around the world. Spain sent 150,000 troops to control the uprising. Popular sentiment in the United States was with the rebel cause. The Hearst and Pulitzer newspapers added fuel to the flames by trying to outdo each other in detailing atrocities committed by the Spanish troops. The situation became grave when, on February 15, 1898, the U.S. battleship *Maine* blew up in Havana Harbor with a loss of two officers and 264 men. The United States blamed it on a Spanish torpedo. Spain said it was an accidental boiler explosion. This later proved to be correct, but passions were high and the harm had been done. "Remember the *Maine*! To hell with Spain!" was the rallying cry.

Less than three weeks after the *Maine* incident, Congress voted $50 million for defense, clearly showing the way the country was heading. Thirty days later, Congress passed a joint resolution recognizing the independence of Cuba and asking Spain to withdraw her forces from that island. President McKinley was given the power to enforce that demand on April 21. This was equivalent to a declaration of war, and Spain countered by declaring war against the United States on April 24, 1898.

Suddenly a great wave of fear swept the east coast of the United States. As a nation, we by no means felt we had great naval power and grossly overestimated that of Spain. Except for a few scattered Indian campaigns to settle the west, we had not been engaged in battle since the Civil War. It did not lessen patriotic fervor to join the military, but the burning questions were: Where was the Spanish fleet? And were they on their way to bombard our cities?

The Spanish-American War of 1898 would be America's last conflict before the era of wireless communications. Marconi's reception of a radio message sent across the Atlantic, from Cornwall in southwestern England to St. John's, New Foundland, was three years away. The telegraph, which had been around for a half-century or more, had revolutionized military operations on land. However, since it required a continuous strand of wire for transmittal and reception, it was utterly useless at sea. Communication from ship to shore, or between ships, required a line of sight signals, usually signal code flags or blinking lights.

The Coast Signal Service of the U.S. Navy was empowered to set up signal houses every forty or fifty miles along the whole length of the Atlantic and Gulf coasts from Maine to the Mexican border. As early as the 25th of April, three sites had been picked for New Jersey. There was one at Sandy Hook, another at Barnegat City and a third at Cape May. With the cooperation of the Lighthouse Service and the weather bureau, each signal house was manned by a skilled telegrapher and connected by wire through Western Union to the Navy De-

ing bunks, telegraph office and a depository for flags, lanterns and instruments. "Good discipline," they went on to say, "is maintained and the establishment is a model of neatness. The magnificent signal pole is ninety-feet in height and, up in the lookout tower, there is a powerful Negus telescope, which is in constant use. At the proper elevation, signals can be deciphered eighteen miles at sea under favorable conditions of the atmosphere."

Vessels passing any of these stations were requested to signal by international code any sighting of suspicious craft at sea, and, likewise, any precautionary news the land station might have was to be communicated to passing vessels within signal distance. It was all in vain; the Spanish fleet never came anywhere near New Jersey. It was halfway around the world bottled up in Manila Harbor in the Philippines, where Admiral Dewey sank it in a grand and glorious, one-sided battle.

*An early photograph of the Signal House, circa 1910. Below, , in the '20s, after the original clapboard was covered in cedar shingles.*

partment in Washington.

The lot chosen for the structure at Barnegat City was not near the inlet but about a half mile below it, at Seventh Street, close to the lifesaving station at Fourth Street. Here vessels could come nearer to shore than the shoals by the lighthouse would allow them. A wood-frame house with a sturdy lookout tower was to be built by Wilkinson G. Conrad of Barnegat under a wartime contract that required completion within ten days.

The new signal house was ready for operation on May 10, 1898, under Quartermaster Charles B. Davenport, who made $55 a month. The young men under his command, all from Hoboken and Jersey City, made $35 a month. The building itself was described in the newspapers of the day as small but very comfortable, well ventilated. It was comprised of two rooms, one of which was used as a kitchen and dining room, the other for sleep-

ing light low on the horizon. "There's Old Barney!" exclaims the helmsman with relief, and all hands know the ship is on the right course and New York is ninety miles away.

The only thing wrong with this scenario is that the phrase "Old Barney" would be an anachronism. It wasn't in use then. Nowhere in the newspapers, books or journals of the 19th century does the term "Old Barney" appear. Certainly there are many references to Barnegat Lighthouse written then, but not a single writer ever called it "Old Barney." It is a completely modern nickname, and that may be why there are a few old-timers for whom it does not sit right (much like someone saying "Frisco" for San Francisco); they prefer the full name of Barnegat Lighthouse.

The nickname "Old Barney" was invented in the of-

*"As dependable as Old Barney" was the slogan for a local milk delivery service until the 1960s.*

The war was over on August 12, 1898, less than four months after it had been declared. The solidly built government structure at Barnegat City, with the huge tower atop it, was strong enough to support several more stories, and they were added in the next decade to give it its present appearance. For many years it was a rooming house. Now a private residence, it has never lost its original name among the local residents and will always be known as the Signal House.

## "Old Barney"

"Old Barney" as a nickname for the Barnegat Lighthouse has no long history, although it sounds like the sort of affectionate term that might have been bestowed upon it long ago in the age of sail. We imagine a schooner, northward bound, hugging the coast in the dark of night with her captain and crew anxiously looking for that single white flash at one-minute intervals that would indicate Barnegat Lighthouse. Suddenly there is a wink-

*The truck is parked at Maryland Avenue in Beach Haven Terrace.*

The title used for Deet's little bit of doggerel was "Old Barney." At about this time a local businessman, Frank H. Klein, who was later to become a Ship Bottom councilman and two-term mayor, was starting up a milk delivery company on Long Beach Island. He chose to call it Hy Vita, and he needed a clever symbol to beat out the big Philadelphia distributors, something that would indicate to everyone that he was purely local. What could be better than a picture of Barnegat Lighthouse on every bottle? Along with it he included the slogan: "As dependable as Old Barney."

Frank Klein's glass milk bottles with the picture and lettering all in red were soon to be seen everywhere and did more to promote the term "Old Barney" than any of the efforts of the Board of Trade. Hy Vita went out of business in the 1960s, and collectors still eagerly seek the bottles.

## Erosion at the Lighthouse

Severe erosion often threatened the base of Barnegat Lighthouse, especially in the 1930s, and when trouble came, people rallied to save it. The following four paragraphs appeared on the front page of The *Ocean County Courier* on September 12, 1933.

### Old Autos Sought in Plan to Save Barnegat Light

*Will Seek Auto Wrecks in Inlet to Prevent Erosion Around Base of Historic Beacon*

Barnegat City residents decided at a mass meeting held at that place last week that perhaps the quickest and cheapest way to prevent tides from cutting into the base of the historic Barnegat Lighthouse and toppling it into the sea would be to place auto wrecks in the inlet.

fices of the Long Beach Island Board of Trade during World War II, nearly twenty years after the light had been turned off forever and replaced by a lightship eight miles off the coast. Jack Lamping, who was the director then, felt that Barnegat Lighthouse, the Island's most enduring symbol, needed some sort of friendly name to attract people to the Island in the war years when gasoline rationing required car pooling. Other lighthouses had acquired such names over the years, and so he began using the term on his weekly radio show and frequently in promotional literature about the Island.

He got a Pennsylvania poet from Downingtown, named H. Vernon Deets, to write a brief poem about the lighthouse to honor one of the keepers who, as a veteran of the Civil War, was buried at Arlington.

"As a beacon of mercy, Old Barney stood
At the edge of the bay beyond the pine wood
Its keeper, I am told was never forward and never bold.
When he died, he was laid to rest among the nation's
 honored best."

According to fishermen and coast guardsmen and others who see the inlet day by day these wrecks that can be secured at junkyards and dumps might solve the problem of saving the famous lighthouse. The men at Barnegat City are willing and will attempt to anchor the wrecks in the swiftly running tides. Some men have offered to use their trucks to go after the disused autos.

Ebb tides are now running within 15 feet of the base of the old tower and threaten to cut under the foundations and undermine the brick structure. Mayor Charles Butler is asking all persons interested in saving the historic beacon where old wrecks can be obtained. The community is soliciting a fund in order to pay the expenses of men donating their trucks for transportation of materials.

There are hundreds of wrecks throughout Ocean County and Mayor Butler is receiving calls daily from people who want to contribute to the movement to save the Lighthouse. Many are willing to deliver these wrecks to the site while others want them collected.

*　　*　　*

The *New Jersey Courier* in Toms River picked up the story, and soon the press had spread the word about the plight of the lighthouse throughout the state. On one weekend near the end of September, as many as two thousand persons assembled at the inlet to lend support and to see for themselves the destruction caused by the outgoing tides. Brush, concrete rubble and old hulks had been dumped in front, and slightly to the left, of the base of the structure. Mayor Butler said there had been no scarcity of old wrecks located for fill; the problem was in getting them to the scene of the action. The amount of $225 was raised to help pay for gas and oil for the local

*A steel "petticoat" was built around Barnegat Lighthouse in the spring of 1934 to halt erosion that threatened to topple the tower.*

The Newark Call, *August 1909*

# Barnegat City, 1909

## Fishermen Find Sport in Plenty At Barnegat City

**B**arnegat City had just nineteen voters at the last election and five of them voted the Democratic ticket. Surf City just below on the sand strip had nineteen also but eleven of them voted that ticket. Harvey Cedars had twenty and fifteen of them voted the Republican ticket. This merely indicates what the winter population is like on that end of Long Beach north of the rail junction and up to the inlet.

Barnegat City is one of the too numerous Barnegats associated with Barnegat Bay, and to get there you have to go by train through the village of Barnegat on the mainland and then over the bay to Barnegat City junction and then north, or you can simply cross the bay by boat. One way is to hire a motorboat or catboat from Barnegat Pier, which is on the bridge over Barnegat Bay from Seaside Park to Good Luck Point. It is a good thirteen and a half miles sail going that way through tortuous channels and only five miles across the bay from Waretown or seven miles from the Barnegat village landing.

It is worth the time and trouble to go to Barnegat City any old way, even by rail. Either the Central or the Pennsylvania Railroad will take you there (in time) by way of Whitings the junction point for Manahawkin, Tuckerton and Beach Haven. Once started from Whitings, there are few stops and only one change of cars, that at Barnegat City Junction, where connections are never missed with the little two-car train which makes the two trips each way every weekday and one trip away from Barnegat City on Sunday afternoon. The railroad is just nine miles long and the trains are run with great care and deliberation, stopping at Surf City, Harvey Cedars and High Point (twenty-two feet above the level of the sea) before reaching Barnegat City, where the line terminates directly across the road from the front of big, old four-story Oceanic hotel. This dignified old building is one of the largest on the coast, barring some at Asbury Park, Long Branch, Atlantic City and some other fashionable resorts.

Barnegat City cannot be called fashionable, as it has no ocean boulevard, no boardwalk and no temptation for motoring. It would be difficult to get an automobile over there and land it, and after it was there it would have only a half-mile of road to run on. Consequently Barnegat City is a place for the motorphobist to visit to get away from the honks and the glare of acetylene lamps but the visitor cannot escape the odor of hot gasoline, as the bay and inlet are alive with motorboats from twelve to fifty feet in length.

The "city" is located on the upper end of Long Beach, an island formed by Barnegat Inlet on the north and Little Egg Inlet on the south, the ocean on the east, and Barnegat Bay, Manahawkin Bay and Little Egg Harbor Bay on the west. The point

*The Sunset Hotel was on the bayside of the inlet.*

*Scenes from Barnegat City in the early 1900s. Above: John Haddock's yard full of "relics from the sea," and at top, the stately lighthouse keepers' house.*

Photo by Fred Thornes
Toms River N. J.

*A view of Barnegat City circa 1914, looking southeast toward the beach. The Oceanic Hotel is the large building with twin cupolas. on the left; the lifesaving station is behind the hotel.*

at the inlet is a quarter of a mile broad and on this enlarged lobe of the Island are perhaps sixty buildings, many of which are quite pretentious summer homes. There are two big hotels, the Oceanic and the Sunset. The former is a temperance house at present and is operated this season by H. Ross Turner. The other one is part of a string of four hotels operated by James Romaine of the American House at Trenton; the Melrose at Belmar and a new hotel at Williamsport,

Pennsylvania. Mrs. Romaine takes charge of the Sunset Hotel, which is at the extreme point near the lighthouse and the landing. Either of the houses could accommodate over one hundred more guests than are stopping there just now, in fact matters are quiet at Barnegat City although the inducements to go there are far beyond those of many previous years. The fishing is wonderfully good in the bay, the inlet and the ocean. There are no mosquitoes there now and the weather is delightful. On the hottest days,

the breeze blows from one direction or another, and the wide bay prohibits the hot land breezes of other coast resorts.

There is one of the finest and safest bathing beaches on the New Jersey coast at the foot of the main street, and it is quite well patronized at all tides and especially at high water. Bathing houses are few, and the custom is to don bathing suits at home and walk through a gap in the sand dunes to the beach. The procession of bathers is one of the interesting features of a stay at Barnegat City. Everything is done in a most dignified manner there and there is never any vulgar display, because there is no flash society there. The visitors are invariably people who seek quiet relief from boardwalk pageants and display and are contented with viewing nature "unimproved."

Barnegat City is truly a primitive place half a mile or so from the cluster of houses. There are no bulkheads, except the dilapidated one at Sunset Park, on the inlet, and a pedestrian may walk twenty-two miles from the lighthouse down the beach to Little Egg Inlet without meeting with any obstructions. There are six life-saving stations on this stretch, and the men attached to this service have to take these walks in sections. There is communication between stations by telephone, and beacon lights indicate the position of the phones. There is likewise a long distance telephone service to all points on Long Beach, so that guests at the hotels can keep in touch with their homes.

Going fishing and coming back from fishing are

The Sunset Hotel.

Edy the Janvis - May Applegate
Morris Jones - Minnie Pedrunth - Bobby Applegate

the chief amusements, but it is enough for many visitors to stroll on the beach gathering shells or to sit upon the piazza with a book and occasionally glance at the ever passing vessels or watch the great white rollers forming on the outer bar and rushing into the inlet in serried rank. This is perhaps the most impressive sight on the Atlantic coast, and visitors never tire of looking at the "white horses" which dash in from the bar even in calmest weather. The tall lighthouse is another object of inspiration, especially when viewed by night, when the revolving lantern casts its rays out to sea.

Perhaps it is all the better for the visitors that Barnegat City is a difficult place to reach, although the hotelkeepers do not feel that way. If it were as accessible as Asbury Park or Atlantic City, the romance of the place would be spoiled for most of the people who enjoy their visits now.

Barnegat City had a nice little harbor a few years ago back of the bulkhead at Sunset Park, but it is shoaling rapidly and is difficult to land there when the tide is down. This will have to be remedied immediately by dredging or pumping. Otherwise, the place may as well be given up as a fishing station. The harbor is the only safe landing at certain stages of the tide and wind, as the current rushing to and fro through the inlet makes that end of the inlet a dangerous landing place except at slack water.

One of the sights of Barnegat City is the home of an old gentleman who has made a fad of collecting relics of the sea. His picturesque house is opposite the Oceanic Hotel and stands in the center of a neatly-fenced garden. The lawn is decorated with figureheads removed from wooden ships which have been wrecked along the coast in the last half century, and on the outbuildings and side and rear fences are displayed the signboards of about sixty wrecked vessels. In front of the house is a large anchor, reclining upon its coil of chain, and behind it is a red and white buoy imbedded in the ground by a white-painted statue of Mercury, which occupies one side of the lawn, and on the other is a carved figure of St. Patrick which was taken from the bow of a vessel. A fountain of bottles and odd flasks rescued from the sea occupies the lawn at the other side of the house. The owner of the place has a poultry yard and a flying cage for pigeons besides several occupied purple martin houses of quaint design. The two lampposts flanking his house on the curb line are red and white replicas of the Barnegat light, surmounted by lanterns.

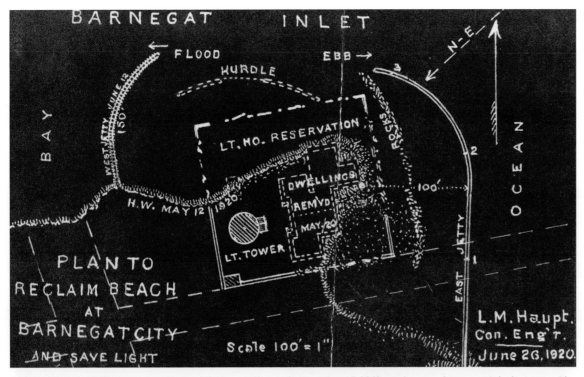

*After a February 1920 northeaster damaged the keepers' house, Army engineer L. M. Haupt drew up plans to encircle the tower with protective jetties. The high water mark of May 12, 1920, shows how threatened the lighthouse was. In 1933, below, junked cars and other debris were dumped into the sands at the foot of the lighthouse in a desperate effort by locals to protect the tower from erosion.*

fishermen using their trucks to haul the old cars.

While the barrier of rubbish had slowed the tidal scour, the base of the tower was now a mere sandy slope exactly a foot and a half from the waters of the inlet at high tide. In the next few weeks, a derelict barge from Atlantic City was towed to the inlet and beached at right angles in front of the tower. It was filled with 2,000 bags of sand. Other hulks were planted along with more old cars.

By late October, it was evident that the sunken barges were working. The fierce ebb tides were sparing the lighthouse, cutting in to the west of the tower near the ruins of the old Sunset Hotel, which had burned to the ground the previous year. The State Board of Commerce and Navigation met in Trenton and awarded a $14,000 contract to a Sea Bright engineering firm to build a steel "petticoat" around the base of the tower.

In the spring of 1934, sand was excavated around the tower to a depth of twenty feet. Into the cut went two heavy steel rings reinforced by thick iron rods and filled with concrete. Finally a 175-foot band of steel pilings, 20 feet out from the lighthouse, was driven to a depth of 30 feet. This semicircular structure was filled with sand, creating a fortress 20 feet above the level of high tide.

The first test of the structure came on November 16, 1934 when a three-day northeaster began, one of the fiercest of a decade of devastating storms. The steel jacket, or "petticoat," held. It has survived every storm since, aided by a number of jetties started by the Army Corps of Engineers on the bay side in the early 1940s. The upper lip of that steel ring surrounding Barnegat Lighthouse may be seen to this day, and the $14,000 spent for it nearly seventy years ago has been more than worth it. It may not seem like much today, but it was an awesome sum in 1934.

## Barnegat City, 1923

Barnegat Lighthouse, from the moment it was put into service in January 1859, was so impressive a structure, rising as it did 160 feet above sea level and casting a beam twenty miles out into the Atlantic, that there was scarcely a newspaper or periodical in the region that did not, at one time or another, send a reporter to this remote spot on the coast of New Jersey to interview its keeper and his two assistants.

Any assignment of this sort was usually treated as an adventure by the writer whether the journey involved sailing across the bay to the Island, or, after 1896, taking the railroad, or finally, by 1920, actually motoring all the way to the north end on the newly completed eighteen-mile "Inlet to Inlet" automobile boulevard.

One of the last in a long line of these interesting visits to Barnegat City was a journey made by automobile in December 1922. It was written up for the *Newark Sunday Call* and appeared in February 1923 under the title "Old Barnegat Light and its Keepers: a Pen Picture."

"A sea gull dipped gracefully to the level of the ocean, and winged again into the blue sky. The faint, even rumble of the surf below was the only sound to be heard high up in the tower. Clarence Cranmer, who has kept the famous light for the last thirty-five years, paused for a moment from his morning work of rubbing the lighthouse window with glycerin to look out. Never had he seen Barnegat City more subdued. It might have been a community of the dead but for the tiny telltale wisps of smoke from cottages discernible above the aged firs. The trees themselves were bent as if weary of forever battling the cruel gales that swept across the inlet."

Cranmer had reason, according to the writer of this piece, to be melancholy. Standing alone atop the light-house he had faithfully tended for so many years, he could not avoid a view of the wreckage of his home far below. The magnificent, three-family keepers' house, built in 1889, had succumbed to erosion in the severe winter storms of 1920 and had to be sold to the highest bidder and torn down. It went for a mere $120.

Thirty-five years of his life he had given up to Barnegat Lighthouse, nearly every day of which he had climbed the 225 steps to the top of the tower carrying a heavy oil can. Now his cozy home at the base had been destroyed by the very waves he had spent a lifetime warning others against. His wife had passed on and he was all alone. Spent and weary and not yet 65, he could not retire on a full pension although a younger man, already his assistant, Andy Applegate, would tend the lighthouse in its final days when it was to lose its great Fresnel lens and become electrified with but a fraction of its former power.

Standing in the ruins of the old keepers' house at the base of the light around midnight and looking up at the great beam of light sweeping the heavens, the reporter encountered a Coast Guardsman on patrol. After chatting about the weather he asked about bootlegging activity in the area.

"Not much of that around Barnegat City," said the patrolman. "Every unknown boat, large or small, slipping into the inlet, is searched by the coast guard as soon as it reaches the town wharf. The new highway stretching

from Barnegat City to Surf City is also closely watched. From the tower of the station all the fishing smacks are visible at sea and their every movement is observed during the day. No chance of any wholesale smuggling on this end of the Island."

Around the base of the tower the next day the writer noticed the bodies of several birds. Cranmer explained that they were unfortunate gulls, which, attracted by the light, had plunged headlong against the wire mesh surrounding it. They were there every morning, he said; after an unusually heavy storm there were as many as thirty or forty various types of birds, ducks and geese. One night, he said, a flock of brant headed for the light and the next morning there were fifty bodies — enough for a month of duck dinners.

"A foolish bird, the brant," observed Cranmer, "a mighty foolish bird. Once he is in the circle of the light around the lighthouse he is doomed. He comes nearer and nearer, like a moth to a flame. Then he whangs right into the wire netting and it's all over."

# A Visit to the Barnegat Lightship – September 1927

You can inquire of the hotel clerk as to getting a boat captain to handle you on the rest of the journey and if you are fortunate he will refer you to Capt. Joe Collins, skipper of the Mar-Sar. Boats like his are built especially for sea fishing, party cruising and hunting on ocean and bay for which this section is noted. These boats are about 12 feet at beam, 36 feet long and draw about 30 inches of water. They are equipped with four-cylinder gasoline motors and can attain a speed of ten miles an hour. They can be hired for a reasonable amount.

Last Sunday we engaged Captain Collins whose Mar-Sar was named after his daughters Martha and Sarah. We headed down Forked River, taking its name from the three forks into which this river divides just off Barnegat Bay.

You will find these captains congenial and full of information, and it was not long before we got Captain Joe talking as we sailed the crooked course of this stream lined with river house boats and pleasure craft. He started by telling us that his busy season starts soon, for, on October 16, the hunting season opens and he had been getting in shape his gunning boxes or sneak scows, a flat-bottom device with a top opening just enough for a hunter to sit in and ride water, marshes etc. They are towed out to the shooting grounds and if placed in marsh, are covered with sea grass, and

if on the beach, with sand with the hunter sitting in it concealed and surrounded with decoy ducks. Captain Joe, incidentally, told of the way to shoot these ducks just as they are spread full wing and about to alight among the decoys, being careful not to hit any one of the airtight wood decoys for they cost real money, and always pick one bird to shoot at and not into the flock.

He explained that the best time to hunt is early in the morning, just at sunrise. The law prohibits shooting before sunrise and after sunset. The law permits the possession of twenty-five ducks, eight geese, eight brant, twenty Wilson snipe and fifteen yellow legs.

You ride along the river into and across the Barnegat Bay in its main channel, marked by cedar sticks on the upper end and by buoys on its lower, with sand dunes between it and the ocean. On your left is the lodge of the Great Sedge Gunning Club of

Trenton and on your right the High Bar Gun Club of Newark. At anchor in the channel is the beautiful power schooner, Osprey III built at Bay Head and ready to start for Bermuda.

You are riding in Oyster Creek channel in the middle of this wide expanse of shallow water and have to follow a winding irregular course. You note, coming opposite, some power boats returning from fishing trips with men cleaning fish and a flock of gulls diving at the parts thrown overboard. Among the fishermen met that day was Mr. Steinway, famous piano manufacturer, who makes Forked River his vacation Mecca.

You now reach a point inside Barnegat Inlet and prepare to ride this treacherous opening from bay to ocean. On the right is a little fishing village of small shacks and a perfect built-in harbor, the headquarters of the pound fishermen, a Swedish settlement with its fleet of open fishing boats for net work.

This is directly in back of the Sunset Hotel and the famous Barnegat Light, which is to be preserved as a memorial as it is one of the oldest lighthouses in the country. The powerful light has been removed and only a weak flash at night serves as a guide to local watercraft.

You are now emerging from the inlet at the flood shoals and the most dangerous place on the Atlantic coast, needing an expert to navigate, as the sandbars permit only a narrow passage and hurl the waters into tremendous waves. You are now safely across into the open sea. The captain puts out the trolling lines in the hope of catching a few bonitos on the run of nine miles to the lightship, the object of the trip.

Out on this open sea you meet more powerboats returning from the ridge, twenty miles off shore. The fishing is done by trolling with stern lines and extended sidelines and results always in large catches. This ridge is the fishing ground for these old timers and is a formation extending from Montauk Point, Long Island to Atlantic City, varying from twenty miles off shore at Barnegat to forty miles at Atlantic City. It is five miles wide and but sixty feet below the surface.

You continue over the ocean waves with a

likelihood of getting seasick and soon you spot a schooner like vessel riding at anchor with the word Barnegat on both sides, the lighthouse of the open sea.

You circle around it, get a friendly salute from the captain and crew and the inquiry, "Have you any newspapers?" And pulling up alongside, you are thrown a rope and pulled to the hull and climb into the port landing entrance where you get a warm welcome from Captain John Carr, Mate Chris Lasdine, Engineer Al Stillwell and friendly nods from the crew. You are at home and amazed at what you see. A perfect picture of cleanliness and discipline with every part shining and in working order. The lightship is known as No. 79, Barnegat Lightship and has been in operation at this location since August 15, when the Barnegat Light was discontinued as a

sea light. It is a new station, just established by the Bureau of Lighthouses under the Department of Commerce.

The crew is composed of hardy experienced seafaring men, twelve in number. They get seven days off every month in the mild weather and are on constant duty the balance of each month. In the winter they get one month off and two months on. A tender from New York picks them up.

You now leave this interesting ship and start the run of nine miles back and over the treacherous bar of the inlet, making an early get-away as it is a ticklish journey in the dark over the bar and through a narrow channel on shallow flats.

Captain Collins said that on his last run to the fishing ridge, he had the thrill of having a fifty-foot whale sport around his craft three times. It was a sight not uncommon to him but one I was just as satisfied to miss.

After a pleasant trip you reach the dock, have a good meal at Forked River and get into your auto for a ride back home, over all good roads. As traffic is not heavy, the ride can be made to Newark in something near two hours. It is well advised before visiting the ship to write to Staten Island, the U.S. Government Lighthouse Service and get permission to look it over and be sure to take plenty of magazines.

— Edward B. Loughran
State Highway Department

# Old Barnegat Inlet

*From the* Ocean County Courier, *August 1931*

By R. G. Collins

The ever-changing channel of the Barnegat Inlet is changing for the worse. As an inlet it gets narrower each year and the water is rapidly nearing the old lighthouse. The channel is now barely navigable for fishing boats with no promise of better conditions as each year sees North Beach [The Island Beach side of Barnegat Inlet — not today's North Beach on the Island] *rapidly coming to the south*. Where a few years ago there was a big basin with good water behind the point of it, North Beach has now become a drive for autoists who can find a good road all the way to Great Sedge.

Years ago, what was known as Sea Dog Shoal, a long sand bar on the north side of the main channel, was often under water at high tide. Some 25 years ago "Dad" Parker placed a few piles of meadow sod on the bar for hiding gunning boats behind them and it was called "Kale's Sods."

Today those few sods are a solid meadow for a mile or more. When the present lighthouse was built in 1858-59, it stood several hundred feet back from the water. In front was a line of hills covered with a growth of large cedars and wild cherry trees. The groves were used for camping parties and picnic parties. Today all these hills are gone and the water is within 25 or 30 feet of the tower on the west side of it. The entire water front from the old Anchoring Point all the way down to the lighthouse has gone in the inlet and where the Sunset Hotel stood 150 feet or more from the water, the tide now washes right up to its foundations.

Ebb tides running swiftly down the channel are rapidly cutting the shore away and in a short time the light must give way to the ravaging tides and fall as the foundation will be undermined. What help is there for it? None, as the government has long since abandoned it to its fate and, with the lightship eight miles off shore, its usefulness is over and the state took it over as a memory of the old days and for the good it had done years back.

Then the government will not spend any money to save it, the state will not spend any more and the borough cannot do it, so what is there to do but await the freaks of the tides? Should the government build a jetty at the inlet, who knows what this may do with the currents? Only time will tell.

Years ago the sea came so close to the Oceanic Hotel that it had to be moved several hundred feet to the west, then shortly afterward this beach built out again about a quarter of a mile. Then, some years later, it again started making inroads until it swept this hotel and several dwellings into the sea. A cottage just across the street from the hotel was so near falling two years ago that a heavy cofferdam was placed around it, and today the shore is several hundred feet out from it. No one can tell what the winds and tides will do, but one thing is true. No one will trust to them doing any good.

If we had several big senators and congressmen living along this part of the coast who were interested, or who had large yachts, you can be sure we'd soon see the sand going high in the air and the sea churned to foam with all the stone being dumped ever so fast.

This is surely a much-needed thing, but if we cannot show a certain amount of commerce, it's a dark sight for us. There are millions spent in some communities on little creeks and mud holes that are hardly frog ponds, but it's as we said they have a "drag" and we haven't. That's the difference.

As to Long Beach, not until about 1880 was there anything except, here and there, an old house between Barnegat Inlet and Beach Haven. Some

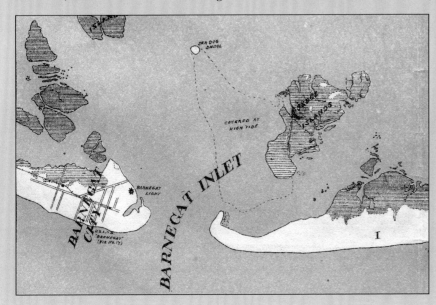

years before this Beach Haven had started to be quite a resort with a steamer running from Tuckerton across the bay. The handsome, commodious, staunch steamer *Barclay Haines* made daily trips from Edge Cove on the arrival of the trains.

Barnegat City started to boom in 1880 and many cottages and two large hotels were built. Three miles below the inlet there was an old boarding house known as the Club House owned by New York people. Years before this was owned by Double Jimmy, proper name James James, then by George Cox, Joseph Ridgway, George Van Note and David Wright (colored). It was abandoned and finally bought by J. B. Kinsey and moved to High Point. Next down was the old hotel at Harvey Cedars, Wesley Truex's old dwelling at Ship Bottom, the Peahala Club, Dr. Tucker's and then Beach Haven and just look at the south end today!

In 1887, there was a large hotel built at Surf City, which was then called Long Beach City and, for a while, Culver's. It was on the west side of the railroad, which was built on the beach in 1886. This hotel was built on the site of the old "Mansion of Health" that was burned down several years before. William Smith built the first house at Surf City near the oceanfront. Next, Isaac Lee built a cottage at High Point and everything we see there today is since 1888.

The beach below the junction has gone far ahead of the north end, as it is now seems like one long city from Beach Arlington south to Beach Haven with hardly an unsettled tract between. The only place on the Island where one can still see the beach as nature made it is between High Point and Barnegat City, and it is hoped that part of this beach will be kept for future generations to see what the old coast looked like years ago.

The old beach is not what it once was, a barren stretch of sand with nothing to break the stillness but the roaring of the sea as it broke against the hills and the shriek of the gull as it flew leisurely along seeking its prey. Today the scream of the gull is seldom heard, and the roar of the sea is drowned by the hum of the automobiles that speed up and down the beach where once quiet and stillness reigned.

# Harvey Cedars

## High Point

The town "High Point" has been gone for fifty years, having been absorbed into the borough of Harvey Cedars in the 1940s. High Point once covered the three-quarters of a mile from Sussex Avenue, in Harvey Cedars northward to Eighty-seventh Street, on the Loveladies line. A driver entering the Borough of Harvey Cedars will note that all the cross streets in the southern half of the borough are named after New Jersey counties. When the county names cease at Sussex Avenue, the streets take numbers starting with Seventy-second Street. Here the visitor will have crossed over into the old High Point section, which runs for another fifteen blocks. This area is the heart of present-day Harvey Cedars, where nearly all of the major businesses are located, including the post office, the borough hall and the fire hall.

High Point was founded in 1887 by a strong, energetic New Englander named Isaac A. Lee. Lee was in his mid-'40s and a powerful figure in the Philadelphia and New York fish trade who took advantage of the new railroad to the Island to set up a pound fishery. The fishery was by no means the first on the coast, but soon to be of great profit to him. He chose High Point as a summer home for his family, enticed friends to join him, and built homes for the men in his employ. He didn't name the town — the location had, since Colonial times, been

*Seventy-eighth Street, looking toward the bay in Harvey Cedars, circa 1908, with High Point Inn at center.*

called High Point, partly due to its huge dunes and partly for its attractiveness as a spot for gunning. It was one of twenty such "points" on Barnegat Bay between Harvey Cedars and Waretown, once well known to local sportsmen who sought them out when the ducks and geese were flying. They had colorful names like Injun Point, Jack's Point, Office Point, South Point, Ram Cat Point, Luke's Point, Whalebone Point and Main Meadow Point.

Within a generation, High Point was not only com-

mercially profitable, it had become a thriving summer colony as well. Both Lee, with his fish pounds, and fellow entrepreneur J. B. Kinsey, with his seaweed industry, had just begun developing and selling building lots. Neighboring Harvey Cedars had become an independent borough in 1894. High Point, though a part of it, was nonetheless to have its own mayor, its own rail stop, and, in 1910, its own post office. Isaac Lee died at his home in Camden on Christmas Day, 1912, at the age of 70, but his

little community lived on.

High Point would remain unofficially a separate village for the next thirty years, long enough to proudly celebrate its fiftieth anniversary on August 8, 1937. In the weekly newspapers High Point always had its own heading for news and social items quite separate from Harvey Cedars. By the 1940s, High Point was quietly absorbed into the borough of Harvey Cedars and its name survives only in the High Point Fire Company.

In 1901, the *Ocean County Courier* reported that "A club house is being built at High Point on the bay at 78th Street by a group of twenty young men from Philadelphia and Camden. It will be used as a hunting and fishing headquarters." Within the decade, as boating grew in popularity and women became active in social activities, the fishing club was incorporated as the High Point Yacht Club. In 1928, after building a handsome new clubhouse and dock two blocks to the south, on Seventy-sixth Street, they applied for membership in the North American Racing Association in order to broaden their scope of activities. They were turned down because their name was in conflict with an existing High Point Yacht Club in North Carolina. They needed a new name, but they never considered calling themselves the Harvey Cedars Yacht Club. High Point had always been, and was still, the name of their community. Their distinctiveness was a matter of pride.

The Racing Association was adamant, so in search of a new name, the club officers looked about and there, on the northern horizon, just three miles away and clearly visible both day and night, was the stately sentinel of Barnegat Light. It would become their symbol and their name. They joined the association as the Barnegat Light Yacht Club and created a new burgee displaying the silhouette of a lighthouse, with flashing rays.

*Camp Whelan, the former Harvey Cedars Hotel, on the bay about 1920, above. At top, Harvey Cedars oceanfront; the pavilion on Passaic Avenue was built in 1898.*

041    Neptune Dining Room, High Point, N. J., E. Dermit, Prop.

In 1932, the club could not anticipate that High Point would one day be totally absorbed into Harvey Cedars or that in 1940 Barnegat City would change its name to Barnegat Light. The Barnegat Light Yacht Club of Harvey Cedars, its name puzzling to some, is perfectly justified historically in its choice. It remains to this day an active organization with over a hundred members.

## The *Sans Souci* And the Perrines

No history of yachting in Harvey Cedars is complete without mention of the role played by at least two generations of the Perrine family of Barnegat, and the story of the *Sans Souci*, the most luxurious schooner yacht that ever sailed the waters of Barnegat Bay.

The *Sans Souci*, built in Barnegat in 1875 by Charles Sprague, a resident of Manahawkin, was two-masted, 100 feet in length, with enough cabin space to accommodate eighteen guests. Her captain and crew of nine were all Barnegat men. Captain Samuel Forman Perrine Jr. (the bearded man standing in the white hat on the hatch in the facing photograph) was one of three generations of the distinguished Perrines of Barnegat. His father, Captain Samuel Perrine Sr., built the Harvey Cedars Hotel in 1837, and was its sole proprietor until his death in 1876. He called it the Connahasatt House and, in all his advertising and stationery, he referred to its location as "Harvest Cedars," not Harvey Cedars.

Samuel F. Perrine Jr. was born in the Connahasatt House in 1840 and, by the time he was 30 years old, in 1870, became the first keeper of the new, fully manned Harvey Cedars Lifesaving Station. His father had been the man in charge of the local house of refuge established at Harvey Cedars in 1850, one of two such units on the Island then. The other was at the south end near Bond's Long Beach House. For all the shipwrecks that there were in those years before the development of sophisticated navigational tools, there were only twenty houses of refuge on the whole coast, from Massachusetts to Georgia. Not one of the stations had a paid crew. The establishment of the U. S. Lifesaving Service mandated and funded at least six fully manned stations on Long Beach Island alone and another on nearby Tucker's Island. During Samuel Jr.'s tenure at Harvey Cedars, he was repeatedly honored for the heroic acts he performed on many dangerous rescue operations.

He stayed on as keeper for several years. To keep occupied in the summer months, he participated in the building of the *Sans Souci* in the Sprague yards at Barnegat. When it was completed, he joined the schooner's crew, working his way up from cook to captain, finally leaving the lifesaving service to become the full-time master of the yacht. As captain, he sailed the schooner as far south as Georgia and the Carolinas, to all the famous sea island gunning and fishing resorts of the day. The winter port of the *San Souci* was Havre de Grace, Maryland, but she returned to Barnegat Bay every spring for refitting.

The ship, which cost $25,000 to build (a considerable sum for that time period), was commissioned by a group of wealthy Pennsylvania iron and coal men, principally John Leisenring of Mauch Chunk (now Jim Thorpe) and Nathan Middleton of Philadelphia. They and their families, along with other shareholders, used it for extensive fishing and gunning expeditions around Barnegat Bay each summer and into the fall. On Saturday nights, they

no auxiliary power.

Unfortunately, the *Sans Souci* was to last only about twenty-five years. By 1908, with most of her original owners dead, the once stately *San Souci* remained out of service along the west bank of Double Creek, near Barnegat Landing. She was eventually dismantled and her priceless furnishings, sails, hardware and portable equipment sold at auction. Before she was dismantled, photographers took her picture for postcards.

Some of her crew were still living in the area, including Captain Perrine, who had held command to the very last days. His son, J. Howard Perrine, was on his way to becoming an acclaimed boat-builder. He would create the world-famous white cedar sneakbox, known as the Perrine, now considered a prized possession by all serious wooden boat collectors.

The *Sans Souci, right, and dining aboard the yacht, above.*

would moor occasionally at the Harvey Cedars Hotel to join in the fun and card playing. In the winter, they sailed the Chesapeake and points south.

During their journeys, the Leisenrings, Middletons and their many prominent guests traveled in high style and lived up to their vessel's name, *San Souci*, which means "without care." The schooner was 135 feet overall with a keel of 89 feet, a 26-foot beam and a draft of 3 feet. The main cabin was 52 feet long and 26 feet wide, with 8 feet of headroom. The large dining room could seat twenty. There was a sitting room and six staterooms, equipped with washstands and water. There was a kitchen, a large storeroom, wine closets and other closets for dishes, lamps, guns, ammunition and fishing gear. There was also an ice chamber, with a holding capacity of five tons, and fresh water tanks able to store several thousand gallons of water. The *San Souci* was schooner rigged, driven by foresail, mainsail, jib and flying jib, with

WRECK OF SANS SOUCI, BARNEGAT, N. J.

*The* Sans Souci *in the early 1900s, abandoned along the banks of Double Creek near Barnegat Landing.*

## The Bungalow on Wood's Island

In 1892, William Henry Sayen (pronounced "Sine") of St. Davids, Pennsylvania, built a large vacation bungalow for his family on a small island in Barnegat Bay. The bungalow was just far enough out in the water to be accessible by a narrow footbridge from the train stop at Passaic Avenue in Harvey Cedars. He'd always entertained lavishly, and, when his wife died in 1903, he converted the place into a hunting club and hideaway for his wide circle of politically influential Pennsylvania friends. For the next two decades these "Bold Buccaneers of the Bungalow," as they called themselves, enjoyed a seemingly endless round of fishing, gunning and card playing.

After Sayen died, the place continued to function as a club until one of its members, Robert W. A. Wood, a wool merchant from Wayne, Pennsylvania, bought it in 1920. He had married Sayen's granddaughter, Katherine Schultz, who, born in 1895, had spent all her childhood summers at the bungalow. It was often referred to in the newspapers as the Harvey Cedars Gunning Club, and in Bayard Kraft's book, *Under Barnegat's Beam*, as the Harvey Cedars Outing Club, but to Sayen's many friends and to the Wood family, who vacationed there for nearly forty years, it was always the bungalow. In the early years they had sometimes called it the "House of the Seven Cedars" for the few gnarled trees remaining on the little island.

"Bungalow" is an Anglo-Indian formation derived from the Hindu word *bangla,* for the unique style of country home used in the Indian province of Bengal. It is usually a single-story structure, with a gently slop-

ing thatched or tile roof, with exceptionally long eaves to shelter a wrap-around veranda from rain and sun. The climate of southern California was ideal for their adoption in America. In the 1890s they were rapidly copied as a design for vacation cottages elsewhere in the nation.

Wood spent a considerable amount of money refurbishing the old club. All through the 1920s the Woods used the bungalow as a private dwelling, although they had many guests. The place had always been equipped for year-round living, but sadly, one night in January of 1933, in a high wind just after a new heating system had been installed, the house caught fire. The flames were visible for twenty miles. So intense was the heat that the local Coast Guard could not approach the house to save anything at all. Many valuable treasures, including a collection of antique pistols purchased at auction in 1920 for $100,000, were lost. Of greater loss historically was the logbook of the Bold Buccaneers of the Bungalow, filled with witty observations over the years. Fortunately, the building had not been occupied at the time.

Katherine Schultz, as granddaughter of one owner and wife of the other, frequented the bungalow for thirty-five years, nearly its entire existence. She described the building as quite large. The broad, covered porch on all four sides was not screened, since there was always a breezy corner to escape the flies and mosquitoes.

There was a large living room at the south end, overlooking the bay, with a dining room at the north end facing toward the Harvey Cedars Hotel. Each of these rather large rooms had a fireplace, and between them ran a long hallway, with four double bedrooms on each side. There were two bathrooms, one for men and one for women. Each was complete with tubs, basins and toilets, all fed by an artesian well, one of the first ever drilled on Long Beach Island. There was a boiler for hot water.

*The bungalow on Wood's Island*

Near the dining room was a large pantry and kitchen with a huge coal range where the club steward, Captain Huey Bolton of Manahawkin, used to make his marvelous clam chowder. He was a kindly, capable man who could guide a hunting party, manage all the boats and cook superbly as well. Bolton liked a nip or two, often joining in with the male guests, but he was always the one able to help the more inebriated of them to bed. An unusual feature of the place was Katherine's grandfather Sayen's bar. It was inside an old-fashioned, roll-top desk, complete with a basin and running water.

Upstairs, above the living room and overlooking the bay through three big windows in the south gable, was a pool table and, near it, a big, comfortable barber's chair bolted to the floor where initiates of the Bold Buccaneers would have to sit blindfolded and drink beer out of a chamber pot. The second floor, despite the dormer windows, could get quite warm in summer and was used for storage. It also served as a dormitory for the help, usually Irish girls. In those days it was the custom for summer guests to bring their help along with them from home to do laundry, clean up, make beds and care

for the children. Every Sunday, in the early years before there was a road on the upper end of the Island, the girls would walk down the train tracks through the empty, narrow stretch that is now North Beach on into Surf City to attend Mass at the tiny St. Thomas of Villanova Catholic Church on Thirteenth Street. It was built and in use by 1898.

Katherine Schultz also described how pleasant life was in Harvey Cedars when houses were few and far between. They would have picnic excursions by train to Loveladies and Barnegat Light, and Saturday dances at the Harvey Cedars Hotel. Everyone used the big pavilion on the oceanfront at Passaic Avenue near the Fenimore house. The pavilion was built in 1898 as a place for bathers to change clothes and, in its upper levels, one could sit in the shade and watch the ocean or, as evening approached, view the sunset over the bay.

James Fenimore, her grandfather's good friend and neighbor, whose palatial home stood on the oceanfront across the railroad tracks, was a great wit. It was he who kept the log book of the Bold Buccaneers of the Bungalow and probably the one who inspired the unique wet bar in the roll-top desk. Fenimore's house and the pavilion near it were destroyed by storms. He once had large land holdings in St. Davids, Pennsylvania, and sold it all very cheaply to friends. He was not a good businessman, but he and William Henry Sayen certainly knew how to have fun in those early days in Harvey Cedars

The Bold Buccaneers of the Bungalow, with all the rituals and trappings of a college fraternity, was made up of mature businessmen of unquestionable ability whose primary interest was Republican politics in Philadelphia and Pennsylvania. Mayors, judges and senators used the place for top-level conferences. When the fun began there was never a more colorful figure than the U.S.

senator from Pennsylvania, Boies Penrose. Born in 1860 to a wealthy and distinguished family in Philadelphia, he was prepared for college by private tutors and graduated *magna cum laude* from Harvard in 1881. He read law and passed the bar, but soon entered politics where his commanding presence was an asset. He was a giant physically, standing six feet, four inches tall, and he loved vigorous sports such as sailing and big game hunting. He served in the U.S. Senate from 1897 until his death in 1920, always vehemently opposed to Prohibition, women's suffrage and progressive politics. He never married.

He was a heavy drinker and great fun to be with in the company of men. His private life and utterances, it was said, brought the pious to indignation. While staying at the bungalow, he would leave for his morning dip in the ocean and return, strolling naked along the narrow boardwalk, like Hemingway on his catwalk at Key West. Women, if any were present, simply had to look the other way. He didn't care what they thought.

Wood's Island, known a hundred years ago as Carver's Island, is greatly diminished today. All that remains of the stately bungalow are a few bricks from the supporting piers and a concrete wellhead in an impenetrable thicket of poison ivy. At the Long Beach Island Historical Museum in Beach Haven, there is an album of photographs from those long-ago summers of 1897 and 1898, showing the family and guests of the Sayens at the bungalow. They are swimming, boating and fishing in the broad expanse of Barnegat Bay. Not a single house but the bungalow can be seen anywhere.

*The bungalow on Wood's Island, in Barnegat Bay off Harvey Cedars, was accessible by a wooden footbridge, or by boat.*

# Beach Haven Houses

## The Cottages

In the 1870s and '80s it was in vogue among the affluent of eastern cities to attach names to their vacation homes at the seashore, not so much in the colorful way that the English named their country estates or southerners their plantations, but rather in the tradition of naming a boat.

Women in the family generally took the honors. In Beach Haven, for some reason, it was invariably a daughter whose name was carved into an ornately shaped board to be hung over the door of a lovely, bowered cottage, while the wife's name would be the one to appear, with no less reverence, on the transom of a graceful yacht.

The practice of giving names to individual dwellings was reserved only for the most elegant of homes. No matter how many servants were required to run them, the sprawling, gingerbread style Queen Annes were always called "cottages" by their owners. This was not out of any attempt at affectation; in the 19th century, the word "house" customarily referred to a hotel or public lodging place. Today people have "beach houses" or "houses at the shore," but in the 19th century, "house" meant something different.

Charles Parry, president of the Baldwin Locomotive Works and builder of the Hotel Baldwin, built another hotel, the Parry House at Beach Haven, in 1874. His palatial dwelling at Coral Street and Atlantic Avenue that he named "All Breeze" was his "cottage."

All Breeze is gone, but many of the beautiful old summer homes from that era are still standing, with names like Florence Cottage, at 127 Coral Street, and right next to it at 123, Portia Cottage with its magnificent twin chimneys. On the north side of Second Street, between Beach and Atlantic avenues, we find Louella Cottage, built by Archalaus Pharo, president of the Tuckerton Railroad. Dating from 1874, the year the resort opened, it is the oldest house in Beach Haven.

Sunshine, wind and sea birds also entered into the naming process. Early summer residents of Beach Haven came up with names such as Curlew Cottage, Saltaire, Sunbeam, Brant, Gravelin and The Dunes. Others were called Elsinore, Penravin, Kathlyn, Wayside, Idylease, Dancer and Thalassa. Even if one of these cottages were to be rented for part of the season to strangers, so well established were the classic old names that no street address was needed. The letter would go into the correct pigeonhole at the Beach Haven post office.

Sometimes the owner's name was reversed. Philadelphia engineer and architect Albert Damon's house on the northwest corner of Norwood and Atlantic in Beach

*Amber Street, looking toward the Baldwin hotel, as seen from the top floor of the Engleside.*
*At right center is the rear of the Portia Cottage.*

*Amber Street, with the three Shakespeare Cottages at right. Behind the houses, to the south, is the Hotel Baldwin, with its recognizable turrets.*

Haven was called "Nomad." That was in the 1920s, and by the next decade there was a great deal of zaniness going on with cottage names elsewhere on the Island. Ship Bottom and Brant Beach were dotted with modest little bungalows and Cape Cods with names like Dun Rovin, Nodaway, Haus Trix, Money-sunk and Bide-a-Wee.

The general rule, however, especially in Beach Haven, seemed to be that if a feminine name were to be attached to a cottage, it was more than likely a daughter's. Florence Cottage, on Coral Street, was named for Florence Brunner, a granddaughter of Charles Parry. Louella Cottage, on Second Street, was named for the two daugh-

ters of Archalaus Pharo, Louisa and Ella.

However, an exception to the daughter rule can be found in the so-called Shakespeare Cottages on Coral and Amber streets. Portia, built in the 1880s on the north side of Coral Street, is named for Portia in *The Merchant of Venice*. Behind it on the south side of Amber Street are three other cottages, built a decade later. They, too, are named for female characters in Shakespeare's plays.

These names are (from east to west), Rosalind (#118), Sylvia (#122), and Audrey (#126). Rosalind and Audrey come from *As You Like It*, and Sylvia is from *Two Gentlemen of Verona*. Portia, on a lot 100 by 100 feet, is one of the largest houses in Beach Haven. Famous for its twin chimneys, it was one of several fine structures around town designed by John A. Wilson, Philadelphia's foremost architect of the Victorian period. Wilson lived at Portia Cottage; it is not certain whether he also designed the other three Shakespeare cottages. With his fondness for the famous playwright, he certainly may have had a hand in naming them, especially since his daughters lived in them.

The name boards of all these fine old homes, which for the most part remain private dwellings, have long since been removed and hung on a wall inside to avoid the houses being mistaken for any one of the numerous boarding houses in the area. It should be noted, however, that the three Shakespeare cottages that face the broad expanse of Veterans Bicentennial Park on Amber Street, though their original names are no longer displayed, are all beautifully maintained bed and breakfast inns today.

## Parry & the Nearsea

When Charles Thomas Parry died in July 1887 at his Beach Haven summer home on Coral Street, his life had, by every standard, been a remarkable success. Born in Philadelphia in 1821, he went to work at the age of 15 as an apprentice in the pattern shops of Matthias Baldwin, who had, only a few years earlier, constructed for the Philadelphia & Germantown Railroad one of the first American locomotive engines to be actually employed

*Beach Avenue, looking toward the ocean along Coral Street. On the corner is the Nearsea Cottage; at the end of Coral is Charles Perry's All Breeze, and next to it is the Drinkers' Curlew Cottage.*

in transportation. Parry became a skilled draftsman and designer, advancing through every level of mechanical labor until, in 1855 at the age of 34, he was appointed general superintendent in charge of locomotive construction.

The firm prospered in the Civil War, and with the opening of western railroads, the Baldwin locomotive became a symbol of excellence. Baldwin died in 1866, and by 1873 the firm took on, in alphabetical order, the names of its three principals — Burnham, Parry and Williams — all of whom, when not traveling and selling locomotives all over the world, vacationed in Beach

Haven. Parry, more than anyone else, was responsible for developing the resort when he opened the Parry House hotel on Centre Street in 1874.

After the fully occupied, 100-room hotel burned to the ground, fortunately without loss of life, on the night of August 11, 1881, Parry, Burnham and Williams began building homes of their own on Coral Street. Parry's own place, "All Breeze," was on the oceanfront at the southwest corner of Coral and Atlantic. Partner George Burnham's huge cottage stood opposite it on the northwest corner. At his death in 1900, it became the Edith Wharton Baby Hospital until it was destroyed in the hurricane

*Pearl Street in the foreground; Coral Street is the next street over. This view is looking north, toward the Engleside Hotel. At right, beyond the vacant lot, is Charles Parry's house, All Breeze. George Burnham's cottage, which became the Edith Wharton Baby Hospital after 1900, is across Coral Street on the oceanfront.*

of 1944. Dr. Edward H. Williams' cottage at Marine and Atlantic, still standing today, is an impressive structure capped with a great onion dome. It has a twin a block to the south, the Converse Cottage, built for John Converse, another officer in the Baldwin Locomotive Works.

Charles Parry generously provided for each of his three married children. For his daughter Adelaide, he built #127 Coral, which she named "Florence" for her daughter. It was, until recently, the summer residence of his descendants, the Barclays. Parry's son, William T., got #135 on the corner of Beach Avenue and Coral, one of the four on that street to be designed by John Wil-

son. Wilson also designed the Nearsea, commissioned in 1884 by Parry for his daughter Ellie. Ellie was Mrs. James Baird, and the mother of Parry's favorite grandchild, Mercer. This rather spoiled little boy would one day become mayor of Beach Haven and bring his father's hotel, the Baldwin, to bankruptcy with his extravagant spending and libertine ways.

Over the years, Nearsea became the home of some remarkable figures in Beach Haven history. In 1907, James Baird's good friend, Philadelphia engraver Charles Beck, bought it and summered there for four years until he bought the old Sherborne estate on Liberty Avenue

and created the fabulous Beck farm, an Island showplace. His grandson, Charles Edgar Nash, the author, in 1936, of *The Lure of Long Beach*, summered at Nearsea as a boy and described it in his wonderfully nostalgic piece called "The Farm."

The next owner of Nearsea was Frederick Ostendorff, who bought it from Beck in 1911. Ostendorff, a highly successful Philadelphia restaurateur, owned the popular German Kitchen at Twelfth and Market Streets. It was always called "Philadelphia's answer to Luchows," New York's own celebrated German restaurant. Ostendorff came to Beach Haven to build, on the eve of the 1914

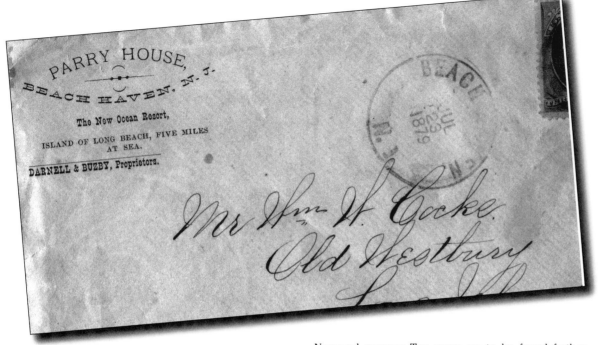

opening of the automobile causeway across the bay, a big brick and steel garage at Pearl Street and Bay Avenue. It would hold 125 cars and was equipped with every modern mechanical device, including an elevator to take cars to a machine shop on the second floor.

## Seven Sister Cottages

In the oceanside streets of Beach Haven, seven large, former summer homes so closely resemble each other in architectural detail that they have been known for decades as the "Seven Sisters." The same contractor built them over a period of several years in the 1920s, from the same plans, with minor variations to suit their locations.

Three of them stand side by side along the west side of Atlantic Avenue, in the block between Berkeley and Norwood avenues. Two more are to be found farther north on Atlantic Avenue, one on the southwest corner of Coral and Atlantic, and another on the northeast corner of Second and Atlantic. The latter, built in 1927, was one of the first houses in Beach Haven to be built on the block east of Atlantic Avenue. Two more of the "Seven Sisters" adjoin each other on the north side of Belvoir Avenue, in the block between Bay Avenue and Beach Avenue. They were the last to be built.

Each house, besides being unusually large, has a single readily identifiable characteristic: a big second-story porch that usually wraps about three sides of the building. The porch is accessed by a wide stairway. All of the houses are cedar-shake and most of them trimmed in white. The hallmark of the "Seven Sisters" is their great size. Most of them take up a considerable portion of the 100-by-75-foot lots they stand on.

On the southwest corner of Atlantic and Berkeley avenues is the first of the "Seven Sisters," built in 1923 for Albert Damon, who had come to Beach Haven after World War I and bought up several lots on Atlantic Avenue, below the Hotel Baldwin. The house was designed by Henry Reed of Philadelphia and built by Floyd Cranmer of Beach Haven. His brother Firman owned the lumber and coal yard on Centre Street, and had just completed the Colonial Theater on Bay Avenue. Within a few years Firman would build an architectural masterpiece, the Beach Haven Public Library on Third Street. Floyd did not know it then, but the Damon house was to become his specialty in the 1920s. There were to be six more in as many years.

Just as the first house was near completion, a close friend of Albert Damon's, a Mrs. Glen of Lansdowne, Pennsylvania, fell in love with the house and wanted to buy it. "Build yourself another one, Bert," she said. "You can do it. You have the land." As the story goes, Albert went to the next corner on Norwood and, using essentially the same plans and the same builder, put up a mirror image of the house. This time he wanted larger porches. This was the house called Nomad, his name in reverse.

Upon visiting him, Damon's friends from Lansdowne were overwhelmed by the quality of the buildings. Jake Verlendin bought Damon's lot between Berkeley and Norwood and had Cranmer build him a house to match the others. They were all built to last. Plumbing and sewer lines were buried deep down in the sand, and concrete was poured on top of them, to form a pad upon which the house rested. Each house was equipped with a coal furnace and a two-car garage. Servants' quarters were on the ground floor. The family living quarters were on the second floor, surrounded by the spacious screened porches. There was a third floor for additional bedrooms and an attic.

In 1927, Joseph Taggart, a Pittsburgh lawyer, ap-

*Coral Street, with the following cottages, from the left toward the oceanfront: Parry's Florence Cottage, architect John Wilson's Portia Cottage, George Burnham's brother's cottage, and Burnham's cottage at the corner of Coral and Atlantic, which became a baby hospital.*

proached Cranmer to build a house similar to the ones he had built for Damon and his friends. With a gambrel roof and several tiers of porches, this sprawling house at Second and Atlantic was bigger than any of them, and also the first dwelling to be built east of Atlantic Avenue, an area hitherto regarded as too close to the ocean.

The next year, James Stevenson of Wilmington, Dela-ware, hired Cranmer to build a fifth house on the south-west corner of Coral and Atlantic. Cranmer was hired again as orders came in from Philadelphia for two more houses, side by side, on the north side of Belvoir between Beach and Bay avenues, the only two of the "Seven Sisters" that are not on Atlantic. More than seven-ty years later, seven are still in remarkably good shape, a testimony to Cranmer's skill. Firman Cranmer returned to running the lumber company and, in 1931, served a two-year term as mayor of Beach Haven. His younger brother, Floyd, continued as a successful building contractor, but there would never be any more additions to the "Seven Sisters." That era had ended.

## Curlew Cottage

Another Coral Street cottage with a story to tell is Curlew Cottage, third in from Atlantic Avenue on the south side of Coral. For more than a century it was the summer home of the remarkably talented Drinker family, whose diaries, letters and journals bring to life a forgotten era.

In 1970, Catherine Drinker Bowen, celebrated biographer of Justice Oliver Wendell Holmes, John Adams and Francis Bacon, turned to autobiography with *Family Portrait*, the story of her own Drinker family of Philadelphia. With four older brothers and one sister, she was the youngest of them to grow up in the opening years of the 20th century. In a chapter titled "Beach Haven," she evokes a nostagia for an earlier time on Long Beach Island with the opening paragraph:

"There was a special smell to the cottage at Beach Haven, indigenous, I think to the Jersey shore. The minute one opened the front door one met it — the combination of dampness, beach sand, old wicker furniture, oil from the guns that stood racked with the fishing rods in the little west room off the hall. Whatever the mixture, to my nostrils it was very sweet. This whiff, this musty breath meant running barefoot on the beach, bathing in the foam of the breakers. It meant sailing on the bay, crabbing from the dock, riding one's bicycle on the wide yellow-graveled streets, easy and free."

In 1889, when Catherine was two years old, her father bought the big, wood-frame house on Coral Street that her mother would name Curlew Cottage. It had been built several years earlier by Joseph J. Pharo, superintendent of the Tuckerton Railroad from 1877 until 1889. Catherine's father, Henry S. Drinker, was a mining engineer-turned-lawyer. After his older children had been raised in a big house on the grounds of Haverford College on Philadelphia's Main Line, he became president of Lehigh University.

The family moved to Bethlehem, but it was always Beach Haven that gave them a sense of permanency. Heading for the shore by train each year in mid-June, with lunches packed, was one of life's great joys for every one of them. All but their father, who took only weekends, would stay until Labor Day — nearly three months of sailing, fishing and gunning on the unspoiled marshes in those magical times of the 1890s and early 1900s. She writes:

"The memories of Beach Haven run all to smells and sounds and sights. At the west end of Coral Street the marshes began, turning soft with color at sunset, pink and lilac and golden green. The ocean beach at low tide lay hard underfoot, wet sand dark below the waterline. On the dunes — we called them sand hills — we played King of the Castle or slid down on our bloomer seats, yelling with triumph and pure joy. The floors of Curlew Cottage, the chairs and even the beds were sandy. Always a lone sneaker sat beneath the hall sofa; by August our city shoes were mildewed in the closets, and the towels were forever damp."

All the Drinkers were prolific diarists. Catherine's brother Harry describes their Beach Haven summers this way: "The cottage was probably ten years old when we bought it and was never a thing of beauty or even of comfort according to modern standards. But Mater always kept it nicely furnished with curtains at the windows, hammocks and rocking chairs on the porch and flower boxes filled with geraniums. A feature of interior decoration was the collection of stuffed birds shot by Pater and us boys. They graced the mantelpieces in the living room and gunroom.

"Although mosquitoes and flies buzzed around in clouds most of the time, we had no screens on the porch and only inadequate half screens at the windows. We used oil lamps, which were cleaned and filled each day by the maid. A cook produced plentiful meals from a coal range. Two other maids swept the sand out of the bedrooms and did the laundry without the help of vacuum cleaners or washing machines. Pater and Mater added the tower room and built the laundry out back with the room above it. One bathroom served the whole household.

"On Coral Street in those years there were no automobiles and plenty of room for playing baseball. Almost every evening boys and girls would make up teams and play until dark. On Sunday afternoons the town gathered on the field between Marine and Ocean streets to watch the black servants at the two big hotels play some remarkably skillful ball while jibing at each other 'I hope de Bald-wins' or 'I'm on de Engle-side.'"

Cecil K. Drinker kept a ten-year journal called *The Log of the Yawl "Gee Whiz,"* which was the name of the sailboat used by all four of Catherine's brothers for fishing and gunning expeditions all over Little Egg Harbor Bay, and for shark fishing outside the inlet. Nearly forty huge, sun-bleached shark jaws decorated the outer walls of Curlew Cottage. Another document is the handwritten *Curlew Cottage Record* running from 1891 until 1951 and filling nearly ninety pages. The early years of the record keep a nearly unbelievable tally of fish caught and birds shot even in the summer months, but no one then had any thought of conservation. Curlew Cottage was sold in 1994 and has, after nearly 105 years, passed out of the hands of the Drinkers.

# A Visit to Beach Haven

The following unsigned piece appeared in the *Philadelphia Mirror* in the summer of 1875 and is of interest for its first-hand descriptions of Tuckerton and Beach Haven.

## 1875

"Having heard of a new watering place on the Jersey coast and having read advertisements about the remarkable sailing, fishing and gaming thereof, I decided to take the cars from the ferry at Camden to find out whether a place for which so many advantages were claimed really existed. We passed through Merchantville, Moorestown, Mount Holly, Lisbon and various other places reaching Whitings in very good time. At this point, the Tuckerton Railroad forms a connection with the New Jersey Southern and when we had changed trains we were quickly transported through Barnegat, Manahawkin and West Creek to Tuckerton.

We found this a very pleasant village, well shaded and having a beautiful lake (now utilized into a pond for mills) lying at the foot of the main street. We were informed that the Indians formerly called this lake, Lake Pohatcong meaning clear water. This appellation is well deserved. I have never seen a more transparent sheet of clear water. To realize its beauty, take a boat and row up the channel at the head of the lake. Here, amid the

dark foliage of the cedars, a scene of enchantment reminding one of some naiad's home suddenly bursts upon the delighted vision. It almost warrants the exclamation of one of the ladies of the party — "This is Fairyland!" The stream runs for a long distance washing through the roots of the big cedars and is justly praised for its palatable and health-giving properties.

Our hotel in Tuckerton was praiseworthy and we will say to the credit of the inhabitants that the prevalent vice — intoxication — appeared to have no votaries here. We passed some days in the peaceful enjoyment of sailing and fishing with fine success.

Upon the arrival of some friends we took the steamer four miles across the fine bay and were installed at Beach Haven in the Parry House, kept by Mr. Robert B. Engle — a commodious hotel, excellently well kept. Being on the sheepshead ground, we had that fish regularly served at the table, not missing a day.

Beach Haven is near the southern end of an island that runs some fifteen or eighteen miles along our coast. It has the advantage of a sea breeze from three quarters of the compass while that from the west must come heavily freighted with the saline qualities of the bay. In this respect, I scarcely know its equal in the vicinity of any of our large cities. In addition it possesses an excellent bay shelter for the yachts and smaller boats so indispensable in the fowling and fishing for which these waters are renowned. I hazard but little when I assert that this place must, at some distant day, be one of the most popular resorts for that numerous

*portion of our citizenship who, eschewing mere fashion and show, desire to spend their vacations in quiet leisure in the house, healthful exercise on the strand, or exciting sport bagging either the feathered or scaly denizens which frequent this place here.*

The following piece, printed here in its entirety, appeared in the *New York Mirror* in July of 1887. Certain words and phrases, after a century, need explanation. The unknown author of this piece mentions, in the third paragraph, talk of the season's coming gaieties, among them "several elegant germans." A "german" was a cotillion of round dances with the frequent exchange of partners. "Euchre" was a popular card game.

Further on there is mention made of "Tuckerton Bay men" predominating in the

membership of the Beach Haven Yacht Club. Note that Tuckerton and Bay are capitalized. The term applied to the many charter boat captains who were not only from Tuckerton, but from West Creek, Parkertown, Manahawkin, Beach Haven and every town south of Barnegat Bay. Tuckerton Bay was an alternate name for Little Egg Harbor Bay in those days.

## 1887

*B*each Haven is justly praised, for it is now one of the most charming coast resorts in New Jersey, having become the favorite abiding place of Philadelphia folks and the resting place of many New Yorkers. Charles Palmer of New York who summers at the Engleside here has tramped, more than forty years ago, over the spot where Beach Haven now stands and is acquainted with every square foot of the ground in the resort. Back then, he says, in the years before the Civil War, it was the favorite hunting ground of New York and upper New Jersey sportsmen but, like other places along the coast once sought out by gunners with their hounds, it has, in later days, become a watering place.

Beach Haven is at the lower end of Long Beach, that narrow strip of sand, some twenty miles long, between Barnegat and Tuckerton Bays and the ocean. Barnegat City marks the upper termination and Beach Haven the lower. The Beach Haven people are mostly summer folks, aristocratic Philadelphians with plenty of leisure and plenty of cash. The great sand dunes have been leveled and, as if touched by the magic wand, have

*A view along Centre Street: the Beach Haven House is on the corner at left and the Ocean House is at right, the third building in. Third Street, at top, has the Beach Haven schoolhouse (with flagpole) at left and the St. Thomas Church at right. The Beach Haven boardwalk can be seen in the distance at upper right*

been metamorphosed into cottages of palatial dimensions and elegant interiors. It is no village of clap-board huts but rather a large cluster of seashore villas and good hotels.

One of the promoters of the place was the late Charles T. Parry, an officer in the Baldwin Locomotive Works of Philadelphia. When his hotel,

the Parry House, burned down in 1881 after only seven seasons, he decided to build a caravansary that would do credit to it and erected the New Hotel Baldwin at a cost of $75,000.

Beach Haven folks are all one big, happy family. They bathe together all summer and keep up a correspondence all winter. While its society is not

exclusive, Beach Haven folks like to know who you are when you arrive. In the pavilion on the beach front where there is a good view of the ocean, there is much talk of the coming gaieties that are to make the season, the biggest ever known. There will be several elegant germans, a yacht race, a lawn tennis tournament and progressive euchre parties.

Dock Road, circa 1900. At left, on the canal that was Mud Hen Creek, is the Hotel DeCrab; the large building in the distance, center, is the Beach Haven House. The Engleside Hotel can be seen to the right.

There is to be an interesting yacht race in the middle of August. The Beach Haven Yacht Club is distinctly "Jersey." The Club Commodore is Charles Gibbons Jr., whose enthusiasm for boating is unbounded and who believes thoroughly in the future of the club he has founded. He sails the yacht Sea Queen. Alfred P. Reager sails the Mart, Samuel Smith the Sea Foam. The prettiest yacht in the whole club comes from Philadelphia. It is the Leucothea and is the property of E. A. Hibbs whose fondness for Jersey waters has made him popular along the coast. The majority of the members are Tuckerton Bay men, who lift oysters during the winter and make pin money during the summer. A number of them own fine cat yachts and work for hire as charter captains.

All officers of the association are uniformed. They have built an elegant dock and clubhouse at the mouth of a tidal creek, now called Dock Road, where some forty spink-spank yachts are tied up. The club dock, which is taken up each winter and reset in the spring, extends in a great curve to the north to enable the yachts to take advantage of the incoming and outgoing tides upon approach to the slips. Every yacht is freshly painted and upholstered every season. There is a rivalry in neatness which is itself refreshing. The skipper of the champion boat in the last annual Beach Haven race is a South Jersey hero

all winter. This year, the regatta promises to attract much attention. It is a twenty mile course running from Beach Haven northwesterly across the bay to West Creek, thence south to the former Bond's Hotel and northward up the channel past the club house and once more around again. Much excitement and betting is generated in the halfway point at the clubhouse.

There is always good fishing and good crabbing in the Tuckerton Bay and a genial atmosphere is the rule here, but the mosquitoes are the first things you hear about after getting "washed up."

Joseph Pharo, the Superintendent of the Tuckerton Railroad, winters in Tuckerton and summers here at his new cottage on Coral Street. He is a relation of Archelaus Pharo, the founder of Beach Haven and President of the Tuckerton Railroad, whose own magnificent cottage stands on Second Street beyond the open lot occupied by the former Parry House. Joseph Pharo is the jolly skipper of the Broad Bill, a yacht of some reputation.

Some of the crack tennis players are here for the summer. Professor Leidy, the well-known naturalist, also professor at the University of Pennsylvania, is summering here. Some of the Philadelphia cottagers are Reverend Dr. Dicky, Cooper Smith, J. W. Lober, George Burnham, J. W. Brown and Joseph Hopkinson, a great grandson of Francis Hopkinson, a signer of the Declaration of Independence. Prosecutor Charles Hedrickson, who ably conducted the prosecution of Agnew, the wife-murderer, is resting here.

*Along Atlantic Avenue, the Williams Cottage is in the center of this photograph, at the corner of Ocean Avenue.*

## Onion Domes in Beach Haven

These graceful old summer cottages are a pair of oddities that seem not to fit the style of that period we now so loosely call Victorian. They were built in the 1880s, nearly identical in structure. Certainly they are as big and richly appointed as all the others of their ilk; what makes them so unusual is their bulbous-shaped, onion-domed roofs, each topped with a tapered wooden spire.

The Byzantine dome is an architectural feature rare in America except on Greek Orthodox churches, where, having no actual function, it is meant to symbolize heaven. Pointed out to Beach Haven visitors as "the onion dome houses," these massive three-story twins, bereft of formal names, have stood side by side on Atlantic Avenue between Marine and Ocean streets for over 100 years. Their once-graceful wraparound porches were enclosed in the 1930s, and their commanding view of the ocean has been gone since the 1960s when houses and

*This panoramic view, looking south from the old wooden water tower, circa 1914, shows a developing Beach Haven. At left is Engleside Avenue; the Engleside Hotel is on the oceanfront. The Hotel Baldwin, also on the ocean, is in the center of the photograph, by the dark water tower. Amber Street, second from left, is followed by Coral and Pearl streets. Bay Avenue, front, has not yet become the commercial center of town., and*

motels started springing up in the once-empty lots along the strand east of Atlantic Avenue.

Summer residents knew these two landmark structures in their day simply as the Williams Cottage and the Converse Cottage as if that were enough — and indeed it was then. Their original owners were very prominent men. Dr. Edward H. Williams was one of three partners in the firm of Burnham, Parry and Williams that would later become Baldwin Locomotive. John H. Converse, a protégé of Dr. Williams and twenty years his junior, was also an officer in the company. He later became the president of the Pennsylvania Railroad, and died in 1925. Williams died in 1889, about two years after he had built

his cottage.

Both cottages were constructed at the same time, and they were designed by architect John Wilson. He and his brother Joseph had a long list of public buildings to their credit, including railroad stations, churches, hospitals, as well as countless big primary residences and ornate stables all over the Main Line. In Beach Haven, they had designed the Baldwin hotel, Holy Innocents' Episcopal Church and half a dozen other big summer cottages built for Baldwin executives on Coral Street and along Atlantic Avenue. The domes on the Converse and Williams cottages seem to have been an architectural flourish and remain a mystery.

## Amazing Medical Footnotes

Nothing stirs the imagination like a house with a ghost or at least a good story. While there may be no ghosts beneath the onion domes, there is a really good story, connected not with the Williams Cottage, but with Dr. Williams himself. Williams had been a medical doctor before he took up railroad engineering. During his brief tenure as a physician he was directly involved in one of the strangest medical cases of the 19th century, that of Phineas Gage and the tamping bar. Here is the story:

Edward H. Williams was born in Woodstock, Vermont

*stretches south into vast undeveloped salt marsh and beach. Beach Haven Construction Co. coal and lumber yard is the large complex above; the long building beyond it is Ostendorff's garage. The small building on the edge of the bay, right, is a drawn-in Little Egg Harbor Yacht Club, which wouldn't be built for two more years.*

June 1, 1824, of distinguished parentage in a big, comfortable home on the village green. It was filled with books and works of art. When steam locomotives were still in their infancy, young Ned became devoted to surveying and engineering and planned to make a career of building railroads. At fourteen he spent a summer in Michigan with an uncle and worked with the crews, planning the route and bridge construction for the Michigan Central Railroad. His youthful imagination had been fired. He returned home to Vermont eager to concentrate on mathematics and start in with the Boston and Worcester Railroad, but he suddenly fell ill with seemingly incurable asthma and recurrent fevers.

There was a medical college in Woodstock, and faculty and students often came to visit him at the big house with its stimulating library. Ned took up the study of medicine, believing it might be less strenuous than engineering, and entered the college. He graduated in 1846 at the age of 22 and moved to the town of Rutland, on the route of the railroad, to become a physician without an established practice. Despite his ill health, he could not tear himself away from any minor engineering project.

On September 13, 1848, Williams was helping his old teacher with a surveying problem along the roadbed. A mile or two down the tracks a workman, attempting to

tamp a charge of blasting powder with an iron bar, accidentally set the explosive off with a spark. His name was Phineas Gage and his unusual accident would make medical history.

The force of the blast drove the four-foot iron bar like a javelin right through Gage's head. It entered just in front of his left ear and shot out the top of his skull. Gage, though dazed and bleeding, with his left eye bulging, could still stand, walk and communicate by pointing. His fellow workmen took him to the town hotel where Williams, the only physician within twenty miles, was summoned to minister to a man everyone thought had only hours to live.

Gage remained alert while Williams began to clean the wound and carefully cut away the broken pieces of skull, watching for signs of infection. Over the next two days infections had to be cut away, and only then could the wound be sewn up. It was a highly sophisticated procedure for so young a man, and quite exhausting for one in Williams' state of health. Gage recovered and went on to become a coachman, often gathering crowds to exhibit his wounds and the iron bar for money. Eventually, he became morose and antisocial, probably as a result of brain damage, but he did live another twelve years after the accident.

His wife donated his skull to the Harvard Medical Museum, where it may be seen today. In 1931, Robert Ripley made Phineas Gage the subject of one of his most grisly drawings for his "Believe It Or Not" feature in the Hearst papers. Readers shuddered at the image of a snow-white skull, pierced from cheek to crown with a black iron bar, and there it had remained, fixed in his head, while the man lived another twelve years after this accident. Believe it or not!

The stress of the Gage case was to have a fateful effect on young Dr. Williams. He had overtaxed himself. Within weeks, his asthma and fevers worsened and at one point he went into a coughing fit lasting several hours. It ended abruptly when he expelled from his vocal cords a beechnut burr that had been lodged there for ten years, ever since his visit to Michigan at the age of 14. Within a very short time he recovered and was cured of all symptoms of what had been thought to be asthma. Now he could pursue his first love, railroad engineering. He would keep his title of doctor all his life, but he would never again practice medicine. His rise in his new field was meteoric. It was one success after another. Dr. Edward Williams became one of the great men of American railroading.

## Beach Haven Street Names

Within towns like Beach Haven, names have also changed over the years. An east-west street called Centre roughly divides the nearly two-mile length of Beach Haven. When the town was founded in 1874, there were only three streets laid out to the south of Centre and two to the north. Now there are twenty-four streets south of Centre and twelve above. All the streets south of Centre have names seemingly chosen by a determined group of Anglophiles. Only half of them are in alphabetical order, making the rest hard for strangers to find. The streets north of Centre, with the exception of Taylor between Eighth and Ninth streets, are all numbered up to twelve. If you walk, jog or bike through the southern streets of Beach Haven, many of which are called avenues, you may have tried to figure out how to memorize their order, because, unlike the named cross streets in Brant Beach and Harvey Cedars, they do not also carry numbers.

*An early photograph of a bedroom in the Portia Cottage.*

Today, the first street south of Centre is called Engleside Avenue. Once called South Street, it was renamed in the 1940s to honor the famous, old hotel that had stood, from 1876 until it was torn down in 1943, on the huge lot now occupied by Veterans Bicentennial Park. The next five streets have a seashore theme. They are: Amber, Coral, Pearl, Marine and Ocean, and, having been laid out and named when the town was young, they are still called streets. Below them, all the cross streets, though narrow, are pretentiously called "avenues."

The English influence that began with the spelling of Centre now picks up with Berkeley Avenue, named for a great castle, and then comes Norwood, a suburb of London. Remember Sherlock Holmes and *The Adventure of the Norwood Builder*? The next eight avenues are all in alphabetical order beginning with "B." They are Belvoir, a castle destroyed in the English civil wars, followed by Chatsworth, one of England's great country houses, followed in proper order by Dolphin, Essex, Fairview, Glendola, Holyoke and Iroquois. Then, instead of continuing with a "J" and a "K," the town planners skipped to Liberty, which is an avenue named for Liberty Price, a bayman who once owned all the bayside meadows south of Mordecai Island and for whom a channel in the bay called Liberty Thorofare is named.

After Liberty comes Pelham, an English prime minister, and then Stratford, an English town. The alphabetical sequence, broken after Iroquois, is resumed for the remaining five avenues. They are Jeffries, a lord chancellor of England, followed by Kentford, Leeward and Merrivale, who was a poet and friend of Lord Byron's. Finally there is Nelson, the last street in Beach Haven. It was named for England's great naval hero.

This nearly half mile of territory on Beach Haven's southern end was once a part of Long Beach Township until Beach Haven annexed it in 1910, at the request of the original landholder, Thomas Sherborne. It was at this time that the easterly ends of all the present-day cross streets, from Liberty to Nelson, were graded and given names. All that remained of the former Sherborne Estate, west of the Boulevard, including his farmhouse on Liberty Avenue, was purchased in 1910 by Philadelphia engraver Charles Beck, who made it into the celebrated Beck farm. The main house was elevated several feet and completely modernized. The vast bayside acreage that once made up the farm is long gone, but the main house remains one of the classically beautiful, old homes of Beach Haven.

Joseph A. Taylor was a former Philadelphia clergyman with good banking connections and a genius for finance who launched a second career for himself developing seashore real estate in the 1890s. He was one of the founders of Wildwood, New Jersey. In 1908, late in life, he came to Long Beach Island and purchased a sizable tract of boggy, unimproved land, from Sixth Street in Beach Haven north to the borough line at Thirteenth Street in Long Beach Township territory. Part of this undeveloped land between Ninth and Tenth streets was being used as a town dump. Here, a big, shallow swamp stretched north as far as Thirteenth Street, near the Dolphin Inn on the oceanfront. It was often referred to as

*At top, a new house at the corner of Atlantic and Belvoir avenues features an old street sign on a wooden post, with a new metal signpost about to replace it – next to a new fire hydrant. Ocean, Berkeley and Belvoir avenues are shown developing, above.*

Dolphin Pond. Partly trapped rainwater and partly fed by springs, it was quicker to freeze in winter than the salt-water coves near it. The town used it for skating parties and on cold nights built bonfires along its edge. In summer, it became a breeding ground for the fresh water mosquito and was eventually filled in with ashes, solid waste and beach sand from the enormous dunes north of Seventh Street.

The only road in the new Taylor tract was a narrow, rutted trail called Beach Avenue, running as far north as the lifesaving station in Beach Haven Terrace. At night the road was lit by kerosene lanterns atop short posts and was known to many as "mosquito alley." The east-west side streets were all named and surveyed, but not yet cleared and graded. The centerpiece of Taylor's new development he named for himself. It was to be a broad boulevard running east to west, from ocean to bay, between Eighth and Ninth streets. Original plans for Taylor Avenue called for a center strip planted with trees and flowers.

Taylor died in the 1920s, before any of his grandiose plans for the construction of homes could be realized. His heirs discovered that his big, empty tract, stretching diagonally southwestward across the wide bay meadows to Dock Road, included the land upon which the Beach Haven Yacht Club had stood since 1884. These heirs, led by real estate broker Robert Osborne, sued, and, in 1930, the New Jersey Supreme Court declared the club to be a squatter. Rather than pay $10,000 for a clear title, the trustees chose to move the building two blocks to the south and put in a new dock.

The land of the Taylor estate remained undeveloped, and by 1937 it had accumulated a bill of $20,000 for back taxes to the borough. In exchange for the cancellation of this debt, the estate agreed to give the Borough of Beach Haven two blocks of bayfront land to build a municipal bathing beach. It was not formally converted to such usage until April of 1950, when a special ordinance was passed to make it a public park. It took another forty-four years to dedicate it and name it after William L. Butler, the town's first mayor.

In the meantime, at least until the mid-1950s, the borough used the area that is now a parking lot and a beach as a town dump. Truckloads of old furniture, bed springs and mattresses were hauled down to the edge of the bay. Old bureaus, with mirrors attached, glinted in the sun alongside bundles of newspapers, automobile tires, old lawn furniture, paint cans, stoves and iceboxes. All of the contents were bulldozed farther out into the meadows, to make the town a little wider. What could be burned was burned regardless of the smoke.

What is not generally known about the municipal beach is the unusual use that the land was put to long before it was a dump. Until 1914, Bay Avenue ran only as far north as Fourth Street. From that point there was a gravel and plank road that crossed the train tracks and ran out over the meadows to the same sandy cove now used as the children's bathing beach. Garbage and spoiled food (but not trash) from the hotels and stores were put into barrels and taken out there to be loaded aboard barges and taken by scow to the mainland to fatten the hogs. This unpleasant location, always foul smelling and abuzz with flies, was known as the "slop dock." A lot of food, in the days before refrig-

FURNISHED COTTAGES

BEACH HAVEN, NEW JERSEY
THE ISLAND RESORT SIX MILES AT SEA

PORTIA COTTAGE
Nine Bedrooms, Two Baths

eration was available, used to go bad, but it was never wasted.

It is purely a matter of nostalgia whether one would prefer to live yesterday in a Beach Haven with a "slop dock" and a smoky trash dump, or in the Beach Haven of today that is all houses and stores and automobiles.

# Beach Haven Merchants

## Cox's General Store and the Surflight District

The Surflight Theatre has been around long enough to be on the historic register, yet the whole complex on the west side of Beach Avenue, between Centre Street and Engleside Avenue, is a relative newcomer. The theater stands in what is the oldest business block in Beach Haven, sections of which were in use the very year that the resort opened in 1874.

This popular theater, on the northwest corner of Engleside and Beach avenues, occupies the site that in the 1870s was a clubhouse owned by Charles Parry, built for his private use and as a place that he and his friends could use in the summer for games of cards and billiards to get away from the women and probably have a drink or two. His hotel, the Parry House on Centre Street, a block away, was a temperance house. The clubhouse, on the other hand, was designed to accommodate gunning parties during the fall and spring.

After the Parry House burned down in August of 1881, Parry built a new hotel five blocks to the south, which he first named the Arlington Inn and later the New Hotel Baldwin. He had established a clientele, so he obtained a liquor license for the Baldwin, and the old clubhouse, where the Surflight now stands, was abandoned. The club's official name, if it ever had one, has been lost, but the building was purchased, in 1883,

*The Parry House clubhouse, at the corner of Engleside and Beach avenues, was purchased by Ralph and Ben Cox of West Creek in 1883 and became a general store on what was then the main street for businesses in Beach Haven.*

by brothers Ralph and Ben Cox of West Creek, who made it into a general store, with room rentals on the second and third floors. A big dining room was added to the west side. The combined business operations were called Cox's General Merchandise and Central Hotel.

Ben was soon the sole owner. By 1895, he had started the first ice business in Beach Haven, in a building located just west of the store and hotel. This was a time when ice had to be cut each winter from frozen ponds on the mainland, scowed to the Island in the cold months, and stored in well-insulated wooden ice houses, packed in sawdust. The supply usually lasted all summer. In those early years, the Baldwin and Engleside hotels each had their own ice houses.

Ben S. Cox went bankrupt in June of 1911, and his ice business was taken over by Elmer King of West Creek. King used modern machinery to make ice, rather than transporting it from ponds. He had the only such place in town, until the Beach Haven Ice and Cold Storage Plant was built in 1920. Back then all meat, as soon as it was brought from the train, had to be put in a salt solution to preserve it. The process was called "brining down." In the summer months, meat and other perishables had to be purchased by households every day from the stores along Beach Avenue. Fish was always cooked as soon as it was caught, but there was still an incredible amount of waste and spoilage.

Cox's store and hotel was bought by Joe Sarner of Tuckerton, who expanded the grocery trade. In 1919, after the war, he sold the store to Calvin Abromovitz of Barnegat. Abromovitz became president, with partner Nate Levison as treasurer, secretary and general manager. The forty-five-year-old building acquired a new name, the Central Provision Market. The upstairs was still the Central Hotel.

*Beach Avenue, in front of Cox's store, at left, included the horsecar railway from the Beach Haven train station to the Hotel Baldwin.*

By 1935, the market had a staff of twelve and a fleet of three trucks making deliveries all over the area. The Central Provision thrived even during the Great Depression. The enterprise could boast the largest electric refrigerator on the Island. It was 33 feet long, 13 feet high and 13 feet wide. The old double-decked porches had been enclosed, and the place was licensed to sell packaged liquor and beer. Out of the more than a dozen stores along Beach Avenue in those years, Central Provision was by far the biggest and most profitable. It was open year 'round, including Sundays in the summer months.

The hurricane of 1944 caused severe flood damage in the store. After World War II, Central Provision closed its doors. Its neighbor in the next block across Beach Avenue, the Engleside Hotel, vacant since 1940, had been torn down in 1943. In a trend that had begun a decade earlier, the business center of town had shifted to Bay Avenue. Of the many meat, produce and dry goods stores that had once lined Beach Avenue, only one, Charlie Cramer's Grocery, between Second and Third Streets, remained open. Upon Charlie Cramer's death in 1963, it, too, was gone.

Just to the north of the building that is now the Surflight, on the west side of Beach Avenue, there was once a little building that for many years was Beach Haven's official post office. In 1930, the service was moved

*Beach Haven's first post office was next door to Cox's General Merchandise, in what was once the town's commercial hub.*

to Bay Avenue, where all the old Beach Haven businesses eventually migrated. The building was torn down in the 1980s.

Next door to the post office, there was once a little newsstand operated by the Potter family. The town gathered here around 5:00 PM every afternoon to wait for the *Philadelphia Evening Bulletin*, which came in on the train. Train service ceased in November of 1935, when the bridge was washed out.

Next to Potter's Newsstand stood a dry goods and men's clothing store operated by John Walsh, a borough councilman and former champion sandlot baseball player from Trenton. Walsh Field, the town's athletic field,

is named for him. John Walsh was one of the first people in Beach Haven to have a radio. He always tuned into the ball games, with the volume turned high, and people gathered on the corner in front of his store to listen.

The whole area around the Surflight was once the commercial hub of Beach Haven. There were several medium-sized hotels on Centre Street early in this century. They could never compare in luxury to the Engleside and the Baldwin, but at least the Beach Haven House, the Magnolia and the Ocean House, on the north side of Centre Street, were in use throughout the year. On the south side of Centre, next to Walsh's Store, there was the famous Grabeldinger Bakery, which later became the

Beach Haven Bakery.

On the southeast corner of Beach and Centre was the Loveland Building. This housed an American Store, a milk depot, and an ice-cream parlor and pool room. The establishment was under the management of Harry T. Willits Sr. when he first came to Beach Haven in the early 1920s. Martin Wida, of Wida's Hotel in Brant Beach, had a meat market in one part of the Loveland Building, between the paper stand and the pool room. Later, the American Store leased most of the building for several years, until it burned down in 1932. The Episcopal church, its immediate neighbor to the south, now the Long Beach Island Historical Museum, was not damaged in the fire. Below Amber Street, on the east side of Beach Avenue, there was Penrod's Store, which was across from Kale's Meat Market.

Cox's old ice house, usually referred to as the "garage," is the only original structure remaining in the Surflight complex. Facing Engleside Avenue, just to the west of the new theater, for more than thirty years it was the home of the theater itself. Filled now with memories of thousands of past performances and the applause of happy summer crowds, it is being used for set construction and the storage of costumes.

## The Engleside Baby Dairy

Beach Haven was only two years old when, in the first week of January 1876, Robert B. Engle began the framing of what was to be the resort's second major hotel, the Engleside. With good weather, an army of carpenters and no plumbing, gas or electrical wiring to worry about, the Engleside was built and open for business by Memorial

*Robert Engle kept three Guernsey cows near his hotel's vegetable gardens, between Amber and Coral streets, for his "baby dairy" — a marketing scheme to attract families with small children. Tending the cows is Tom Gifford.*

Day, then called Decoration Day. It was a success from the start, particularly due to Engle's experience of having run, for two summer seasons, the nearby Parry House, the town's first big hotel. The rest was due to his sound Quaker business sense.

Engle chose to attract families to his new place. Until then, the primary clientele of any of the hotels on the remote barrier beaches of New Jersey had been the sporting crowd. Mostly men came in the off-season for the gunning and fishing. In the summer months, their wives often accompanied them, but rarely were young children brought along on these vacations. A major consideration had been the unavailability of fresh milk. Although cattle were once raised on the barrier islands to keep them from wandering, the milk the cows produced was not very palatable. They needed sweet grass. There was plenty on the mainland and good milk could be purchased there, but, being raw, it spoiled in the heat of

summer in about the time it would take to sail to the Island.

Recognizing that health-conscious families of the post-Civil War period were getting used to having fresh farm milk brought into the cities by train and that they were willing to pay for it, Robert Engle established a "Baby Dairy" for infants and older children. It was a brilliant marketing scheme. Engle advertised the Baby Dairy in the Philadelphia papers. He was soon able to attract people who might never have ventured out onto an island for a lengthy stay, at least not with small children.

There were cows on the mainland, not far from the landing at Edge Cove near Tuckerton. Milk could have been brought across the bay on the steamboats. Steamboats were used for some time, even after the railroad trestle to the Island was built in 1886. But the milk might be already a day old. How would the milk be kept fresh until the dinner hour, and then how good would it be

the following morning at breakfast, with an ice house as the only means of refrigeration?

Robert Engle, who had at one time been a farmer near Mount Holly, brought three Guernsey cows into Beach Haven. He kept them near his vegetable gardens, located on the whole block between Amber and Coral streets, east of Bay Avenue. The cows were placed in the charge of local resident Thomas E. Gifford, who milked them twice a day and saw to it that they had the proper forage. Some of it was essentially the same diet that the half-wild cattle of Colonial times had had on the barrier beaches, but it was supplemented with fresh clover and hay, brought over by boat, to improve the taste of the milk.

Even after a railroad bridge was built to the Island and tracks laid to Beach Haven, making good farm milk available, Engle kept his Baby Dairy in operation for at least another decade. He found it was good for business.

Engle continued his advertisements in the Philadelphia papers:

"Delicate children often come to the Engleside, whose only need is fresh air and pure fresh milk. For these we keep three Guernsey cows upon the premises, whose milk is for the babies alone, and this is so much appreciated that we shall continue the Baby Dairy. The regular supply of milk and cream comes daily by train from one of the finest farms in Burlington County."

Near the kitchen he had a wooden icehouse filled with big cakes of ice cut each winter from a frozen pond in Holgate. They were well packed in sawdust and the chilly interior was not put into use until late May. The supply of ice usually lasted until September, when the hotel closed for the season.

## Kapler's Drug Store

The advent of the automobile in 1914 started the slow shift of Beach Haven's business center away from Beach Avenue; it moved westward one block, to Bay Avenue. Before then Bay Avenue had been little more than a trail along the edge of the tide-washed meadows. Bay Avenue was widened and graveled to become a part of the new road to the causeway. Promotional literature of the Beach Haven Realty Company called the improved road an "automobile speedway through the heart of the resort."

It was, of course, no such thing. Cars didn't go that fast and besides, for at least another generation, the true heart of the resort was still Beach Avenue. Here were the town's two major hotels — the Engleside and the Baldwin — the town's three churches, the post office and at least a dozen groceries, meat markets and dry goods emporiums. But it was all coming to an end.

*This Spanish-inspired building, later to become Kapler's, was built in 1927, and survived many storm tides, including the one, top, in 1933.*

*The commercial center of Beach Haven moved a block west from Beach Avenue with the advent of automobile traffic on the Island. In 1934, Lester Paxson began operating his new pharmacy on the ground floor of Downing's Real Estate building at the corner of Bay Avenue and Centre Street.*

By the mid-1920s, Bay Avenue and Centre Street had become the new town hub. The oldest establishment at this choice location was a hotel called the Beach Haven House. It was built on the northeast corner of the street around 1874. The other three corners were vacant land until 1912, when Jacob Britz built a barbershop and ice-cream store on the southwest corner. His son, Milton, was to make it into a tavern. It was another ten years before a movie theater was erected on the northwest corner. In 1927, Elmer Downing established a real estate office on the remaining corner of Bay and Centre. It was a solidly built structure of Spanish design, with room for three businesses on the first floor and two apartments on the second floor.

Elmer Downing, who also ran a profitable amusement arcade on the boardwalk at Centre Street, kept his real estate office in the east end of the building. In 1934, he leased the rest of the space to pharmacist Lester Paxon, who since 1920 had been operating a drugstore and ice cream counter in a building adjoining the Engleside Hotel. It was called Horace Spackman's Seaside Pharmacy, a longtime favorite with the summer crowd.

Paxson's new drugstore, in the Downing building, would be the fourth such place in a chain he ran. He had a pharmacy in Tuckerton and another in Ship Bottom. Until 1940, the Engleside Pharmacy was kept open in the summer months only; his other three were year-round operations. Paxson kept a very busy schedule until his retirement in 1946. He then opened a candy store in Beach Haven, which he kept until his death in 1960 at the age of 74.

Amos Kapler and James Bower, of Tuckerton, bought out the Paxson chain at the end of the 1946 season. Their partnership, formed in 1943 at Somers Point, was dissolved in 1951. Kapler took over exclusive operation of the Beach Haven drugstore. Kapler's Drug Store also had a first-rate lunch counter along the south wall, serving Dolly Madison ice cream and at least thirty different kinds of hot and cold sandwiches. It was the town's most popular lunchtime gathering place until well into the 1960s.

*Before becoming Kapler's Pharmacy, it was Paxson's. Lester Paxson is wearing the tie. He had operated the drugstore and ice cream counter in a building adjoining the Engleside Hotel since 1924.*

# Tucker's Island & Holgate

## Purkey's Pond

**M**achinery for the making of ice, through the processes of compression or evaporation, was not commercially available until the late 19th century. Until then the old, traditional methods were still in use. Ice was gathered and shipped from higher altitudes; in northern latitudes it was cut from frozen ponds and lakes in the winter months, packed in sawdust and stored in well-insulated ice houses and even shipped to the tropics. It was a major industry in New England.

The cone-shaped frames of ice houses, once as common as barns and corncribs in the rural landscape, dot 19th-century paintings and drawings of the New Jersey Shore regions. Other than salt, there was no better way to preserve food. The *Ocean County Courier*, in the winter of 1898, made note that "200 tons of eight-inch ice were brought over from the Mainland to Beach Haven and put into the Engleside ice houses: while Butcher Cale filled his house with a load of six-inch ice from Holgate's Pond."

The first hotels used local ponds, when frozen, as a source of ice, and they all had ice houses for storage. Robert Engle of the Engleside Hotel in Beach Haven got his ice from a site called Purkey's Pond, in what is now Holgate, and transported it by horse and wagon to his icehouse behind his Beach Haven hotel. The origin of

*A graceful, arched footbridge crossed Purkey's Pond in Holgate and was in use until 1924. Ice was cut from the pond until 1910.*

the name Purkey has been lost, but not its location. It lay just east of the present Long Beach Boulevard at Inlet Road in Holgate. Severe erosion, beginning in the 1920s, has left barely a strip of land east of the Boulevard today, but at one time the beach and several ridges of dunes extended nearly a half mile between the road and the ocean.

The first Bond's Lifesaving Station # 22, established in 1871 near a former house of refuge built in the 1840s, was on the beachfront due east of Purkey's Pond. This station nearly washed away in the winter of 1886, and an entirely new, much larger structure was erected a thousand feet back. It is possible to pinpoint its location because its distance from Station # 21, at Maryland Avenue in Beach Haven Terrace, was computed in 1904 with a huge measuring wheel twelve feet, three inches in diameter. This surveying device was rolled down the beach to the Bond's station, and the distance proved to be exactly 3³/₄ miles. The Maryland Avenue station has never been moved. If you drive a car south from there today, that very same distance, you will stop at Inlet Road in Holgate. Look east another quarter of a mile to the sand bar out beyond the breakers; that's where Bond's station stood from 1886 until 1924. The beach there has eroded over a half mile in the last hundred years.

Purkey's Pond was just to the east of the old dirt road that ran south from Beach Haven to Tucker's Beach and Tucker's Island. It stretched for several blocks and was crossed by a footbridge at what is today Inlet Road. Bayberry bushes tall enough to break the wind surrounded the water so that there were seldom any ripples when it froze, making the surface as smooth as glass, just perfect for ice skating. The bridge across it ran east and west so that the Coast Guard could get out onto the north-south road (Long Beach Boulevard) that led up to Beach Haven.

It is this first bridge across Purkey's Pond, with its graceful arch, that Robert Frye Engle, the photographer son of Robert B. Engle, found so intriguing that he took many pictures of it. After 1910, ice was no longer being cut from the pond, but the bridge remained in use until 1924, when the Coast Guard station was moved from its oceanfront location at Inlet Road down the beach a quarter mile to Janet Avenue and across to the bay side of the Island.

## '44 Hurricane And the Lovetts

Storms are a fact of life on a barrier island. In the late afternoon of September 14, 1944, Long Beach Island was hit with the full force of a huge hurricane known ever afterward as the Great Atlantic Hurricane of 1944. There was damage nearly the full length of the Island, but Holgate, where 100 out of a total of 119 houses were totally destroyed, bore the brunt of it. Most of the destruction was caused less by the ocean than by the swiftly rising

*The Boulevard in Holgate after the '44 hurricane; a bulldozer has cleared one lane.*

*Destruction from the '44 hurricane near Bond's Coast Guard Station in Holgate.*

ner of Jacqueline Avenue and the road along the bay (Bay Terrace). John Lovett was sixty-five in 1944; his wife was sixty-three. They had been married for forty-four years. He had retired in April 1944 as head of the machine shop at the John B. Stetson Hat Company where he had worked for thirty-seven years. They had owned the house at Holgate since 1931. It was one block north of Bond's Coast Guard Station.

"Joy Lovett and I were married in 1949. Grandpop Lovett (as I think of John H.) talked to me twice about his experience in the hurricane. John R., his son and my father-in-law, was a morose man at best, and it was acknowledged by the family that he would never talk about the hurricane.

"When the storm started, two women in a nearby

waters of the bay after the eye of the storm had passed. There was a sudden, unnatural calm as the water began to rise above second-floor windows, and then came the full backlash of the wind from another direction. Houses were rocked right off their foundations and, crashing into each other, wound up as tons of splintered wreckage in the bay meadows.

Some people ignored Coast Guard warnings and tried to ride out the storm in their houses, and a few didn't make it. It was at Holgate that the only drowning deaths on the Island occurred. There were four in all — three elderly women and a 3-year-old child, whose

body was never found. Her mother spent the rest of her life looking for that child, obsessed with the notion that she had somehow survived, was in the care of another family and had lost all memory of her early childhood. Two of the women found dead had lived in oceanfront houses, which they refused to leave despite the urging of the Coast Guard. The other dead woman was Kate Hagy Lovett.

Here, in the words of her grandson-in-law, is the story.

"The house of John H. Lovett and his wife Kate Hagy Lovett was swept away in the September 14th hurricane, and she was killed. The house was on the southeast cor-

The '44 hurricane left this house in Holgate standing, as well as Bond's Coast Guard station, below.

house, one with two small children, came over to the Lovetts' more substantial building. The water rose, and men rowed over from the Coast Guard Station and offered to take the six to the station for shelter. Grandpop insisted that they would be all right and the Coast Guardsmen left. Soon afterward, the water came into the house and they went to the second floor. The house was soon shaking mightily as the waves pounded it, and Grandpop could hear the refrigerator downstairs floating about, smashing into walls and jarring the building.

"Finally, he decided they should swim to the Coast Guard Station. (It was only 200 yards to the south.) He and his wife were excellent swimmers and all four adults had life vests. The Lovetts tied each one of the children to themselves and they all started for the station. The water was now at the second floor window levels. Grandpop, the child with him and the two women made it, but his wife and the other child were lost. The child's body was never found. The names of the other people are gone from my mind. I remember my mother-in-law saying that the mother, a Philadelphian, never would believe that the little girl was dead, was convinced that she had been rescued, that 'somebody had her,' and spent much time and effort on wild goose searches for the child.

"My father-in-law, John R. Lovett, drove down to the Island the next day. He was stopped at the mainland end of the causeway; police were not letting any non-emergency vehicles on the Island. He walked all the way across and down to Holgate. The house was gone, and there was no sign of his parents. He began the walk back, and a National Guard truck stopped him and the soldiers questioned him. When he explained himself, they offered him a ride, but apologized that there were dead bodies with the soldiers in the back of the truck.

*Surveying what is left, after the '44 hurricane, in Holgate.*

He said that was all right, climbed in, and one of the bodies was his mother.

"Grandpop bought a lot on the corner of Eighteenth and Waverley Street in North Beach Haven the next year, much farther up the Island and presumably safer. He had a foundation poured and single-handedly built a small house for himself where he spent his final years. He died on Christmas Day 1950. The house is still there but greatly modified and expanded.

"The event of the hurricane had an awful emotional impact on the family. They still went to the Island to visit Grandpop, but Joy was never comfortable. We vacationed there after we were married, but after Grandpop died , the family sold the house and Joy never wanted to go to the Island again. Then in 1962, as she sat reading accounts of the March storm, she suddenly said, "Maybe we should go to Beach Haven for our vacation next summer." I saw that as a breakthrough and agreed without comment. We began spending a few weeks there annually, but she always refused to go south of the Beach Haven borough. Then one year, she said, "Let's go down to the end of the Island." We drove down and she pointed out where the old house had stood. It was about twenty-five years from the hurricane to that final emotional closure. She died a few years later at the age of forty-one.

"The Jacqueline Avenue lot stood empty for years, and the water went through there in the '62 storm. Since then, three houses have been built on the lot. Let us hope that the storm gods are through with the site."

James Smart, Philadelphia
September 1999

## Rafinesque

Constantine Samuel Rafinesque, born in Constantinople of French and German parentage in 1783, emigrated to Philadelphia in 1802 and lived most of his life in America. Now recognized as one of the world's preeminent naturalists and horticulturists, he missed genuine recognition in his lifetime by being too diversified in his interests, some of which bordered on the eccentric. He was an insatiable discoverer and collector of plants, shells, fish, birds and animals, devising over 6,000 scientific names in the field of botany alone.

He began writing at 19 and at the time of his death at 57 in 1840, he had authored some 220 books, pamphlets and tracts in English, French, Italian and Latin. The best known of his works was the document he produced in 1836 called the *Walam Olum*. This purported to be a translation of an early Leni-Lenape account of their origins, from the crossing of the Bering Strait 4,000 years before to their conquering of an earlier mound-building people who had already settled in the Midwest.

Rafinesque claimed to have worked eleven years translating the painted wooden tablets called the *Walam Olum*, but said they had been lost and he had only a notebook copy. It mattered not. His discovery soon became, to credulous scholars, as significant an ancient record as the Bible or Homer's *Iliad*. Only in recent decades has it been proven to be a hoax, one of the really great ones of the 19th century. Why he expended so much effort on it is not known. It may have been an attempt to get the attention he so desperately craved all his life. It may also have been done to poke fun at Joseph Smith's contemporary discovery of a Mormon Bible, the original tablets of which were also "lost." Rafinesque had declared that whole episode to be a hoax, but its subsequent success may have inspired him to attempt a similar text.

In the summer of 1802, Rafinesque recorded the following trips taken with a fellow horticulturist, Colonel Forrest of Philadelphia.

"We took several excursions together in Pennsylvania, and had even intended to go over the Allegheny Mountains as far as Pittsburgh; but instead undertook a journey through New Jersey to the Sea shore. We went in a cart through the Pine Barrens to Tuckerton and Egg Harbor. I made an ample collection of fine and new plants at Quaker Bridge in the barrens, and on Tuckers Island: I discovered many new Plants on this Island such as *Drosera filiformis, Ameranthus pumilus, Gerardia maritima,* &c."

*Drosera filiformus* is the sundew, an insect-eating plant related to the pitcher plant. Plants of this sort are independent of the soil for nutrition and would thrive on the sandy barrier beaches. It has a small yellow flower, but its name, sundew, comes from the glistening droplets at the ends of hairs growing on its narrow leaves. They shine in

# Tucker's Island Visit

When Edgar Smiley Nash, founder and editor of the short-lived Beach Haven summer weekly, the *Breeze,* paid a visit to tiny Sea Haven, on Tucker's Island, in July of 1907, its days as a seaside resort had been over for nearly a generation. Only the lighthouse and the lifesaving station remained, along with the families of the men needed to maintain them, along with a few diehard summer residents. Sea Haven's decline began with the arrival of railroad service to Beach Haven in 1886. For one reason or another no attempt was ever made to run the tracks another five miles southward.

Firsthand accounts of visits to Sea Haven are rare and invariably sparse in detail. This piece from the *Breeze* is no exception, and the reader must examine every sentence for information. Nash used a gasoline-powered motorboat on his journey down the bay. These early, thumping "one lungers" were in their infancy then, having first appeared on Little Egg Harbor Bay in the late 1890s, much to the dismay of the sailing crowd, who called their owners "stinkpot sailors." Soon they were everywhere.

Nash visited Bond's Lifesaving Station on his way to Sea Haven. The station had a dock on the bay at Janet Avenue, but getting to the station itself was a half-mile hike over the dunes to its ocean-front location. It would not be moved to the bay until 1922, in the era of the rumrunners.

Nash mentions an investment group interested in developing Sea Haven and selling lots. This would have been the St. Alban's Investment Corporation, which a generation earlier, had lent lighthouse keeper Eber Rider the money to build the St. Alban's Hotel. It had only a few good seasons before it failed. By 1905, the lenders had foreclosed and taken all the land on the north end of Tucker's Island, the former Sea Haven. They planned to call their resort St. Alban's but it never got off the ground. All that ever came of their dream was the change of a name. It was St. Alban's, not Sea Haven, that remained on the books until the badly eroded, abandoned island was removed from the tax rolls of Long Beach Township in the 1930s.

## A Cruise in The Breeze Press Boat

from the *Breeze,* July 1907
by Edgar Smiley Nash

*There was heavy sea running in Little Egg Harbor Bay when the* Breeze *press boat, the* Tomatokan, *warped to the dock to receive us, and we threw our souwesters into the swaying craft and climbed aboard with camera and plenty of plates. We were soon underway and our Bridgeport engine never missed a stroke as the stiff little craft, with Captain Beers at the helm, plowed swiftly out through the channel and soon showed her teeth to the white capped breakers of the bay itself. Ten knots she was making with the tide and we soon left Beach Haven astern.*

*Tucker's Island Lighthouse*

*The schoolhouse on Tucker's Island. The teacher, standing at left, was Florence Morss.*

Every wave rolled over her but we were all snug aboard, dry in our water-proofs, and the camera, with its brilliant Zeiss Tesser, safely wrapped in an oilskin. Two miles at ten knots is but a stroke, and in seemingly no time we were moored at Holgate's and off for the lifesaving station, where on the way we passed Purkey's Pond with its pretty fringe of golden flowers like "fair yellow daffodils stately and tall." The lifesavers at Bond's have many a praiseworthy deed to their credit, and, now, after the perils of the winter's gales, they are taking a well-deserved holiday until August.

The length of the annual service has been gradually extended. At first, in 1871, it was only during the three midwinter months and slowly increased until, for the last ten years, the crews have been on duty all the year except June and July. The men at present are a little fearful lest it be further increased to include even these summer months, as this is their only opportunity of being with their families for any length of time.

Bond's Hotel, now a bit of interesting history, was nearby and with it the many tales we have heard — such good ones too — of hospitality, fun and all the rest. We now thought of it as a dear old ruin, something to be seen to be appreciated. After bidding good-bye to Enoch Grant, who has charge of the Bond estate, our engine again thumped towards Sea Haven, where in the land-locked cove was the Alert, one of the three of the Government's new power life-boats. It is a marvel of boat building with double planking of mahogany and air-tight compartments for righting her. She's self-bailing, of course, has two masts, spray hood and a ten-horse power explosive engine. Uncle Sam invested $8,000 on this boat and wisely, we think. She can go some too, according to one of the crew. "We took the Lieutenant on his last inspection across the inlet, sails all set, and engine full ahead, and the seas a spillin' over her. Gee, she looked just like one of them porpoises."

We landed at Sea Haven in the Captain's dory, which was offered to us. These observing men know your needs, and their generous hearts grant them before you think of asking. The lighthouse where Captain Arthur Rider now has succeeded his father, who kept it for nearly forty years, was open to us. High above the tide it sheds its warning of red and white to the endangered mariner at sea, much may be told of lighthouses but not at this time. Just below the light is the Little Egg Harbor Lifesaving Station where Captain Jarvis Rider had been in charge for thirty-eight years. The log shows many hard days and nights of service, much credit to captain and crew.

Enterprising capitalists have acquired property at Sea Haven and are about to develop it along the most improved lines. Streets have been laid out at North Sea Haven and the ready sale of building *sites indicates the founding of a large cottage settlement on that desirable portion of Long Beach. It is purposed to greatly widen the Island at this point and consequently deepen the bay by the use of dredges. Here is room and reason for one of the greatest seashore municipalities on the Atlantic and it is apparent everywhere that good seed is being sown.*

*Sea Haven is well worth a visit. You will find a lifesaving station, a light, a schoolhouse with a big bell which they can use for a fog bell. If you are lucky you will see, as we did, issuing from the ruined hotel a smiling old patriarch nearly ninety in years looking at us through his fingers, but only in fun about the camera. "'Twere the old man Lippincott," the lifesaver said.*

*Tides and a railroad train commanded us homeward and we made for the new life-boat. Picked up the* Tomatokan *and the captain took back his dory. Headed back to Beach Haven through the cove and into the open bay, past a sea bird perched on a spar buoy rocking in the swells. We made port just in time for our Philadelphia guest to satisfy the craving of his appetite and catch the smoky train for the sultry city.*

the sun, and when tiny insects land on the sticky droplets and are caught, the hairs turn inward and digestive juices exuded by the leaves absorb food from the bodies of the insects. The other plants that he mentions are not unusual and grow in the salt marshes from Maine to the Carolinas.

The next year there is the following passage:

"In July I took an excursion of 15 days through New Jersey to the sea shore and sea islands, to study them better still. I went by Burlington, Mount Holly, Vincentown and Buddtown to the Pine Barrens, which extend here about 30 miles to the sea, intermingled with Cedar swamps. I passed through the Grouse plains, without trees; the soil is gravelly, covered with bushes, and has no value, although healthy and with good water. There is no village in these sandy pinewoods and gravelly plains. I stopped at Cedar Bridge to botanize and found many plants.

"This spot is 9 miles from Barnegat and 10 from Manahawkin villages near the sea. I went to the last which has 60 houses and a fine pond of clear water 3 miles around, but colored like all the waters here. I remained 5 days in the neighborhood to explore the woods, swamps, salt marshes, meadows, &c. I spent 6 days on the great Island of Long Beach, 24 miles long, but often cut up by the sea in storms. It is frequented for the sea air and the sea baths, and has a whale fishery in the spring, for whales coming near the coast.

"Like all other litoral islands, it is a narrow band of sand mixed with shells, downs (dunes), bushes, holly groves, salt marshes and ponds. I collected 25 kinds of seashells, some very rare such as 3 species of golden amonias, grooved, smooth and dilated. I returned in stage by the same road. This small journey of 150 miles had furnished me many materials."

## Little Egg Harbor Light

Despite the incredible number of shipwrecks along the coast of New Jersey in the late 18th and early 19th centuries, the federal government was slow in getting lighthouses built anywhere but at the entrance to New York Harbor. Barnegat Lighthouse, on Long Beach midway between New York and Cape May, wasn't built until 1837, and even then it was only a 50-foot tower of brick and masonry with a fixed light at night. Another dozen years would pass before a similar light was built twenty miles to the south of Barnegat at a place known alternately as Short Beach or Tucker's Beach. The light was officially named the Little Egg Harbor Light and, were it still standing, it would be about five miles below the center of Beach Haven.

The Little Egg Harbor Light was a mere 40feet high, capped in red and with a fixed light of limited range. It wasn't much better than Barnegat, which in those early years was capped in black, but the differing color characteristics of the two lights were meant to be an aid to mariners in clear weather. At night, however, both lights were so feeble that they were often mistaken by smaller coastal vessels for another ship closer to ashore.

The Little Egg Harbor Light was improved in 1854 with a better lens and alternating red and white flashes. The equally inadequate Barnegat Lighthouse was, by the middle 1850s, acknowledged to be doomed due to erosion and a whole new tower three times taller was already under construction with funding provided for a first-class lens and light. Another such light was being built at Absecon in Atlantic City and so, unneeded, Tucker's Light was abandoned in 1859.

The new 170-foot, red and white tower of Barnegat Lighthouse was ready by 1859. Though both it and Absecon were first class lights, they were still too far apart to overlap, and so the Little Egg Harbor Light would have to be re-lit. The Civil War delayed this, but by the summer of 1866, Congress appropriated $5,000 to restore the Little Egg Harbor light and build a single-story keeper's house nearby. The new light cast its red and white flashes at night. If it had only a ten-mile range in haze, it still made a useful navigator's mark between Absecon and Barnegat.

Where was the original Tucker's Light and what happened to it? It was no more than a 40-foot tower. We know that it was built in 1848 on the high ground that had been the site of Tucker's Hotel, and that it was abandoned during the Civil War, until the new one, the white dwelling with the square tower atop, was built. Actually that original lighthouse has been right under our noses all these years. Nearly every photograph of the Little Egg Harbor Light shows a round, white structure of immense girth just to the south of it. It is usually described as an oil house and, in fact, was used to store cans of kerosene fuel, but it seemed grossly out of proportion if that was its only purpose. The lighthouse inspector noted that it was eighteen feet in diameter at its base, with walls two feet thick and the ceiling sixteen feet high. This solid brick and mortar structure was the base of the original light built in 1848. There it had been all along until it, too, fell into the sea in 1927.

These structures and everything else in Sea Haven were all built on sand. Tucker's was, after all a barrier island, just like neighboring Long Beach Island. Beach Haven, five miles to the north, was the closest stop for mail and transportation. The Green Street wharf at Tuckerton was nearly eight miles away by boat. The only source of fresh water came from rain procured from the roofs of dwellings through downspouts into rain barrels and cis-

*Arthur Rider, son of Eber Rider; for 60 years they were the father and son keepers of Little Egg Harbor Light on Tucker's Island.*

terns. The salt water table on the Island was high. There were two cellars under the lighthouse, and the inspector noted that one of them was filled with water half of the year.

The only real road on the Island was made of hay and crushed clamshells. It led to a wood-framed boathouse about 1,500 feet from the light. The boathouse, built on pilings, was equipped with a hoist. There were wooden boardwalks between out-buildings all around Sea Haven, and a low bridge crossed the narrowest point of the slough near the lifesaving station at the south end of the Island, and led over to Tucker's Beach. The crews

hauling lifesaving equipment to the site of wrecks on the beach used this bridge.

There was no wharf or boat landing near the premises of the lighthouse. Small boats entered an arm of the bay, called the slough, just east of the light and landed on the beach. Across the slough was a wide stretch of sand known in later years as Tucker's Beach. It was a five-mile walk from that point across from the lighthouse to Beach Haven and actually six and a half miles from the bridge across the slough. Residents of Sea Haven did their grocery shopping in Beach Haven, usually at Penrod's Store on Amber Street. Amanda Rider Penrod was a

# Guardsmen Quit Station in Storm

## Sea Haven, New Jersey Coast Guard Base Wrecked and 18 Men Take to Boats

From the Ocean County Courier, *January 26, 1933*

Eighteen members of the Sea Haven Coast Guard Station on Tucker's Island seven miles south of Beach Haven, today abandoned the station which was wrecked by pounding seas and a northeast gale during the night.

The majority of the guardsmen at the isolated station, which threatens momentarily to topple into the sea, were brought to Bond's Coast Guard Station on Long Beach Island at 2 o'clock this afternoon in three power surfboats. The remainder of the crew got away safely at noon and reached shore near here in two of their own boats.

The Sea Haven station, its doors and windows battered in by the 60-mile gale and torrential rain, is so badly undermined that in all probability the station will have to be abandoned permanently.

Before abandoning the station the guardsmen rescued nearly all the valuable equipment and their pets, including two cats and a dog. The surfmen at Sea Haven, under Chief Boatswain's Mate Frederick Parker waited until help arrived from the Bond's station, three miles away before deserting the beleaguered frame station on the tiny island, washed by both the Atlantic Ocean and Barnegat Bay. It has been buffeted by several recent storms and its security imperiled by undermining of the sea.

It was after the crew sent out a dot and dash "SOS" call at 5:00 AM today that the Bond's Station went to their fellow-guardsmen's rescue in a powerboat. When the rescuers reached the little island, it was awash, and the station plainly showed marks of the storm's fury. The crew, except the few who had gone to Beach Haven, were standing in the flooded rooms in hip boots, the water gradually mounting higher.

The remaining two boats were not sufficient to get off all the equipment and men and there was a shout of delight when the Bond's boat, in command of Surfman Nottingham, hove into sight. Then Skipper Parker gave the command, "Abandon Station," and the three boats were launched into the tempestuous sea.

The Sea Haven crew will be housed at the Bond's Station in Holgate temporarily pending orders from Washington as to whether the Government will attempt to build another station at Sea Haven or order the crew to be assigned to other stations.

The Sea Haven Coast Guard Station on Tucker's Island was lost to storms and tides in January 1933.

*When the Little Egg Harbor Light fell into the encroaching sea on October 12, 1927, the keeper's residence portion of the building was set afire. At left is the base of the original 1848 Tucker's Island lighthouse, which was replaced by the wood-frame structure after the Civil War.*

sister of Arthur Rider, the keeper of the lighthouse, and a daughter of Eber Rider.

Eber Rider, a resident of Tuckerton, was appointed first keeper of the new light on May 29, 1867. He and his family and one assistant had to live in the new structure with only two rooms, an attic and a detached kitchen. This semi-private mode of living went on for a dozen years despite repeated pleas for better quarters, and it should be noted that Eber Rider and his wife were a couple who eventually had twenty-two children. Only five of them, however, survived to adulthood. Finally, in 1879 the building was expanded to another story and a 10-by-10-foot wooden tower was placed atop the roof.

The light was not much higher than the former brick tower, but conditions for tending it were improved. The old tower was taken down and the substantial masonry base of it was converted to an oil storage room. The bricks from the upper part were used to make piers for a new porch. A later addition behind the keeper's house soon provided for another eleven rooms for the growing Rider family.

On March 22, 1906, after thirty-nine years as keeper, Eber Rider retired and his position was taken over by his son Arthur H. T. Rider. Arthur was, like his father, a dedicated man and a delightful character. He looked, talked and acted just the way a lighthouse keeper ought to and

was always being visited and photographed by members of sailing parties. Beach Haven was only about six miles north of the light; until 1920, all boaters desiring to get out into the ocean had to go around Tucker's Island to use the wide, deep Little Egg Harbor Inlet two miles south of the light. It was all to change radically after the great storm of February 4, 1920 when "Old Inlet," shoaled in since the 1870s, reopened between Holgate and the northern tip of Tucker's Island.

As it grew wider and deeper, the inlet became a boon to fishermen seeking a shorter passage from Beach Haven to the outside. These were the golden years of the party boat captains, who renamed it the Beach Haven Inlet. It was not a boon for Tucker's Island, now being stalked each year by ever-worsening erosion. The worst year was 1927; it would also be the last.

Keeper Arthur made the following report to his superiors at the Third District office after a severe northeast storm on the 20th of February 1927: "Nearly all of the foundation was washed away from the front of the building. The old hotel (the St. Alban's) that stood about 200 feet away and another house 500 feet away were washed down and totally destroyed." On August 28 the keeper wrote: "Front porch of this station was washed down and carried away by the sea yesterday afternoon." A month later on September 30, 1927, the Little Egg Harbor Light was discontinued and Arthur Rider was retired from the service. Together, he and his father had been keepers of the same light for a total of sixty years, a record unequaled by any other American lighthouse

On October 10, 1927, he wrote: "Tucker Beach Lighthouse is so much undermined that it has started to sag and lean toward the ocean." It fell over on October 12 and on the next day, October 13, he wrote: "Tower and dwelling except dining room and kitchen upset in the surf yesterday and was broken up and washed away by the sea." The following day he wrote: "The dining room and kitchen of the Tucker Beach Lighthouse, which was badly wrecked when the main part of the building pulled from it and upset in the surf, was completely destroyed by fire yesterday afternoon."

His grandnephew, Paul Rider, was there to take a dramatic sequence of four photographs showing the lighthouse's slow fall into the sea. The next afternoon he was still there to turn his camera onto the burning of rest of the nearby structures.

It has been said by some that the remaining badly damaged buildings were set on fire by vandals who sneaked out there under cover of darkness, but it now seems certain that orders came from the Third Coast Guard District to destroy them so as not to confuse passing mariners. Unfortunately, Rider never made a note that he had followed orders in setting the fires himself. The fact that Paul Rider was on hand to photograph the buildings burning in broad daylight is some indication that it was an official act, and not arson.

## Beach Haven Inlet

In the 1930s, the beaches at Holgate — nearly a half mile wide — were solid and clean enough to accommodate a Beach Haven Inlet Airport. Small planes found room to land and take off in any kind of wind — north, east, south or west — it didn't matter. The deep, ever-widening inlet was located right where the parking lot at the end of the Boulevard is today, and the whole area was dotted with the tents of fishermen throughout the 1920s. The only fresh water available had to be carried in buckets from the artesian well at the Coast Guard station on Janet Avenue. Sanitation was an obvious problem and tenting on the beaches was proscribed after 1937,

*This unique structure was a water tower near Bond's in Holgate. It was moved across the bay to West Creek, and can now be found on Route 9. It is known as the "chair house" for the straight-backed chair that has remained on the peak of the roof for more than half a century.*

giving a boost to the trailer camp enterprise.

Different sections of the south end, before the great March Storm of 1962, acquired different names such as Venice Beach, the Smith Tract, Silver Sands, Beach Haven South, Beach Haven Heights and, for the area around the Coast Guard station, Bond's. Beach Haven Inlet was the one name actively pushed by Long Beach Township Commissioner William DeFrietas, who in the 1930s owned a bar on McKinley Avenue called the Inlet Inn. He also had a boat livery, and it served his interests to promote fishing in Beach Haven Inlet, which in those years was only a few blocks away, just south of Cleveland Avenue. The new water tower, built in 1938, had the name "Beach Haven Inlet" emblazoned on it. This was all at the behest of William DeFrietas. After his bar was destroyed

in the hurricane of 1944, DeFrietas built a new one in the middle of the Island and continued to call it the Inlet Inn despite its new location miles from any inlet. This is the same bar that is now Kubel's Too.

The inlet's name remains on the water tower, but the inlet itself began to drift southward in the 1930s, and a huge stretch of land, now the Holgate Unit of the Edwin B. Forsythe National Wildlife Refuge, began to accrete behind it. Beach Haven Inlet, after years of use by canyon-bound fishermen, began to shoal up so badly that in 1984, the channel markers were removed by the Coast Guard, who urged the use of the safer Little Egg Harbor Inlet a mile to the south. Beach Haven Inlet is still used by smaller boats but, for all practical purposes, it is gone and, except for nostalgia and a love of history (who can

# Tucker's Light, 1907

In November of 1907, a lighthouse inspector from the U.S. Department of Labor and Commerce made a routine visit to the Little Egg Harbor Light on Tucker's Island, five miles south of Beach Haven. His observations, contained in a sixteen-page form that he filled out that day, came to be of great value as the lighthouse is one of more than a dozen such historically important regional structures built as replicas at the Tuckerton Seaport, a re-created maritaime village.

The Little Egg Harbor Light, known alternately as Tucker's Light or the Sea Haven Light, has been gone since 1927, but there are enough photographs of it to serve as models for a reasonably faithful reproduction of its exterior. The discovery of this document, along with the original plans for the building itself, has enabled the Seaport to place bedrooms, closets, hooks, trap doors and stairs all in their proper places.

No one seems to have a color photograph of the Little Egg Harbor Light, which seems to have been completely overlooked by the makers of hand-colored postcards early in the century. It is not as if this official document of 1907 contains such a picture, but the inspector notes that the shutters were green, something that has never been mentioned before. It has always been known that the outer walls of the dwelling were painted white and the light tower on the roof was black because navigational charts in the era of the light's existence labeled these two colors as its characteristic for identification by daylight. The minor detail of the color of the shutters was not important then, but it certainly became so to the designers at the Tuckerton Seaport.

H. Bamber, assistant engineer — that was the name and title of the inspector — noted that the operation of the light by night was a white flash lasting a full minute followed by six consecutive red flashes, each of ten seconds duration. Probably because it was outside the purview of the report, the inspector does not mention why Tucker's Light would blink red for a full minute and then white for another. The reason was that the inlet just to the north of the light — the one that the first light had been built to guard in 1848 — was already known as "Old Inlet" because another wider, deeper one called "New Inlet" had opened two miles to the south of the lighthouse. "Old Inlet" became completely sanded in by 1870, just after the new light had been built. It was too late to move the light, and besides, the ground near New Inlet was too low and marshy. So the red flashes were a warning to mariners to consult their charts for the safer inlet not very near the light.

At the time of its construction in 1869, the tower on the roof — which, incidentally was square and measured 10-by-10 feet — was painted red instead of black, but such a combination of colors could, in hazy weather, cause it to be confused with Barnegat Lighthouse twenty miles to the north. (No matter that Barnegat was more than three times higher.) Red and white may have been the colors for the original Tucker's Light because the first Barnegat Lighthouse, built a decade earlier in 1834, was a 50-foot white tower with a black crown.

Tucker's (also called Sea Haven, or Little Egg Harbor) Light was originally a 40-foot-high tower, built in 1848. Its base is shown here to the left of the wood-frame structure, which replaced it in 1869.

quarrel with that?), it should have little practical meaning as a place name for residents of the south end, unless another inlet is cut through in the same place by another storm as powerful as the blizzard of February 4, 1920.

## "Along Our Jersey Shore"

*A writer and an artist from* Harper's New Monthly Magazine *took the train to West Creek in the summer of 1877 and then sailed to Long Beach Island. Together, they produced a journal called "Along Our Jersey Shore," from which this is excerpted.*

Long Branch, that fashionable resort had no inducements strong enough to detain us who were in search of the picturesque, and we continued in the cars to Whiting's some thirty-six miles down the coast, where we transferred ourselves from the New Jersey Southern to the Tuckerton Railway, by which we arrived at West Creek.

There is an implication of remoteness and queerness in the very name of West Creek. The traveler who finds it in his timetables is quite sure not to make the mistake of supposing that it is much of a town, or a mushroom outcome of a real estate speculation. It is old, probably its inhabitants are fishermen and the sea washes up to it through a slough in one of the wonderfully green salt water marshes. That is the idea that the name would convey, and it would not be very much out of the way.

The inhabitants are fishermen, farmers, and boatbuilders properly, but in the course of a year they turn their hands to the harvesting of salt hay and ice, the cultivation of oysters and clams, or to almost anything else that will yield an honest penny. Many of them are old sea-captains, who in their day have taken large vessels on voyages to the farthest countries, and who, because

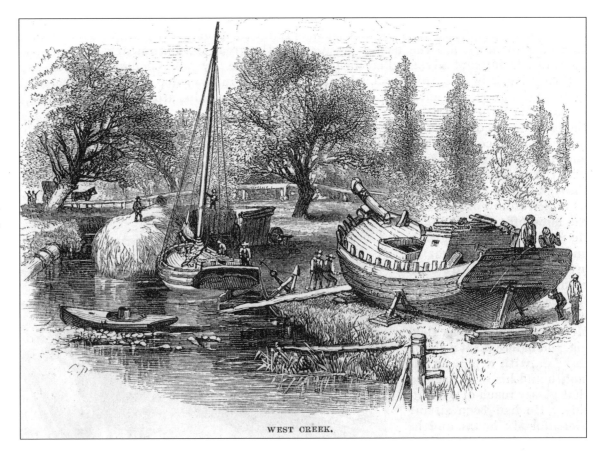

WEST CREEK.

the sea when it once takes hold of a man never wholly relieves him of its charm, or allows inland life to be endurable, are satisfying their lingering cravings for the element by short and safe yacht cruises, spiced by the small profits and gentle adventurousness of bluefishing. Others have been fishers from babyhood, their cradles seines, and their mother's apron strings trolling lines. By thrifty living the best of these have acquired the proprietorship of small cat-boats or sloops and are enabled to exist comfortably and respectably. The ne'er-do-wells divide their attention among a variety of pursuits and though they may never have possessed an unbroken dollar in the straitened course of their impecunious careers, some

ingenuity has made them the owner of a boat — a crazy old thing usually, which has been condemned by their more prosperous neighbors, and so dexterously patched that it will just float and bear a ragged strip of sail.

There is one salient trait in the men of West Creek — they all wear trousers, which in itself is a fact sufficiently obvious to debar the claim of novelty; but the trousers are of such structural peculiarity that they form a new scheme in the philosophy of clothes ceasing to be nether garments simply, and extending far above the hips to the armpits, under which they are braced with a firmness which conveys a suspicion that the rest of the body is suspended from the shoulders. A few inches more of the length and a pair of sleeves added would make any other article of costume superfluous, except for ornament. Another thing that attracts the observation of the stranger is the superiority of the women in education and social refinement, which is so marked that it suggests a new force in civilization. An old and prosperous settler with a large family takes the boys and brings them up as he had been brought up — in freckles, toil, untidiness and ignorance, or at least ignorance of schooling; if their desires are realized, they become keepers of the village store or hotel, or fishermen, or farmers, and they attain manhood with some independent property, a good deal of shrewdness, but without any polish of mind or appearance.

The girls, on the contrary, are sent to school and liberally dressed; and when the father builds a fine new house, with a piazza and a Mansard roof, they are adapted by education and training to grace it; and should a visitor sit down to dinner with them, and see their male relatives, unshaven and not fastidiously clean, eating in their shirt sleeves, he might wonder at the strength of the domestic tie which holds such difference together in contentment. When the pleasantly furnished parlor, decorated with many little feminine arts is occupied by the girls in the evening, who are reading or sewing, and their brothers come in with acquaintances who are quite incapable of responding to any of their intellectual needs, the oddness of the phase is greater and the contentment seems impossible.

To understand the geographical position of West Creek, it is necessary that the reader should know one remarkable and uniform feature of the Atlantic coast. From Long Island southward to Cape Fear, a distance of some six hundred miles, the main-land is separated from the ocean by a belt of dazzling white sand, intersected and broken into islands by narrow inlets, and at the portals of New York, Delaware and Chesapeake Bays. In some places this outer beach is no more than a quarter of a mile wide, the surf almost drenching it from side to side, and in other places it is five miles wide. The sea encroaches upon it or extends it from year to year, widening here and shortening it there, and sometimes leaving dangerous shoals still farther out, upon which the waves break in terrific tumult. Few of the inlets are navigable and most of them are constantly changing positions, new ones appearing after violent storms, and others being suddenly filled in by sand. The water between the beach and the mainland is navigable to small vessels, and when the sea is heavy outside, it affords safe sailing to the many sloops and schooners trading between village and village along the coast. On the inner border, the main-land meets it with a long, low, melancholy fringe of salt meadows which retreat into cedar swamps and firmer ground.

From the dusky cedars and through the meadows West Creek flows, and on its banks where it is not more than twelve feet wide, the foliage stands, the fresh water of such land-born streamlets, mingling with the salt of the ocean, and the flat reaches of sedge and rushes, make a paradise for birds, and in the gunning seasons sportsmen from the city drop into the village, but other visitors are seldom seen.

Aside from its population, West Creek has not much

LITTLE FISH PEDDLERS AT WEST CREEK.

to show. It has several wide streets over which some good old trees form an ample canopy and between the cottages there are sturdy vegetable gardens or fields of corn. Were it not for the seines which are spread in front of some of the houses or in the fields and the salty invigorating air, it would have nothing to distinguish it from an agricultural settlement. We are forgetting, however, the old hotel with its long line of hitching posts under the piazza, and its invariable menu of bluefish, mackerel, oysters or sheep's head and we are also forgetting the small-boy peddlers, who hawk fish from house to house in baskets, wheelbarrows or other available conveyances.

Leaving by way of the creek, the village looks its prettiest. Its white houses are compactly knotted in a clustering wood and above the topmost waves of green a church spire impales the sky. It resembles an island, the low meadows pressing against it without a shrub or tree among the tall, rank grasses, whose swaying is the only relief to their prostrate verdancy. Drifting through those meadows on a brilliant August day in the smallest of sloops; a warm sun and a sapphire dome of sky; the heat of the sun modified by a sea breeze, and the blue feathered with distant waifs of cloud, a pile of salt hay strewn in the stern for comfort in reclining — such were the accessories that made idleness sweet, exertion vanity, and care a vapor, as we hoisted sail at the little landing and moved toward the ocean.

The artist had been quiet so far but now he burst into rapturous exclamation of delight at the colors, the shadows and the forms, exacting attention to this object and that, as an artist will when he strikes a phase of nature to which his imagination is harmoniously responsive. The creek is zigzag and its straight reaches are so short that in whichever direction the wind is, the tacks must be fre-

boastfulness; a good deal of a certain kind of knowledge; a clear perception of what is wrong, and a total inability

Bill Pharo.

conversation covered a wide variety of subjects; it was his opinion that what is now New Jersey was recently, geologically speaking, part of the bottom of the sea, and in proof thereof he adduced the fact that oyster shells had been found very much farther inland than the present coast-line.

We passed out from the mouth of the

LANDING AT BEACH HAVEN.

quent and abrupt. Each turn brought something new in view to arouse the enthusiasm of my artist friend and one moment he eagerly directed my observation to a queer sail of a passing sloop and its flickering reflection in the water, or to the indolent attitude of the sun burned man at the tiller; the next moment an old battered scow lying against the muddy bank with the long grass hanging over and trying to hide its unloveliness; the next to a mass of driftwood washed into a little bay, upon which the sun, breaking through a bed of rushes, cast long yellow bars; the next to the village wrapped up in the foliage, that was now quite distant; the next — but his discoveries were continuous and his raptures inexhaustible; what had been abandoned as useless, and things

that would have been eyesores to nine people out of ten, the play of the waving grasses and the reflections were caught by him and declared to belong to the problematic region of the picturesque. Meanwhile a whole fleet of fishing boats was passing us on their way to the village and our captain, sitting astern was talking to us incessantly.

We passed out of the mouth of the sinuous creek into Little Egg Harbor Bay, separating the outer beach from the mainland, and sailed across to Beach Haven, the newest of the watering places, where we proposed to spend the night. Behind us was that emerald expanse of meadow limited by a broad line against which West

Creek village rose; a fleet of small sailing vessels was in sight, and beyond the beach, which threw off a blinding reflection from its intensely white sand, was the ocean, with larger sailing vessels gliding north and south.

The landing at Beach Haven is inviting but its promise is not fulfilled by a more intimate acquaintance with what is called "the only practical seaside resort in America." Pleasure boats with white hulls and high, slender masts are harbored around the wharf, and more serviceable sloops and schooners find anchorage in the adjacent waters. The beach is not more than half a mile wide and it fronts on the bay with an edging of salt meadows, which are half submerged and redolent of brine. A long path leads up to three overgrown caravansaries — these, with a row of bathing-houses, comprising the settlement which is unique in several ways. It is called a "practical seaside resort" because it is actually on the ocean, and the bay removes it from anything more than a mere suspicion of land air. The surf on the outer beach is boisterous, the waves throbbing in overwhelmingly, and the wind spends itself over the low reach of sand, without a tree or elevation of any kind to break its force. For the first few hours of a visit, one is amazed at the unaccountableness of the taste which brings people in search of such a pleasure. The light is intolerably glaring; the shore is flat and verdureless; in times of storm the hotels are bleak and unsheltered, and in calms they are filled with mosquitoes. It is not accountable at any time indeed, unless we give the visitors credit for a keener susceptibility to a very subtle and poetic form of nature than most watering place habitués have.

What most visitors came for and stayed for were the evening hops, the bathing and the yachting, all of which are much better at many other places we could name; and it is in view of this fact that Beach Haven is unaccountable.

We arrived on a Saturday evening. Fiddles were scraping and feet shuffling in the halls of the big hotels; the broad piazzas were crowded with loungers and promenaders, mostly fair maidens and stately matrons in refrigerant summer dress that reached their necks in diaphanous snowy muslin; the men were happy in a surfeit of tender attentions; and at the close of day, all the yachting parties having come home to supper, the wharf on the bay was left to us.

The sun was setting on the brilliant plain of sedge as we looked landward, and beheld the spires of West Creek and Tuckerton rising out of the distant woods which changed from blue to purple to a smoky crimson until a great globe of fire sunk well behind them and left them a chilly black. But before this, the whole sky was transformed into a sea full of flaming shoals; a mass of cirro-cumuli had become detached and the fragments floated against the pearly blue of the sky and burned with the reflected glow. Green never before seemed so green, or capable of so many shades as it did on the marshes, which, as the sun disappeared behind the woods, were momentarily tipped with gold, and then left to brooding green and blue. In the far north a storm was bursting of tumultuous clouds which had also caught some of the rosy magnificence of the sunset, and were laced with the vivid thrusts of forked lightning, the night came upon us, advancing from a tender pearl blue to an unsympathetic gray, which grew darker until the last light from the west had been extinguished, and the stars pierced the sky with incisive brilliancy. The myriad stars that shone in the opaline moonlight night were as nothing compared in numbers with the gnats and mosquitoes; but who would not have endured even greater torments for a sight so memorable? It was such a sunset as can be seen nowhere else than on those plaintive marshes and barren sands of the Jersey coast.

The sandy strip upon which the "practical seaside resort" is situated is nearly twenty miles long, and is called Long Beach, its northern extremity being formed by the Barnegat Inlet, and its southern extremity by the Little Egg Harbor Inlet. The next island south is called Brigantine Beach; the Barnegat shoals are northward. Along this desolate coast so many vessels have come to grief, and so many bodies have washed ashore, that it is known among fishermen as the Graveyard.

Treasures from many lands are gathered from wrecks, and a fisherman's family is often helped through a trying winter by the provisions, that the sea casts up. When an orange schooner is wrecked, there is dessert after every meal in the cottages or should the cargo be prunes, that fruit becomes a common article of diet. A visitor is sometimes surprised to see foreign brands of olives and canned stuffs in the shelves of the village stores; he learns that they have been secured from a wreck; and the host of one inn at which we spent a night had some excellent Maria Benvenuto claret, labeled, with grim suggestiveness, "Imported direct via Barnegat Shoals."

Fashionable summer resorts are new things to the outer beach. Formerly a small house was erected here and there for the accommodation of sportsmen and parties of fishermen, who came over from the mainland with their wives, daughters and sweethearts for an evening dance. The gaiety at one of these gatherings at Harvey Cedars was eclipsed by the startling announcement that ship had gone ashore and was making signals of distress; whereupon the whole company made for the beach, including the women in all their holiday finery, and not a ribbon or a flounce was thought of until the last man had been landed from the wreck.

# The Mainland

## Edge Cove

Until 1871, when the twenty-nine-mile Tuckerton Railroad opened up, southern Ocean County and Long Beach Island (then called Long Beach) were still an unspoiled wilderness of massive dunes, broad marshes and teeming wildlife. It was a sportsman's paradise. Aside from the descendants of early whaling families, the owners and staff of scattered hotels catering to hunters and fishermen made up most of the Island's thin, permanent population. The U.S. Lifesaving Service, with its chain of seven stations, had just been established.

Beach Haven opened in June of 1874 and, with its grid of streets and steamboat wharf, it became the first planned community on Long Beach. All the materials for the construction of three hotels as well as for the scores of new summer cottages springing up around them had to be floated across the bay in barges. It was an ancient method of transport known locally as "scowing."

Summer people began arriving at Tuckerton in great numbers from West Jersey and Philadelphia and had to hire any available sailing craft to get themselves and their baggage across the bay. It was the traditional method of getting to the Island, but new, steam paddle-wheelers like the *Barclay*, and later the *Pohatcong*, were soon ready to take them in comfort and style from a wharf at Edge Cove, near Tuckerton, to another wharf at the end

*Tuckerton Creek, point of departure for passengers and materials bound for the new resort of Beach Haven.*

The following piece is from a typewritten manuscript found among the papers of the late Charles Edgar Nash in the Beach Haven Library. It may never have appeared in print.

A graduate of Haverford College in the 1920s, Nash began as a writer of technical manuals for Bell Telephone. In 1935 he used the skills acquired there to revise and expand the Island's first history, *The Lure of Long Beach*, at the behest of his grandfather, Charles Beck of Beach Haven. Nash's ability to combine technical information with pure nostalgia is clearly evident here and in the wonderful chapters he wrote on the Tuckerton Wireless and Barnegat Light in *Lure*, and, in his later writings on the Barnegat Lightship, Texas Towers and submarine cables. This short piece on the long-ago excursions from Beach Haven to Tuckerton is drawn from memories of his youth.

# Cross-Bay Sail

by Charles Edgar Nash

Catboats at the Beach Haven Yacht Club.

In the first quarter of this century, or certainly as far back as I can remember, one of the pleasantest and most relaxing experiences for young and old alike among those who summered on Long Beach was a sail to Tuckerton and back on one of the big cat-boats belonging to any one of the many members of the Beach Haven Yacht Club, who sailed or guided fishing parties as a means of livelihood.

These craft were strictly a local design admirably adapted to their bayside environment, being of shallow draft, too broad beamed to upset in any normal blow, and usually running from nineteen to twenty-three feet in length. They sported big centerboards in centerboard wells amidships, which could be raised or lowered according to the depth of the water, giving them very good "reach" on a tack when the board was down.

Most had cabins that sheltered the forward part of the cockpit to protect occupants from too much sunburn in the salty and often spray-filled air, or from rain if a storm blew up. The wide semi-circular combing around the open rear cockpit behind the cabin was invariably topped with a conforming plank seating arrangement about eight inches wide and

an inch thick. Passengers usually sat here atop cushions taken from the cabin.

A tall mast with a gaff rigged fore and aft sail, resplendent with three or four horizontal lines of reef cords, provided the motive power. As I remember it, a jib was seldom used or thought necessary. It was fun for youngsters or even oldsters, to sit in the cabin and look down the center board well into the crystal clear, green water to see an occasional fish or crab swim past as you listened to the unforgettable music of the water tinkling, singing and gurgling against the hull

*A beamy Barnegat Bay catboat, a captain and sailing party.*

which magnified the sound like a bass drum.

These cabins were comparatively low roofed. A grown up, standing on the floor boards, could see over them. They had a long curving bench or bunk on each side that conformed to the shape of the boat. On these you could lie half under the deck of the boat if you didn't feel well, or if you just wanted to relax and enjoy the lapping of the waves. Underneath the benches were long rows of bulky, canvas-covered, cork life jackets with canvas shoulder straps and tie strings ready for instant use if ever needed.

In the center of the cockpit, a few feet behind the centerboard well, there was invariably a fish box made of tongue and groove boards with a heavy, canvas covered lid that could be lifted to put fish

It was no cinch to sail all the way up Tuckerton Creek, with its many twists and turns, and the captains took great and justifiable pride in their ability to navigate all the way up to the headwater without running aground or smacking into a boat sailing out. Here they docked and their passengers debarked near some of the town's graceful and beloved willow trees along the creek, then walked a short distance to the main street and across it to Blackman's famous ice cream parlor for some much needed refreshment.

Blackman's was near the old Tuckerton Friends' Meeting House with its luscious large-fruited mulberry trees, and both the ice cream parlor and the Meeting House were only a stone's throw from Tuckerton's gem of a lake, which had been created by beavers before the white man came. During the warmer months the lake was a floating garden of pink and white water lilies as far upstream as the eye could reach.

The Leni-Lenape Indians had named the lake Pohatcong and it contained cedar water so pure and delicious that it retained its sweetness for months even in a ship's water casks. For that reason coastal mariners had favored it for over a century and a half when we first arrived in its vicinity.

At a time when most ice cream emporiums served only vanilla or most only vanilla and chocolate, Blackman's took pride in making and serving all the natural flavors that the fruit and berry seasons provided and these made from real cream obtained direct from local dairymen. The selection ranged all the way from wild strawberry and swamp huckleberry to cultivated peach, apricot and cherry.

The prices were reasonable, being five and ten cents a serving, if my memory is correct and, in later years, I never found any ice cream that could even approach this, save possibly Italian spumoni, also made of cream, or Basset's at Philadelphia's Reading Terminal. There was also home made sponge cake and iced cup cakes if your appetite dictated. But I will never forget the big glasses of ice cold cedar water direct from the cooler, chilled by chunks of the previous winter's ice harvested from Tuckerton Lake.

It was virtually a natural uncarbonated root beer, crystal clear and with a rich coloration almost like sherry wine from its impregnation with energizing extracts from the roots in a chain of cedar swamps upstream, connecting with what scientists have called one of the greatest natural reservoirs of pure germ-free water in the world. Today the major portions of this great underground water supply are encompassed by the famous Wharton Estate, which fortunately is state owned.

For years, in the early 1900s, after every big freeze in winter, cedar-water ice was harvested in blocks on Tuckerton Lake and stored in cedar-shingled icehouses on the lake shore where it lasted all though the summer under thick layers of insulating sawdust until it was needed. For you must remember there were no electric refrigerators in those days, and no electric lights either, but they managed to make out all right anyway. Without this ice there would certainly have been no Blackman's ice cream with its accompanying glasses of ice-cold cedar water. Blackman's Ice Cream Parlor is gone

in to keep them out of the sun or to take them out after a fishing excursion. This was about thirty inches high and made a nice seat for as many as four people.

Cabins could get hot, so some were built with rectangular windows forward that could be lifted for ventilation or portholes that opened on the sides. Some cabins were no more than vertical posts supporting a solid roof but with rolled green and white striped awnings along the sides that would allow almost any degree of ventilation or protection needed. The presence of awnings usually characterized an older boat than those with portholes.

*now, but this is the same family that left perhaps a more enduring legacy in Leah Blackman's historical writings, which are destined to live on through time.*

*Those were the days of simple pleasures and complete relaxation, which we cannot seem to duplicate today. Just the thought of a sailing trip of perhaps 12 or 15 miles across the bay and back and up and down Tuckerton Creek with its innumerable twists and turns, requiring much tacking may seem boring to a hotshot modernist, especially if the goal, or end, in view was only a plate of ice cream, a glass of water and perhaps a piece of cake.*

*There was no thrilling speed and no particular excitement except the knowledge that you were sailing through history. On the meadows going up and down the creek you passed what has been called the largest prehistoric Indian shell mound on the east coast north of Florida. This was perhaps ten feet high, twenty feet wide and one hundred and fifty feet long. It had a dozen red cedars growing on or around it, the five on top having weathered many a coastal storm. Over the years mainland farmers have used tons of its clam and oyster shells to lime their fields and, in the early days, whole barge loads of the shells went into the mix of the hungry iron furnaces back in the pines that helped arm and equip our armies of independence.*

*And up and down this same serpentine creek an endless parade of shipping brought so many supplies, necessities and luxuries after the Revolution that, on March 21, 1791, President George Washington commissioned the town as the third Port of Entry of the United States, preceded only by New York and Philadelphia. The latter was then the largest city in the colonies. It seems almost inconceivable, but in those years Tuckerton was one of the busiest trade centers in the new nation.*

*Hundreds of ships were built locally, especially schooners which became popular all up and down the coast and many of these operated out of Tuckerton as their home port. And as for food, raiment and all the conveniences of those days, the ladies of Tuckerton took a "back seat" to no one.*

*So scoff if you will at such a sailing trip but anyone of us who ever made it will never forget it.*

of Dock Road in Beach Haven, where they boarded horse-drawn carriages to their hotels and cottages. There would be no rail transport across the bay for eight years, until a trestle was built in 1886 and tracks laid to both ends of the Island. The following passage from an 1883 newspaper illustrates what the steamboat passage in this interim period was like:

"The journey here is one of the most delightful trips in the State of New Jersey. You travel via the Pennsylvania Railroad as far as Whitings, forty-two miles from Philadelphia. There you change into the cars of the Tuckerton Railroad, which take you to the borders of Tuckerton Bay. You then leave the cars and embark on board a little steamboat, which gives you a delightful voyage across smooth water, lasting about three-quarters of an hour, to Beach Haven. The bay is full of sharks and sometimes you catch a glimpse of the monsters following in the wake of the steamboat. On arriving at Beach Haven you have your choice of two hotels…"

Barges could arrive any time. Piled high with barrels, bales, crates and lumber, they were usually floated on the next high tide up the canal along Dock Road to the firmer ground at what is now Long Beach Boulevard. Their cargo was then loaded aboard ox- and horse-drawn wagons to be transported along the rutted sand roads for deliv-

*Charles Beck near Edge Cove, Tuckerton.*

# Cedar Bogs

At the beginning of the 19th century, Alexander Wilson, American ornithologist (1766-1813), described the cedar bogs of South Jersey as follows:

These swamps are from half a mile to a mile in breadth, and sometimes five or six in length, and appear as if they occupied the former channel of some choked up river, stream, lake or arm of the sea. The appearance they present to the stranger is singular: a front of tall and perfectly straight trunks, rising to the height of fifty or sixty feet without a limb, and crowded in every direction, their tops so closely woven together as to shut out the day spreading the gloom of perpetual twilight below. On a nearer approach, they are found to rise out of the water, which, from the impregnation of the fallen leaves and roots of the cedars, is of the color of brandy.

Amidst this bottom of congregated springs, the ruins of the former forest lie piled in every state of confusion. The roots, prostrate logs, and in many places, the water, are covered with a green mantling of moss, while an undergrowth of laurel, fifteen or twenty feet high, intersects every opening so completely as to render a passage through the area laborious and harassing beyond description; at every step you either sink to the knees, clamber over fallen timber, squeeze yourself through between the stubborn laurels, or plunge to the middle in ponds made by the uprooting of large trees, and which the moss concealed from observation,

In calm weather the silence of death reigns in these dreary regions: a few interrupted rays of light shoot across the gloom; and unless for the occasional hollow screams of the Herons, and the melancholy chirping of one or two species of small birds, all is silence, solitude, and desolation. When a breeze rises, at first it sighs mournfully through the tops; but as the gale increases; the tall mast-like cedars wave like fishing poles and, rubbing against each other, produce a variety of singular noises that with the help of a little imagination, resemble shrieks or the groaning of beasts of prey.

ery at several destinations.

The logistics of transport on the Beach Haven side of the bay are generally well known. Much has been written about Dock Road and its canal — busy in the early days, declining slowly after the arrival of the railroad and ending when it was filled in with sand and gravel to widen the street when the automobile came to Long Beach Island.

What is not known, because it seems never to have been written about, is what was happening at Tuckerton in the 1870s, the departure point for the people and freight destined for the beaches. We do know that earlier in the century, visitors to the resorts on Tucker's Island and the Philadelphia Company House (later Bond's), at the south end of Long Beach, boarded roomy catboats at the Green Street wharf in Tuckerton and either paddled, drifted with the tide or were towed down the creek out into the bay where their captains set sail eastward.

When the twenty-nine-mile, single-track Tuckerton Railroad was competed from Whitings and the cross-state line between Camden and the Amboys, hordes of new people started coming to southern Ocean County in the summer months. To get all these vacationers and freight out to the new resorts, the railroad built a spur track three quarters of a mile long from the terminal in Tuckerton eastward to a large and moderately deep indentation on the bay called Edge Cove.

Edge Cove was a safe anchorage, but it had never been used much for the transport of goods and people because its distance from town would be equivalent to fifteen city blocks across meadow and marshland, a terrain not very suitable for horses and wagons. A rail track out to the cove, however, made it a simple matter to roll passenger and freight cars out to a waiting steamboat and all the many barges and catboats waiting for hire.

But did the heavy locomotive itself go out to the very edge of the bay where there was no way to turn around? People would disembark at once, but the freight cars could never be unloaded quickly enough for the train to be on schedule for the return trip to Whitings. Perhaps the cars were backed out there by the engine once the train had reached the Tuckerton station, and then the freight cars could be unhooked and unloaded into barges and scows over the next 24 hours. Trains running backward were not unusual.

The rails and ties were laid on well-drained meadow sod without a supporting roadbed of gravel. The tracks would be strong enough to support loaded cars but perhaps not the excessive weight of an engine, the loss of which in this soft terrain could have been disastrous. Using horses to get the passenger cars out to Edge Cove would not have tied up the train, and people of that day were well used to the smooth ride of horse cars on rails.

In every city in the 1870s and '80s until the invention of the electric trolley, horse cars were state-of-the-art transportation.

The spur to Edge Cove was no longer used by the railroad after the rail trestle was built across Manahawkin Bay to the Island in 1886. By 1892, the Tuckerton Railroad leased the track to Horner & Co of Tuckerton for the transportation of clams and oysters from the bay to the terminal in town. They used horse-drawn cars and, so it has been said, for a few years in the 1890s — until pranksters wrecked it — the legendary "Clamtown Sailcar." Much has been made of this vehicle and it has become part of local lore. It's a device that has been tried from time to time elsewhere in the world, usually on abandoned straight tracks and without much success.

The first sailing-car in America, and probably the world, ran briefly on the tracks of the Baltimore and Ohio in the 1830s. The "Meteor" drew enthusiastic crowds for its few short excursions. Despite its light wicker sides and large wheels, it required a good gale from behind to drive it. Head winds brought it to a stop, and any strong side wind would capsize it or blow it off the tracks. Mishaps like this occurred so frequently that the Meteor became just an amusing toy.

## Tuckerton Wireless

With but an hour of sunlight left on the bitterly cold afternoon of December 27, 1955, the great steel tower, 773 feet high, remained pointed at the wintry sky over southern Ocean County. The wind, unsteady since mid-morning, finally stopped shifting and blew hard out of the west. The chief of the demolition crew gave the signal, and his men, who had been standing by for several hours, made the final cuts with their torches on two of the three great cables supporting the massive structure.

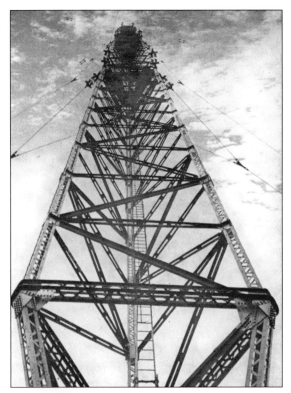

*In 1913, the Tuckerton Wireless, at 820 feet, was the tallest structure in America. In Europe, only the Eiffel Tower surpassed it.*

A third cable had been attached to a huge winch on a truck parked safely some 1,500 feet to the east. As its reel turned, the cable wound tighter and the tower, no longer with any support from behind, was pulled forward. With a slight assist from the west wind, it tottered and then leaned toward the waters of Great Bay and the Atlantic Ocean. A hundred feet of its topmost section, precut and weakened earlier that day, buckled backwards and then, with a heart-stopping rush, the entire 800 tons of steel girders and two miles of antennae wire crashed to the earth.

The shock of the crash, softened somewhat by the marshy ground around it, could nonetheless be heard and felt a mile away, but not quite the four miles into

Tuckerton, where the mighty radio tower, known to the world as the Tuckerton Wireless, had been a source of pride for forty-two years. No one was hurt in the demolition project, but the crews, all men from Brooklyn and Connecticut, agreed that it was the most dangerous wrecking job they had ever attempted. "One puff of wind from the wrong direction at the wrong time and there would have been a very expensive mess," the foreman is quoted as saying.

The tower, at the forefront of radio technology in 1913 when it was completed by the German government as a twin for its other tower across the Atlantic in Germany, had become outmoded. No longer of practical use to its new owner, the Radio Corporation of America, which had shut it down in 1949, it was sold and had to be demolished to make way for a $55 million resort center on the 1,800-lot tract of land in Great Bay. The development, about four miles south of Tuckerton, is known as Mystic Islands. The remains of the once awe-inspiring Tuckerton Wireless can be seen to this day in three strategically placed, steel-reinforced anchoring blocks for the three guy wires that supported the tower, and, of course, its heritage is apparent in the name "Radio Road."

The visits by the Germans to Toms River and Tuckerton in June of 1912 began in secrecy. The rival Marconi Company Ltd., with a transmitting tower in London, England, had already purchased marshland near Shark River in Monmouth County to put up its own tower. But Professor Rudolph Goldschmidt of the High Frequency Machine Company for Wireless Telegraphy had unlimited funds at his disposal. He had developed a tower, of his own invention, that, by necessity, would have to be higher than any radio tower ever built and rest on an absolutely flat base unobstructed by any solid object. Even a tree stump or a large rock, that might possibly

*1954: Built by German engineers in 1912, the Tuckerton Wireless was a high-tech marvel of its day.*

create interference. It could not be built on a mountain. It had to stand at sea level, near the water, on ground solid enough to support its great weight. After exploring the entire coast for a site, he chose Hickory Island, four miles south of Tuckerton and made his purchase in June of 1912.

Goldschmidt found the remote location to be an advantage in keeping away trespassers. Hickory Island was a knoll, or hummock, rising out of miles and miles of surrounding salt meadow. Although the logistics of supply and transport would be difficult, German efficiency prevailed. All of the material for construction had to be transported to Tuckerton by railroad, reloaded and carried to the site by truck. The motor trucks employed were the largest ever seen in South Jersey. The operation was a great boost to the local economy. Workmen got better wages than clamming and oystering would ever bring them. As many as seventy-five of them were

bringing $2,000 a week into the local economy. Horse and mule teams and drivers were also in great demand. Visitors were not encouraged lest the Marconi people send spies.

Westinghouse, an American company was building the power plant and installing the engines and dynamos. By January of 1913, most of these buildings were in place, including the boiler with a stack 150 feet high, almost as high as Barnegat Lighthouse. It would soon be dwarfed by the spider web of girders rising beside it. The work of building that huge tower was the German half of the operation, and it was taking longer than expected. Planned to be 820 feet high, it had, by January of 1913, reached only 200 feet. With characteristic German thoroughness, Goldschmidt's High Frequency Machine Company required all the interlocking parts to be tested to fit at the plant in Germany and then taken apart and shipped to the United States.

The base of the tower was made of three steel trestles, in the shape of an inverted pyramid, tied together at regular intervals so that the weight was centered a little above the ground on a huge ball-joint of solid steel encased in concrete. The great height attainable by the tower was based on a new German principle — using

three steel guy wires attached to three giant concrete anchors sunk twenty feet into the ground, and rising another twenty-five feet above it, with enough weight to give the tower the rigidity to remain upright, and with some flexibility to withstand wind pressure. Every stay and every guy wire was insulated with glass again and again; Goldschmidt's design permitted no interference whatsoever. Halfway up the tower the framework telescoped to allow the base of the upper half to fit inside the top of the lower half. Again, everything was insulated

By September of 1913, the Tuckerton Wireless, at 820 feet, was the tallest structure in America. In Europe, only the Eiffel Tower surpassed it. Two months earlier when the tower was only 640 feet tall, messages were already being received from Hanover, 3,700 miles away in Ger-

# 'Hawkin Bear

In ages past, when the nighttime woods on the mainland were dark, deep and mysterious, there was a pervasive belief that a bear was living there. Like a creature in a fairy tale, it was always a solitary bear. It never left tracks. It never had a mate. Sightings of it were sometimes years apart and never very reliable, but it became a matter of civic pride among several villages in southern Ocean County as to whose woods the bear had chosen to make its home. Manahawkin and West Creek were always at odds with each other over this, and citizens of each town claimed several sightings over the years. Manahawkin actually had the best location for the elusive bear with its famous "'Hawkin Swamp," a vast and nearly impenetrable cedar bog that lay between the bay meadows and Route 9 and ran northward into Barnegat. Present-day Hilliard Boulevard runs through what was once the thickest part of the former 'Hawkin Swamp. Though still a shady and tangled forest, its great cedars have long since been cut down and even the ancient windfalls sunk deep into the muddy ooze were all mined early in the 20th century.

Journalists of the day had a lot of fun with these so-called bear sightings and what follows here is an amusing piece, written tongue in cheek in an old fashioned, colloquial style from the *Ocean County Courier* in the spring of 1909.

## Steve and Lee Tree the Bear
### It Gets Away in the Dark

### Another Bear Story Comes From the Depths of the 'Hawkin Swamp

*Hist! The Great Black Bear has been seen again (at least it would have been seen if it hadn't been so black, the swamp so thick and the night so dark) in 'Hawkin swamp. For the third time, this Bear has made himself known, and this time Manahawkin is strutting and pluming itself over West Creek, Staffordville, Mayetta, Cox's Station, Little Gloucester and Cedar Run as having been the stalking place of Ursus Major.*

*For be it remembered that, in its last two appearances, it was only to West Creek men that the Bear made himself known. As was fitting and proper, he first showed himself five years ago to John Salmons, the West Creek school teacher. John was riding down the road on his wheel and thought it was an approaching vehicle. He and the Bear*

*Main Shore Road, now Route 9, West Creek, in front of J. B. Cox's General Store during the winter of 1896.*

just quickly passed each other going in different directions. The Bear evidently figured that while Professor John's business was teaching the young he probably wasn't much of a hand with fire arms, and so he picked him out as the man to carry the news that he (the Bear) had arrived.

The next time the Bear made an appearance, it was to C.D. "Neal" Kelly of West Creek to whom we are indebted for the only authentic account of his appearance. Neal, you recall, was on his way home from church one night and walking alone down the snowy main street of town. For a moment he thought he was in the company of a big black dog and here it was the Bear trotting alongside him as peacefully as if he too had been to prayer meeting.

West Creek, after this sighting of the bear, sorter bridled and sidestepped, and made up her mind that she was number one in these parts. After all, didn't she have among her citizens Oscar Parker, who was the only man who knew how to build a road, and Charlie Cox, who was the best man any town ever had for Sheriff? And don't forget John Holman, who had all the rest of the cranberry growers in Jersey, on Cape Cod and in Wisconsin, all skinned to death with his new two-horse cranberry harvester.

West Creek's been number one for five years now because nobody outside their town ever actually seed the B'ar. But West Creek ain't ace high just now on bear stories: No siree. 'Hawkin has a straight flush. Dave White says so, and that's all there is about it. 'Hawkin has the Bear!

The Bear has deserted West Creek and is making his home in 'Hawkin swamp.

Steve Johnson and Lee Hazleton know this is so for they are the two who, with four dogs, two guns, two axes and a lantern, treed the Bear.

And what Steve and Lee say must be so — Ain't Lee on the grand jury and ain't Steve a brother to Sam Johnson and ain't Sam a court officer, and didn't Steve's house get struck by lightning when Steve, himself, dodged the bolt, and ain't Lee and Steve both known as mighty hunters and ain't? — but what's the use of going any further. Everybody knows that either Lee or Steve knows a Bear when he sees him, and wouldn't mistake him for an automobile like Professor Salmons did, or for a big, black doggie like Neal Kelly did. So when Steve and Lee say they saw the Bear, or when Lee and Steve say it, it must be so whether it is so or ain't so.

It happened in this way. It was a nice night and Lee and Steve took their fox dogs out for a run. The dogs took off into the swamp. The swamp was black and dark. The dogs treed something and everyone knows that the kind of dogs that Lee and Steve own wouldn't fear to tackle anything the size of a bear or a panther, and as there ain't been no panthers around hereabouts in a dog's age it must have been the Bear they treed for you can't get away from that logic. It proves itself like adding up a column of figures t'other way, and at any rate the dogs wouldn't quit barking and they wouldn't come out of the swamp, and whatever it was wouldn't come out either.

So Lee and Steve went home and got their guns

and their axes and borrowed a lantern that had some John D. illuminant (kerosene) in it cause both of their own was empty. They went way into the swamp but the dogs had by now gone farther in yet. It was dark in there and the farther they went the darker it was and the louder the dogs barked and the bigger the Bear got. Leastwise both Lee and Steve say so, and as they was the only ones there but the dogs and the Bear, and the dogs and the Bear won't talk, why we have got the word of Steve and Lee for it.

So they shot and shot and called the dogs. "Sic 'em Towser, good dog, go get him. Gee whiz Steve, you go. No, Lee you go. You're biggern I am anyway. I think, Steve, you're just the man to kill that Bear. Think how nice, Lee, it would be to have his hide for a rug. I don't want any bearskin for a rug. Besides bear meat wouldn't be any good this time of year anyway. Let's wait till he's fat in the fall, Steve." — and so they had to come home without the bear.

But the Bear is in 'Hawkin swamp. Don't you believe any of those backbiters from West Creek who are going around saying that the dogs treed a possum. Don't you believe it at all. I guess 'Hawkin is just as big as West Creek and has a right to get the Bear once out of three tries. So there! And we can prove it by other solid Manahawkin citizens like Doc Hilliard and Henry Cranmer and Tom Sprague. All three say it was the Bear.

many. By the end of the year, with costs of construction already nearing one million dollars, Goldschmidt was receiving messages from the Marconi station at Clifden in Ireland and other wireless stations on the European continent far less powerful than his sister station in Germany. A receiver he invented could take in one hundred words a minute. The electrical impulses could be photographed on a long reel of sensitized paper and read at leisure; otherwise the dots and dashes were, to the human ear, no more than a continuous hum. All such messages were translated from the Morse code of dots and dashes and relayed by telephone to New York and Philadelphia. The tower was designed only to send and receive messages in an easterly direction out over the Atlantic. Goldschmidt charged eight cents a word.

As soon as the tower had been completed and was fully operational at the end of March, 1914, Goldschmidt got rid of all American employees and had the place fully staffed with Germans. In August of that same year, war broke out in Europe. Although America remained neutral until 1917, there was widespread distrust of anything German in those years. When the British liner *Lusitania* was sunk by a German submarine off the coast of Ireland on May 7, 1915 with loss of American lives, it was rumored that the order to sink her had come from the Tuckerton Wireless in the terse message "Get Lucy."

None of this was ever proven but it remains a popular notion. Such a message, however, would not have been necessary. Prior to the sailing of the *Lusitania* from New York on May 1, 1915 the German Embassy in Washington placed clear warnings to Americans in the shipping sections of every New York paper that any vessel flying the flag of Britain, or her allies, was liable to destruction in the war zone. The *Lusitania* deliberately disregarded the warnings. The sinking, however, was one of the reasons

America abandoned its neutrality and entered the war. When it did, the German staff was removed from the Tuckerton Wireless for the duration.

Other than the story of the *Lusitania*, which is probably not true, few people today know anything at all about a radio tower in southern Ocean County that was once known all over the world. One of the problems with the Tuckerton Wireless is that, unlike nearly all other tall structures such as lighthouses, obelisks, skyscrapers and its nearest rival in height, the Eiffel Tower, it was the least photogenic of landmarks. Old photographs and postcards do little for it, either close up or from a great distance. It was simply too narrow and too tall,

even after it lost its topmost sixty feet in a storm, to be suitably framed so it could be seen all at once.

## The National Hotel

The National Hotel, empty for several years, was declared to be a fire hazard and torn down in the 1970s. Once one of Manahawkin's best-known landmarks, its former site was just across from Manahawkin Lake on Route 9. There are still many who remember the old National in its heyday.

It was a substantial wood-framed, three-story, year-round hotel in the architectural style of the 19th century. It never had much of a lobby, as its entire first floor was a tavern. A big, circular bar took up most of the space, along with tables, shuffleboards and the area needed for a dartboard. Upstairs, each high-ceilinged, narrow room had a radiator and walls that were either papered or bare, white plaster. Most were furnished only with a single framed picture, a wooden chair and double or twin iron bedsteads. Some had sinks, but the cheaper rooms were not outfitted for plumbing and still employed the standard washstand with bowl and pitcher, just like the old days. Men's and women's bathrooms were at the ends of the halls, exactly what, at one time, every shore visitor was used to. Top-floor guests at the National were no doubt comforted by the sight of knotted ropes tied to the radiators and coiled under each window for use in the event of fire.

It was part of another era. For the National Hotel of Manahawkin, that time period extended all the way back to the American Revolution, when it had been a stage-coach stop and a gathering place for patriots. In the 19th century, any trip across the state took nearly a whole day. Those visiting Long Beach Island who chose to cross the plains into Manahawkin, instead of taking the normal route into Tuckerton, would usually need a night's lodging before the sailboat ride across the bay. The National Hotel was where they stayed.

After the twenty-nine mile, single track line of the Tuckerton Railroad was completed in 1871, the Manahawkin depot was no more than a few blocks from the hotel. It was at a meeting in the hotel as early as 1872 that a group of investors first discussed building a rail trestle across Manahawkin Bay to the island of Long Beach. It would not happen for more than a dozen years, but the plans for it began at the National Hotel. By then,

the exterior of the hotel was being changed. Its porches were enclosed with row after row of double sash windows, and a third story was added. As always, the roomy tavern on the first floor was its biggest drawing card.

Like most public houses, it had a stable out back; in the age of the automobile, it was cleaned up and converted into a dance hall called The Red Barn. The former horse stalls around the wide, wooden floor were converted into privacy booths with tables. As a local nightspot it became very popular during and after Prohibition. In the early 1930s, Ben Crane of Tuckerton led a small band, with two fiddles, a guitar, an accordion and a harmonica. They entertained at the Red Barn with such tunes as "That Silver Haired Daddy of Mine," "May I Sleep in Your Barn Tonight Mister," "Red River Valley" and "Let Me Call You Sweetheart."

In the early 1950s, it was the bar of the National that became popular for its country and western music on weekend nights. It was the one mainland bar that drew people from Long Beach Island. In those days, barhopping on the Island was nearly a nightly ritual. No one thought anything of leaving Britz's Bar or the Antlers at Beach Haven and driving all the way to Kubel's or Hans' Tavern next to the lighthouse. There were no traffic lights and few cars. The entire north end was a dark ride, but nothing was ever as dark as Manahawkin at night. Once you crossed the old causeway into Mud City, the whole shoreline south of the causeway, now edged with the bright lights of a thousand homes, was as black as pitch. The mainland's single stoplight was at the intersection of Route 9 and Bay Avenue, and the only places open at night for business were two neon-lit diners, Horner's Esso Station, and, of course, the National Hotel. Beyond Manahawkin, pine forest lined both sides of the road all the way westward to the Four Mile Circle. There was no

Garden State Parkway and no hospital — nothing for twenty miles but Clayton's Tavern and Frankie Mayo's Halfway House.

The National Hotel was always packed on Saturday nights with fun-loving local men and women from up every sand road along Route 9. They were all there for the draft beer, socializing and country music; sun-tanned Islanders in khaki trousers, crew cuts and plain white T-shirts stood out a little.

By day the National Hotel bar was a convenient place to wait for friends arriving on the New York to Atlantic City bus. Passengers debarked in a graveled lot across the street on the edge of the lake and usually headed right for the bar for a couple of quiet drafts and a sandwich before the drive over to the Island. The whole operation was owned and managed in those years by Nick and Geneva Visco. Because of all those wonderful country and western Saturday nights, everyone on both sides of the bay called it "Frontier Play House" after the very popular 1950s television show. It was a name that stuck.

## The Pinelands

Not until after the American Revolution, when the woods of central New Jersey were cleared of the notorious Tory sympathizers called "pine robbers," was it safe to cross the state without an armed escort. One of the most important arteries of travel in those years was the Tuckerton Stage Road. In its heyday, from about 1790 until the 1840s, it ran for fifty-nine miles almost in a straight line from Camden through Haddonfield, Taunton and Atsion to the coast. It was along this road that the old stagecoaches carried both passengers and mail direct from Philadelphia to Tuckerton and back.

Renewed hostilities with the British in the War of 1812

# An Outlander's View of the New Jersey Pinelands

*From the* Newark Call, *October 1923*

New Jersey's wilderness is the pine plains of Ocean and Burlington counties, not the rock-ribbed section in the extreme north end of the state. It is natural to regard the mountainous country as wilder than flat land, but the percentage of population and cultivation of the soils is much higher in the mountain lands of Passaic, Sussex and Bergen Counties than it is anywhere between Lakewood and Cape May. These conditions have seen comparatively little change in a century.

Twenty-five years ago only 13 percent of Ocean County was cleared and most of the cleared land was in one or two townships, and in Burlington County the cleared portions of the pinelands did not represent more than 10 percent of the whole. It is doubtful if any considerable improvement has been made since except the vicinity of several popular resorts, such as Lakewood, Toms River, Island Heights, and Forked River. Brave efforts to bring South Lakewood and Barnegat Park into prominence have not succeeded as yet. Along the main highway following the river shore of the bay and along the lines of the Southern Railway of New Jersey, there are some habitations in little clearings near the marl deposits, but these do not represent more than 2 per cent of the territory, most of which is given up to pine barrens, cedar swamps, shallow ponds and here and there a secret oak bottom or a wide expanse of cranberry bog, whether cultivated or allowed to run wild for lack of energy.

Here and there are narrow roads, deep with white sand and barely wide enough for a wheeled vehicle to clear the tree trunks. Some of the roads are merely kept as a tradition; they are relics of a time when the manufacture of iron from bog ore, found in the swamps, was an important industry in this region. They were then important highways though never good roads. Now they scarcely retain a reason for existence except such as thread their way through the pines from one little clearing to another, or lead from a railroad station to some isolated settlement. In driving over these woods roads, one comes occasionally upon an old forge site where iron was made from the soft bog ore with the charcoal furnished by the surrounding pines. Again an abandoned village will be found, relic of an unsuccessful venture in glass manufacture in the heart of the wilderness.

An awesome silence prevails except for the soughing of the winds through the trees or the occasional blast from a distant locomotive whistle. Upon the stranger this silence is likely to have a depressing feeling, but the pines are really jolly in comparison with the cedar swamps, where the closely matted branches shut out the sunlight and give only a few glimpses of the sky, where the ground is ever wet and covered with fallen logs. In the depths of the cedar swamp there is absolute silence as well as gloom, and to get lost in one of these places is likely to turn a timid individual's brain, or at least give him a bad fit of nerves. There is little animal or insect life in the pinelands and far less in the cedar swamps. Here and there, crude corduroy roads have been built by the lumbermen bent on getting out their standing cedar but there is little indication of any effort in Ocean County of getting out the great prehistoric monarchs of the forest, which are buried far down in the mire. In other parts of southern New Jersey there is quite an industry in mining the ancient cedars.

Most of the streams in Ocean County flow through, or have their source, in these cedar swamps. It is regarded as health-giving water, although it neither tastes nice or looks inviting, it having a decided bitter taste and a dark amber hue. The streams in many cases are not confined strictly to their channels but straggle in little rills hither and thither over a broad expanse of swampland made up of porous peat, layer upon layer of fallen trees, the accumulation of perhaps thousands of years of successive growths. Percolating through this mass of wood and decayed vegetation, the water takes on its pungent cedar taste and its brownish color.

Cedar swamps are not the only dense and almost impenetrable places in Ocean, Burlington and Atlantic Counties. There are many swamps growing oaks, beeches, gums, poplars and birches, with underbrush of magnolias, swamp huckleberries and a thousand other growths, amid a tangle of creeping vines and brambles, which *make progress almost impossible for mankind.*

*It must not be supposed that all of the roads through the pinelands are deep in sand. The county roads are all quite good and some really admirable. These roads are made of the clayey yellow gravel much like that with which the paths are dressed in the city parks and are easily kept in repair with light road machines. They do not require much repair because they are so porous that they do not hold water and, as a consequence, are seldom muddy and never up heaved by frost. Most of the roads around Lakewood are of this character, and there is a fairly good and almost straight yellow gravel road from Lakewood to Toms River, and from the latter place the main highway is constructed in the same manner down to and through Barnegat village. From this road several similarly graveled offshoots lead to the railroad stations and to the boat landings at Forked River, Waretown and Barnegat.*

*It is pretty hard in dry weather to get any satisfaction out of farming in Ocean County except in a few favored spots. Favored localities are those where there is some clay and hard pan at a reasonable distance down in the white sand to prevent the rains from sinking down to feed the artesian wells near the Eocene region. Really, there are places in the county where the sand is 125 feet deep before clay is struck. In other places clay is found so near the surface that the seeds of corn and vegetables can reach moisture at all times. Where the sand is deep, there is little satisfaction in trying to raise crops even in wet weather, because the water sinks down far below*

*the roots and carries the fertilizer with it, no matter how liberally it may have been spread upon the surface. Marl answers a double purpose as a fertilizer and to form a cement with sand to enable it to hold a fair percentage of water which falls from the sky but even this will not do much good in certain kinds of sandy soil.*

*In that part of Ocean County where the marl is plentiful and close to the surface, or where there is a bed of hard clay of any kind within a few feet down, good crops of corn are raised and there are a number of productive peach orchards. In favorable seasons potatoes, melons and beets are raised upon the white sand farms, but such places are few and far between and are valuable oases in the pine barrens.*

*Pineland country is undoubtedly healthful. Some years ago a hotelkeeper was taking a guest around the country in a buggy, with the idea of showing him a desirable piece of land to purchase. After looking it over the visitor said that it would make a fine cemetery because it would be easy digging and the water would not give any trouble to the tenants. The hotelkeeper remarked to his guest: "We have no use for any cemeteries down here. Nobody ever dies."*

*Half an hour later, they came across a funeral cortege consisting of a hearse and a string of queer vehicles.*

*"Hullo!" said the visitor. "How is this? It looks very much like a funeral to me."*

*"It is," said the hotel man. "The man in the casket is the local undertaker. He died of starvation."*

again slowed traffic to the shore. Once it was over, seaside resort destinations like Tucker's Island and Horner's on the south end of Long Beach were an easy sailboat ride across Little Egg Harbor bay from Tuckerton. The first known regular stage service across the state was run by Isaac Jenkins, whose ads first appeared in 1816, although he may have been in business earlier than that.

Occasionally, a traveler's account is enhanced with a delightfully clear image of what life was really like long ago. In a letter dated July, 1827, a Philadelphian passing through the swelteringly hot pinelands on his way to the shore notes the extreme coldness, sweetness and darkness of the cedar water at a stream where they stopped to rest and how thoughtful it was for some vacationer, homeward bound, to have left, on the edge of the bank, "a dozen sun bleached clam shells as big as dinner plates that a hot and thirsty traveler might use to dip into the current to splash himself or take a drink."

The Pine Barrens, comprising nearly one third of the whole state, fully deserve the name. The earliest settlements in New Jersey were along the banks of the Delaware River where the soil was productive. As the colonists pushed eastward into the pitch pine woods, they found the soil to be virtually useless for crops and dubbed the whole vast territory "the barrens." Few would ever settle there. A thinness of soil made for a thinness of population, but an incredible number of things other than food crops grow there. It is not by any means a desert.

One part of the Pine Barrens is an eerie stretch of dwarf trees covering many square miles in Burlington and Ocean counties along another major east-west road, Route 72, a branch off Route 70. Here the stunted pine and oak grow not much more than two to five feet high, although normal pine forests border them.

Old records tell that, early in the 19th century, in the

fall of the year farmers from West Jersey and people from Philadelphia used to drive down to the plains and load their farm wagons with heath hens that populated "the Plains" in such numbers no one hunting them even bothered to shoot them. Their flight was so slow and labored they could be killed with sticks and clubs. Related to the western prairie chicken, these birds, extremely noisy in their mating season, were ground nesters. Farmers, who slaughtered them by the thousands, took wagon load after wagon load back to the markets on the Delaware until, by 1830, the entire population had been eliminated in New Jersey. A hundred years later, in 1932, the very last one died at a controlled nesting site on Martha's Vineyard. The heath hen, like the Carolina parakeet and the passenger pigeon, is now extinct.

Route 72, which now runs right through the "Plains" into Manahawkin, was, until 1950, known as Route S40, an extension of Route 40. It was not paved for automobile use until 1935. By 1950, a new highway (Route 72), wider and considerably more level, was built alongside it. The old, undulating roadbed of S40 is still there, a few feet to the south of 72, and is used today as a dirt bike trail. Long before these routes were automobile roads, they were busy wagon trails across the state from Manahawkin and Barnegat to the river ports on the Delaware. For most of the 19th century, it was not at all unusual for farmers, headed eastward with their wagons, to encounter (mostly in the winter months) one or two men in nautical garb on foot, headed westward to Burlington and Camden where they could sign up for work. They were sailors who had survived any of the great number of shipwrecks along the barrier beaches in those years. If they couldn't be hired, or find ready passage to New York aboard a vessel sailing out of one of the little villages on the creeks of the mainland, they chose to hike sixty miles to the other side of the state.

# Shipwrecks & the U.S. Lifesaving Service

When the U.S. Lifesaving Service was inaugurated in November of 1871, shipwrecks were commonplace, and New Jersey was by far the most dangerous stretch of coastline in the United States. Along its desolate barrier beaches from Sandy Hook to Cape May, forty-one fully manned units were placed approximately every three miles. These new station houses were of uniform design, 18 by 40 feet, and windowless on three sides. They were painted reddish brown and devoid of any ornamentation save a cupola, lightning rod and large white numerals on their seaward walls. They resembled big barns or garages in the dunes. Locally they were called "red houses."

Each station was to be manned by six men and a keeper who would live in the stations from September through April, when there was the most danger from storms. Each man was paid $40 a month, and the keeper got $60, which was a good wage then for baymen with seasonal income. These men had fished, clammed and gunned in local waters all their lives, and they knew how to operate boats in the surf. Besides their obvious skills, they were chosen for their resourcefulness, courage and integrity. It was a proud service.

When the Lifesaving Service was active, from 1871 until 1915, there were six units on Long Beach Island. They were at Barnegat Inlet, Loveladies, Harvey Cedars, Ship Bottom, Beach Haven Terrace and Bond's, at what is

now Holgate, on the south end of the Island. Beach Haven was skipped as a location because the community did not exist in 1871. Three miles south of Bond's there was a seventh unit officially known as the Little Egg Harbor Station, on Tucker's Island. Of the stations from that era only three still stand today in their original locations — Loveladies, Harvey Cedars and the Long Beach Station at Maryland Avenue in Beach Haven Terrace. The

# Ocean County's Lifesaving Stations, 1892

From the *New York Mirror,* October 1892

"The stranger, who for the first time visits our coast, will notice nestling among the hills and dunes of shifting sands, quite near the ocean's shore, little red, barn-like structures at intervals of four miles. Or perhaps, at some gay summer resort, he will see a more pretentious building, surmounted with a cupola and a flagstaff, with a wide door at the sea front as though it were the engine house of some fire company. A closer scrutiny will show him that all these units are strung together like beads upon a string, by a telephone line, erected upon iron poles along the beaches and buried beneath the sand and mud where it crosses the water at the inlets.

"If his visit is made during the stormy months, between the first days of September and late April, he will see patrolmen start from their stations, at regular hours, each wearing a blue jersey, with the blood red legend "U.S. Lifesaving Service" on his bosom and likewise a similar device in gold on his cap. Should curiosity lead him to enter one of the buildings, he will find, to the landsmen's eye, a curious medley of mysterious implements — prominent among which will be the life boat and a villainous looking brass mortar, or short Parrott gun, but inquiry will soon set at rest any misgivings and the stranger will learn that he is at one of the Lifesaving Stations, which originated on the Jersey shore, but now, strewn all along the Atlantic, Pacific, Gulf and Lake coasts of the United States, have developed the best and surest protection against loss of life and property by shipwreck to be found anywhere in the world."

Following is a list of the stations and their crews in southern Ocean County in the year 1892, beginning at Forked River, and then crossing Barnegat Inlet onto Long Beach and running south to Tucker's Island and Little Beach.

## FORKED RIVER

D. L. Yarnell, keeper, Oscar Brinley, Martin McCarthy, Reuben Tilton, Charles P. Cambren, Samuel B. Predmore, Jesse S. Penn.

## BARNEGAT (Barnegat City)

Joel H. Ridgway, keeper, C. D. Thompson, A. S. Chandler, T. B. Predmore, G.H. Birdsall, B. S. Ridgway, A. F. Falkinburg

## LOVELADIES

C. J. Grimm, keeper, J. T. Mills, G.W. Peterson, Alfred Fox, S. Ridgway, E. A. Falkinburg, J. R. Cox.

## HARVEY CEDARS

Hudson Gaskill, keeper, B. Martin, S. B. Elberson, G. E, Bennett, H. L. Hazleton, J. H. Throckmorton, S. J. Johnson.

## SHIP BOTTOM

J. W. Truex, keeper, I. W. Truex, B. P. Pharo, G. P. Inman, S. D. Crane, W. H. Stevens, W. Pharo.

## LONG BEACH (Beach Haven Terrace)

James Sprague, keeper, C. E. Seaman, J. A. Spragg, Thomas Shinn, H. S. Jones, Charles W. Rutter, F. M. Sprague.

## BOND'S (Holgate)

John Marshall, keeper, H. Ireland, Joel H. Sprague, James A. Morris, Otho Brown, Samuel A. Jones, Eber Rider Jr.

## LITTLE EGG (Tucker's Island)

Jarvis B. Rider, keeper, J. H. Riley, C. E. Jones, James Marshall, Samuel Andrews, James A. Cranmer, Lewis J. Cranmer.

## LITTLE BEACH

James Ridel, keeper, George W. Horner, Alex C. Falkinburg, Samuel H. Jones, Lambert H. Parker, Clayton Berry

stations at Barnegat Inlet and at Holgate (Bond's) were moved in the 1920s. The Ship Bottom station was torn down in the 1960s and the Tucker's Island Station (Little Egg Harbor) washed into the sea in 1931.

For most of the men in the Lifesaving Service on Long Beach Island in the 1870s and 1880s, it was a lonely existence and often a very dangerous one. There was monotony, but the men were seldom idle. They had their watches at night to perform. Every four hours two men left the station house at once. One would walk north on the beach and the other south to meet the patrols from the adjoining station houses, exchange a brass token and return. Then there were routine drills, the maintenance of buildings and equipment, and of course waiting and watching for shipwrecks — their purpose was to save lives.

In foul weather it was impossible to see the entire beach from the tower, and patrols sometimes had to be run throughout the day as well as the night. The meeting and exchange of tokens was required only on contiguous beaches. In a snowstorm, all that could be seen to guide the patrol might be the blurry edge of gray water, or white, churning surf, or the hard sand at low tide. Many an obstacle — a ship's mast, lumber, an old wreck, or even a huge dead fish — might cause the patrolman to stumble in the dark.

In the early years of the service, the men traditionally wore civilian clothing, dressing much like the fishermen and baymen that they were. In 1899, right after the Spanish American War, the service decided to adopt a naval uniform largely as a consequence of the recent role they had played in coastal defense, as sentinels looking for the Spanish fleet. It was not that the enemy fleet was ever much of a threat, but the public perceived it as such.

Reading down a list of the names of the men in the service at the six stations on Long Beach Island in the 1890s, one finds that almost all are from the oldest families in the region: Perrine, Soper, Ridgway, Inman, Truex, Cranmer, Sprague, Rider, Rogers, Birdsall, Gaskill, Shinn, Parker, Hazleton, Crane, Falkinberg, Pharo and Rutter. This was to be true for several generations.

By the middle of the 1880s, the railroad had come to the Island, bringing with it ease of transport and supply, and, of course, more people. Within the next decade the stations, formerly hidden in the dunes, were all redesigned and enlarged. The sturdy, old-time "red houses" suddenly became little more than storage sheds beside the new, greatly enlarged modern stations, all decked out in handsome white clapboard with big lookout towers and halyards strung with colorful flags.

All of this was happening just as the need for the lifesaving service was declining. Steam power and better aids to navigation had greatly reduced the number of ship strandings. By 1915, the U.S. Lifesaving Service merged with the Revenue Cutter Service and became the U.S. Coast Guard. The advent of Prohibition in the 1920s kept all the stations on the Island busy chasing rumrunners, but that exciting episode was all over within thirteen years. By 1935, most units were decommissioned until the advent of World War II, when they were all reopened and overflowing with new recruits. At war's end they all went inactive but for two. Bond's was moved to Beach Haven and shut down a few years ago. Today the only station left on the Island is at Barnegat Light, the last one in a distinguished history of 130 years, a history filled with stories of danger and heroism.

## Architecture

In a forty-year period, from 1880 until about 1920, the U.S. Lifesaving Service and its successor, the U.S. Coast Guard, commissioned the design and building of some of the nation's most architecturally tasteful structures ever paid for with government money. They were the more than 200 lifesaving stations set every three or four miles, mostly on our eastern seaboard and on the Great Lakes. Nearly all of them have been in private hands for decades; because they are so unique and generally well cared for, they are as eagerly sought after as lighthouses when they appear on the market. Many have been made into attractive restaurants or gift shops, but most are dwellings.

The Lifesaving Service was formed in 1871 and, while the first manned station houses were outwardly not that impressive, their replacements in the 1880s and '90s were true works of art — each in perfect harmony with sea and sky. Lonely outposts in the dunes, usually red roofed, with gleaming white sides, these two and one-half story structures came in several designs, but all had, jutting out of the roof, the characteristic sash-windowed watch tower, so often imitated in seashore cottages built in the 1890s. At least a dozen Queen Anne cottages in Beach Haven once had such towers, where one could open a door in the attic and climb to a fourth story to view, in solitude and comfort, an endless parade of sails on the horizon.

Of the six classic, wood-framed lifesaving stations on Long Beach Island, all were decommissioned after World War II except for the one in Barnegat Light. This was replaced by a new, larger unit in the 1960s, as was Bond's Station on the south end of the Island. In 1964, all Bond's personnel were moved to a new station at Pelham and West avenues in Beach Haven. That, too, has recently been decommissioned and now Barnegat Light has the only Coast Guard station on the Island.

Of the original six buildings, five still remain. The Ship Bottom station on Twenty-sixth Street was, despite neighborhood protests, demolished in 1950. It could have been bought for $30,000, but it badly needed a new roof. Architecturally, with its octagonal tower, it was one of eleven such stations built in the "Jersey" pattern at the turn of the century. The style was duplicated at Mantoloking, Toms River, Tucker's Island, Brigantine and other coastal resorts in New Jersey.

The Loveladies station, in seashore-Queen Anne style, is a duplicate of the Bond's station at Holgate on the south end of the Island. Rebuilt in 1887, it was closed, for lack of funding, in 1917 and reopened in 1924. Then the Coast Guard needed every available unit on the coast of New Jersey to hunt down the rumrunners who were boldly landing whiskey on the beaches at night. When Prohibition was over, it shut down in 1935, only to be revived for the duration of World War II.

Bond's, like Loveladies, was rebuilt in 1887, but in those days Bond's was at least a half-mile east of its present location, out on the beach at Inlet Road. An earlier 1871 structure had been even farther east. Bond's was moved southwesterly to the bayside location on Janet Avenue in 1924 to be nearer to its power boats. In the Prohibition years, much contraband whiskey came through the new Beach Haven Inlet, then no more than six or seven blocks south of the station. Bond's, from its inception in 1871, was never closed until 1964, and then only because the entire unit moved into new, larger quarters in Beach Haven. The old Bond's station on Janet became a private dwelling.

There is another set of twin buildings on Long Beach Island. They are the Harvey Cedars station, which became a fishing club, and the Long Beach station at Beach Haven Terrace, in private hands. Both were decommissioned in 1946, and both owe their style to a station first built in far-away Minnesota in 1894. Harvey Cedars, rebuilt in 1901, and Long Beach, rebuilt in 1904, are both known as "Duluth-type" lifesaving stations. Twenty-eight of them were built, all on the Great Lakes and the East Coast. There are other Duluth-style stations at Forked River and Absecon.

Twenty-eight Duluth models were built around the nation between 1890 and 1908. Impressively large, all have very tall, rectangular lookout towers. Twelve were built in New Jersey, two on Long Beach Island.

## Rescue of the Abiel Abbott

From the 1890s into the early 20th century, despite all the advances in marine engines and better aids to navigation, there were still enough shipwrecks to warrant the rebuilding and modernization of nearly all our nation's lifesaving stations. All of the units on Long Beach Island and nearby Tucker's Island and Little Beach were brought up to date with brand new structures, a vast improvement over the primitive "red houses" of the 1870s and 1880s. The men did not change. They were still held to the same high standards as before, and the U.S. Treasury Department continued to reward heroism and self-sacrifice with the presentation of gold medals for valor.

Each of these heavy, coin-like decorations was worth about $100. Rarely, however, were they kept as a memento to pass on to descendants. After posing for a photo-

graph, the wearer of the medal usually turned it in for its cash value to buy necessities for his family. It would be worth around $1,600 in purchasing power today. The surf man made $40 a month or, taking inflation into account, about $600 in today's dollars. In the summer months, these men lived off the land and water just as their ancestors had.

On June 4, 1904, the U.S. Treasury Department addressed the following letter to Surfman J. Horace Cranmer of the Ship Bottom Lifesaving Station. As it was summer and the station would not have been open, it was sent to his home address in Manahawkin. The keepers and each of the surfmen of both the Ship Bottom and Long Beach stations who participated in the rescue of the remaining crew of the *Abiel Abbott* got gold medals and letters identical to the one that follows:

"Sir:

"Transmitted herein is a gold life-saving medal of honor awarded you under the provisions of Acts of Congress approved June 20, 1874, and May 4, 1882, in recognition of your heroic conduct on the occasion of the rescue by you and your comrades of five men from the wreck of the barkentine *Abiel Abbott,* under the following circumstances, as shown by the testimony of eye witnesses.

"On the 20th of January, 1903, the *Abbott,* while on her way from Turks Island, West Indies to New York City, heavily laden and drawing 17 feet of water, went aground on the outer edge of the Ship Bottom bar, coast of New Jersey, at about 8:15 o'clock in the evening. As soon as she stranded she showed a signal of distress which was answered by Patrolman B.P. Pharo of your station, who burned his Coston signal in promise of assistance if possible. Pharo then made his way as fast as he could to the station where he arrived at about 9 o'clock, the weather having constantly increased in severity. The night was intensely dark, the wind and sea were very high, and a heavy rain storm had set in.

"Immediately upon receiving from Pharo information of the disaster Keeper Truex telephoned to Keeper Falkinburg of the Harvey Cedars Station on the north, and to Keeper Mathis of the Long Beach Station on the south, requesting their aid, and then with his crew hastened to the scene. As soon as he arrived the Lyle gun was placed in action, but the first projectile did not quite reach the wreck, as stated by those on board who heard the shot fall a little short in the water. A second projectile, however, landed on board, but nevertheless they could not avail themselves of it because it fell about amidships, while the sea was so rough as to confine all hands to the extreme aft part of the vessel. The whole hull save the quarter deck was submerged and the waves were rolling deeply over it. Two more shots were fired, but the wreck could be located only by the faint glimmer of light in the rigging, which was scarcely perceptible, and whether the projectiles landed on board or not, the

shipwrecked men were unable to leave the little area of comparative safety which still remained to them.

"The night was now so dark that only the break of the waves close on the shore could be seen, and all the conditions were so adverse that no sane man would have attempted to launch a boat before daylight. So, the survivors testify was their own opinion, although they fervently prayed for assistance. Under these circumstances you and your comrades of the three crews now assembled were obliged to wait and fret inactive on the beach until there should be sufficient light to justify an attempt to push out into the heavy breakers among the dangerous masses of wreckage which already encumbered the water. Between 3:00 and 4:00 in the morning the mainmast fell, but hung alongside for an hour or more when the fore and mizzenmasts also gave way.

"With the fall of the mainmast one of the sailors madly jumped into the water and was never seen again. When the other masts went, the remaining eight men were dragged overboard but by means of the tangled spars and rigging still attached to the wreck five of them managed to struggle back to the top of the cabin. Three had perished.

"At the first sign of dawn, while you and your watchful comrades were straining your eyes seaward, trying to pierce the fog, a faint outcry from the wreck was detected, and instantly all hands, as one man, jumped for the boat. Five of your own crew and one man from the Long Beach Station grasped the pulling oars, while Keepers Truex and Mathis took places in the stern to handle the steering oar and direct the movement. Surfmen stood in the water on each side of the boat to keep the wreck stuff clear, and an opportune moment succeeded in shoving her out without damage from the planks, timbers and general debris, which were thrust about by

the waves with deadly force. Mr. Jones, a wreckmaster who was present, says that, when the launch was made, he thought the chances were ninety-nine in a hundred that the boat would be smashed. Nothing daunted, however, by dint of powerful work and skillful handling she reached the bar sufficiently near the wreck to make out the five men still on board, but although every effort was exhausted by the sturdy oarsmen she could make no further headway, and battered and scarred, but fortunately still seaworthy, was obliged to return. The Captain of the *Abbott* states in his testimony that he was sure you could not reach the wreck.

"The gun was again resorted to, but just as the second shot was being fired the cabin top, to which the men were clinging, broke adrift and became involved in the great flood of wreckage from the *Abbott,* which was now swiftly going to pieces. Again, you and your comrades leaped to the boat and shoved her off.

"Every man present was eager to have a part in the rescue, and in the rush two from the Long Beach Station found places at the oars, while Keepers Truex and Mathis again stood in the stern at the steering oar. With consummate skill and faultless courage the boat was driven forward, happily without serious injury, until it reached the five almost exhausted sailors and took them in. A landing was soon safely effected, but not long after Frank Laven, one of the rescued men, expired from an ugly wound to the temple.

"The launching of the surfboat,' says the investigating officer, Lieutenant Bertholf, R.C.S., 'twice that morning through the heavy surf, filled with timbers and all sorts of wreckage, bristling with nails and spikes and bolts, was a feat that the Ship Bottom crew and the Lifesaving Service have reason to be proud of.' Captain Hawkins of the *Abbott* crew says, 'I did not think it possible for them to get to us, but somehow they did, and got us ashore, and I think it is a miracle that I am alive to tell the tale. No man could have done more than the Lifesavers did.' That every man who went in the boat on either occasion freely imperiled his life is apparent beyond question.

"It affords me great pleasure to act as the medium for the award of the accompanying medal in testimony of so heroic an achievement vouched for by experienced Surfmen amply capable of estimating its merits."

## The Wreck of
## The Kraljevica

The surfman walking the beach on the midnight watch was the only one to see the brilliant flash out over the ocean. In the heavy cloud cover it looked like lightning, which is not that rare in winter storms. He stopped and, holding a gloved hand to his face against the sleet and wind-driven spray, he began to count. The light faded in forty seconds; there was no thunder, and it was not repeated. It was a distress rocket from a ship grounded on the shoals.

As he hurried back to U.S. Lifesaving Station No. 17 at Barnegat Light, his quickened pace would be the first in a series of steps leading to what would forever be known as the *Kraljevica* tragedy, after the Austrian bark whose rocket he'd just spotted in the darkness at 1:30 AM. Before mid-morning of that day, February 10, 1886, three brave men would drown in a futile attempt to reach the ship stranded on the Barnegat shoals, and — unbeknownst to them — already abandoned by her captain and crew just after the firing of the rocket.

The sighting was reported to station Keeper Joel Ridgway, who at once went out onto the beach with John I. Soper, but they could see nothing until the first light of dawn. Then there it was: a three-masted bark on the shoals a half mile to the southeast of them, too far to shoot a lifeline from the station's cannon. Ridgway sounded the alarm and ordered the surfboat rolled out of the boat room and down to the water's edge. Then he made a telephone call to Keeper Grimm of the Loveladies station to advise him and his crew to stand by on the beach while he and his men took the boat out.

Keepers Grimm and Ridgway were both from the mainland village of Barnegat, where they were neighbors and lifelong friends. In fact, nearly all of the men at both stations hailed from Barnegat. Ridgway had no hesitation whatsoever in heading out into the stormy surf. His boat crew was considered the best on the coast and they had nothing to fear. This sea, however, was far worse than any they'd ever seen. Here are Captain Ridgway's own words in the Keeper's Log:

" … several times the boat would stand almost on end and it seemed as though she would go end over leeward. Twice we were thrown about with so much force that if I had not been under my steering oar nothing would have prevented me being hurled yards from the boat. We avoided several seas going out, either one of which would have swamped us completely. It was all we could do to make any headway against these seas. If any man were to ease his pull on the oar just the slightest the boat would stand still or go astern. When at last we succeeded in getting through the break on the bar we found the current had taken us 400 yards south, or to leeward of the wreck. The sea was increasing rapidly as it was driven before a rising wind."

Ridgway and his men had expected to find the water smoother beyond the bar but it was not, and the struggle to get closer to the wreck brought his men to the breaking point. It was only then that they discovered that the vessel had been abandoned. In violation of one of the laws of the sea, her distress flags were still flying. Ridgway nonetheless urged his men to pull harder. If they could get to the ship they could tie up and rest for a while. It was to no avail; the wind and the current were too much for them. Ridgway now had no choice but to return, despite the condition of his men, and, after first valiantly trying to back the skiff in so the waves would lose their power against the pointed bow, they decided to turn and run with the seas, hoping for the best. At about 400 yards off the beach, one great, towering wave, so hollow they could not rise to it, crashed down atop them with tons of icy water. The boat, swirling like a chip, tossed the men in all directions and turned completely over. The Loveladies and Harvey Cedars crews were standing helplessly by on the beach. The storm was far worse than it had been early that morning.

Of the six oarsmen, two of them, Solomon Soper and his nephew John Soper, were seen to slowly cease swimming as the men on the shore watched and shouted but were unable to get to them. They were drifting outward in their cork life jackets and may have succumbed to the cold water. Perrine, the third man, had, it was later discovered, been struck in the face by the boat or an oar, and probably could not have saved himself anyway. All three bodies were found far down the beach late in the afternoon. Captain Ridgway and three others made it to shore and were pulled out of the surf by the men of the Loveladies Island Station. William Inman required two and a half hours of intensive work at the station to bring him around. Cornelius Thompson, also unconscious, was restored right on the beach. Henry Reeves and Ridgway were the only ones able, with a little help, to stand.

The fourteen-man crew of the *Kraljevica* lost nine

The following piece appeared in the *New York World* in the spring of 1894.

# Jack Tar's Terror

## Long Beach's Death Roll; Terrible Record of Wrecks On the Storm-beaten Shore About Barnegat Light

### Upward of 500 Lives Lost on the Beach Where Pleasure Reigns in Summer

Long Beach — there is nothing of the tragic in the name, but the narrow strip of storm-beaten land that bears it, bears also the terrible reputation of being the scene of more wrecks and loss of life than any other similar piece of sea coast on the merciless Atlantic shore — Sable Island alone excepted — from Labrador to Key West. To the summer visitor it looks safe and harmless enough as he treads its beach — smooth and glistening — or as he bathes in its gently swelling surf. But speak the words to the old seaman, whether coaster or long distance voyager, and it conjures up before his mind visions of the dread Barnegat Shoals where the winter winds blow fiercer even than at Hatteras, colder than at Cape Cod, and where the soft and yielding sands are more cruel to poor Jack's craft than even the rocky islets of Maine.

Long Beach is a narrow island, twenty-two miles long and almost two miles wide at some points. At others, so narrow that the stormy Atlantic's mighty breakers rush in roaring torrents between its sand hills and lose themselves in the scarce quieter waters of Barnegat Bay. At the north end, Barnegat Light rears its high tower, warning the incoming mariner that land is ahead and that he must shift his course while at the southern extremity, Little Egg Harbor Light tells him of the shoals that are almost as much feared as those at Barnegat.

On the ocean shore the Island shows a firm hard beach, where in ordinary weather the gentle surf breaks. Then come the ever shifting dunes of sand covered with coarse grass in summer, fragrant wild roses, bayberry bushes or tangled thickets of cat briars which hang out their grape-like clusters of blue berries in the fall, with here and there a clump of stunted red cedars, gnarled, old and storm beaten, the branches invariably twisted to the south by the fierce north winds of many winters. On the bay front are many islets whose lush growth of salt grasses, higher than a man's head, are used by the eager sportsmen to build the blinds from which a perpetual fusillade of shot is kept up as long as ducks and geese remain on the bay.

Nesting among the sand hills are seven government lifesaving stations manned by worthy descendants of the brave and hardy fishermen of a century ago and a half ago, whose daring work as wreckers — wresting from the very teeth of the relentless sea its half swallowed prey — rather than any act of blood or violence, won them the name of the "Barnegat Pirates." Strange to say, these Life Savers went off duty on May 1 this year of 1894 without once being called to face the dangers of a wreck — the first winter in many years.

Prior to the last twenty years — in a period for which there are no authentic records — more than five hundred lives have been lost on this beach. Since the building of lighthouses and the later development of the Lifesaving Service, there have been many wrecks in which all hands were saved. Up until recent years the beach has been practically deserted, and it mattered little whether the shipwrecked tar perished in the sea or was dashed ashore to die from hunger, cold or exhaustion in his vain efforts to reach food and shelter on the mainland, several miles distant. But now, flourishing little summer villages, with large modern hotels and cottages of the inevitable Queen Anne architecture of the city man's country home, break the long stretches of its wilderness at Barnegat City, Harvey Cedars, Long Beach City and Beach Haven.

The first wreck on the beach for which a record is now extant, was that of a British transport, bound from Halifax for New York with troops for the garrison there. She came ashore near the south end of the Island on January 23, 1779. How many lives were lost will never be known but thirty dead bodies were picked up on the beach, many of them being British officers belonging to Lord Howe's regiments in New York. The natives gallantly rescued all they could — and sent them as prisoners of war to General Washington at Morristown, to be exchanged for the husbands, fathers, sons and brothers who were languishing and dying in the prison hulks of New York Harbor.

Another armed vessel, the British privateer schooner, Cock, went ashore trying to make Little Egg Harbor in a storm. She had been captured, and of her prize crew of thirty Yankee sailors, twenty were lost; the other ten swam ashore. That was Feb. 23rd, 1781. The Spanish brig La Tigre, taken as a prize by the Buenos Aires schooner Constitution, met with the same fate on the night of January 11, 1820 on Barnegat shoals. Her crew of eight men was drowned. In the interim between these two dates — 1781 and 1820 — fifty vessels, large and small, were wrecked on this beach.

In the next score of years seven men were lost from the wrecked schooners Emmeline, Betsy and Caroline and the brig Samson. The Powhattan struck on the shoals, was sighted and the wrecking crew was on the way to her assistance, when, while Captain Myers was shouting to the wrecking master on the shore, a huge wave swept over her and not a life was saved, so suddenly did she break up. The same day, Captain H. S. Fields and four of the crew of the schooner Manhattan, which had struck on the beach, decided to stick to the schooner but she broke up and only one man made it to shore alive.

Two years later on January 5, 1856, when the schooner Pacific and the bark Duke de Braganza both came ashore in the same storm, twenty-five more were added to the list of Long Beach victims. The next December, four of the brig Tasso perished, and with them John F. Jones and John Parker, two gallant wreckers, who lost their lives in trying to save the shipwrecked mariners. Since then, in the last thirty-seven years, seventy-six seamen have been lost.

Is it any wonder, with this known roll of over five hundred victims that the bluff captain of a coaster turns a "little pale about the gills" when, with his schooner scudding before a nor'easter, with no canvas but a storm jib, he sees through the mist and rain the flashing light of Barnegat looming up on the lee bow, and in the lulls of the shrieking gales he hears the thunder of the breakers on the shores of Long Beach? Or is poor Jack to be blamed if, when homeward bound from around the Horn, or mayhap from the East Indies or from the Baltic, after a week of dead reckoning, he sights this same revolving light rising out of a bank of fog dead ahead — is poor Jack to be blamed if under such circumstances he says his prayers with greater alacrity than is his wont? Nor would you think so were you to visit the churchyard of any one of the hamlets that fringe the "main" shore back of Long Beach and see the many nameless graves and hear the explanation given in response to your question.

of their number. They had been bound for New York from Marseilles with a cargo of salt when they struck the shoals. They had departed in the night in the ship's longboat. By the time the storm had carried them as far south as Brant Beach, their boat capsized in the surf and only four men and the captain made it ashore alive. By a stroke of luck they had found a gunner's hut behind the dunes, well stocked with food and fuel, where they fell into an exhausted sleep and were not discovered by the Ship Bottom patrol until they wandered out when the storm was over two days later.

The bay was full of ice, so the bodies of the drowned surfmen were taken across the inlet in boats and carried by horse cart up the beach to Seaside Park, where they were put on a handcar, taken to Toms River and then sent home by train, reaching the village of Barnegat at 8:30 PM. The people of Barnegat, alerted earlier in the day by telegraph, turned out to honor the dead heroes. The following Sunday, funeral services were held at the M.E. Church and the three were buried in the Masonic Cemetery, where afterward the U.S. government, by special act of Congress, erected to each a tall marble shaft telling of the circumstances of their deaths. Solomon Soper, age 62, left a widow and two grown daughters. John L. Soper, age 47, a nephew of Solomon, left a widow and two young children. S. Firman Perrine left only a widow.

The Austrian government took note of the affair and a year later, through the Austro-Hungarian Ministry in Washington, sent a fund of $460 to be divided among the families of the dead surfmen.

Of the four survivors, Inman never recovered from the exposure. He was made postmaster of Barnegat, but he soon went blind from the effects of hypothermia and died within a few years of either consumption or a lung ailment aggravated by that experience. Reeves and

## Ship Bottom Wrecks

An incident in 1817 gave Ship Bottom its unusual name. It happened so long ago that lack of any official report, or even name for the ship involved, almost relegates it to the realm of legend. The elements of the story remain consistent, however. A young woman was rescued from the hull of an overturned ship that had become stranded, possibly in fog, on the outer bar. When she was brought ashore, she knelt and made the sign of the cross in the sand. She spoke no English. Her language, said her rescuers — all men from Tuckerton — was either Spanish or Portuguese.

That cross in the sand marked the spot that forever after would be known as Ship Bottom. "Ship's Bottom" was a form dropped from accepted newspaper usage around 1912, but some old-timers were still saying it in the 1940s. The name Ship Bottom had become permanently inscribed on maps and charts in 1871, when the location was chosen as the site for one of the U.S. Lifesaving stations on Long Beach Island.

We don't know the name of the woman involved in this miraculous rescue, but we do know the name of the leader of the rescue party. He was Captain Thomas Willet of Tuckerton, who, sailing south along the coast in heavy fog, was looking for the inlet just below Long Beach. Some twelve miles north of that inlet, he is said, in some accounts, to have heard cries for help from a shoreward direction. He anchored and, taking a small boat closer to the beach to investigate the source of these shouts, found nothing but an overturned hull in the surf. Upon climbing aboard to investigate the wreck, he and his men heard a frantic thumping coming from inside. They fetched axes to chop a hole in the planking and soon found a lone survivor — a woman, cold and wet, but

Thompson were still hale and hearty twenty years later, as was Captain Ridgway who remained in command of the station until a few years before his death in March of 1908.

In the history of the lifesaving service, the *Kraljevica* tragedy became one of the rarest of instances: a surfboat with an experienced crew, unencumbered by panicked passengers, was overwhelmed by the sea and lives were lost. It was one of those things that just did not happen. Clearly the extreme fatigue of the men, coupled with the rising intensity of one of the 19th century's most powerful storms, had much to do with it. There are other factors to consider. If the captain and crew of the *Kraljevika* had lowered the distress flags when they abandoned her, Captain Ridgway might not have struggled that extra

hour to get closer to a ship that was clearly breaking up, and his men might have had the reserve strength to return and make the kind of landing they were trained to do in the roughest of seas.

And then, if the captain of the doomed *Kraljevika* and his four men who made it to shore with him had not had the good luck to take shelter in a fully provisioned gunner's shack immediately upon landing, they would have been found within a half hour by the Ship Bottom patrol. This patrol would have telephoned all the northern stations on the Island in the middle of the night to alert them that survivors of a wreck were on the beach and that no one was aboard their stranded ship. This call would have stopped Captain Ridgway from launching his surfboat at dawn.

otherwise unharmed. The source of the voices in the fog was never discovered.

Imagine the plight of this woman, who, until that moment, was crawling around over loose cargo in the pitch-black hold of a ship that was slowly filling with water. The hatches beneath her were either closed or buried in sand, and the only pockets of foul air were now in what had been the very bottom of the ship, near the keel. It was about to be her tomb, for on that wintry coast there was not a soul for miles. The crew and fellow passengers, if any, had been washed overboard and had already perished in the icy water. How long she was in there is not known, but when she heard Willet's men clambering onto the barnacled hull over her head, she began tapping and thumping with whatever was at hand.

She was carried at once to the beach, where the men built a fire and she was given warm clothing. After her rescue, this unknown Spanish woman, who marked a place called Ship Bottom with the sign of the cross in the sand, disappears into history. Where she went, no one knows; she may simply have boarded another of the numerous craft plying the coast in those days and left the region. Some say she married one of her rescuers and lived out her life in Tuckerton, but had she done so, we would have a more complete rendering of the story and would surely know her name.

This speculation that she went to the mainland to live has gotten mixed up with another remarkably similar incident that took place on the Barnegat shoals, near the lighthouse, some thirty years later. On September 10, 1846, the sloop *Adelaide* or *Mary Adelaide*, out of Manahawkin, encountered a severe gale, struck the bar and capsized. Captain James Lamson and his crew perished almost instantly. The vessel, still bottom up, drifted toward the beach, where it was spotted by Barnegat Lighthouse Keeper John Allen, former Keeper Garret H. Herring, and Charles Collins.

Around dusk, just before the tide would turn, two of the men determined to inspect the *Adelaide*, which they knew belonged to natives of Barnegat. They wanted to see what could be salvaged. At almost dead low water, they climbed aboard the slippery hull. She was rocking and scraping in the sand as the surf rolled in and out. Treading carefully along her keel, they heard a knocking noise. They stomped with their heels and it got louder and more insistent. Someone was alive inside and answering back.

Herring and Collins jumped off and ran back to the lighthouse. It was getting dark and Allen was already in the tower, tending the light. They got axes and a lantern, and returned to the wreck. It had taken twenty minutes, and by now, spray was dashing over the hull with the incoming tide. As they chopped into the location of the knocking, the *Adelaide* began to roll under them, but they soon had an opening large enough to look inside. In the light of their lantern, they saw a young girl, in her teens, almost frightened out of her wits. It was Captain Lamson's daughter. She very nearly drowned as the water began pouring in, but they pulled her to safety.

Miss Lamson, greatly grieved by her father's death, went back to the mainland, where she soon recovered and, some time later, married a family friend, a fisherman named Worden from Forked River. They had a daughter named Katherine, who lived until 1925 and often told the story of her mother's miraculous rescue from the hull of an overturned ship.

This exciting story of the *Adelaide* incident in 1846 is fully told in Edgar Rowe Snow's *Famous Lighthouses of America*, published in 1955 by Dodd Mead. It is a strange parallel to the Ship Bottom story, but it differs in that the names of every person involved, including the name of the girl from Barnegat trapped inside the hull of the ship, are known. It may explain the notion, held by some, that the unknown Spanish woman, found at the place named Ship Bottom in 1817, wound up living on the mainland.

In the long history of the age of sail, women passengers were often sent below in stormy seas for their own protection. The hatches would be secured to keep the water out. If the ship capsized with all hands lost one can only shudder at the fate of the poor soul trapped inside such a derelict until it finally sank. It is only the rescues that are unusual.

In January 1910, the Italian bark *Fortuna* ran aground in a fog, ten blocks north of the Ship Bottom Lifesaving Station. There was no loss of life, but the ship, which could not be pulled off, soon capsized and became a subject for postcards, doing much to reinforce the name Ship Bottom. Since no picture of the 1817 namesake-wreck existed, the 1910 photograph became the borough symbol.

Margaret James Jennings was born July 3, 1844 in Manahawkin when it was still a part of Monmouth County. Her family moved to Barnegat and she entered school just before the formation of Ocean County in 1850. Her father was James James, who was born in 1813 in Dover, Pa., and died in West Virginia in 1871. Her mother was Martha King, born February 7, 1811 in Manahawkin. What follows is an account of her early life, drawn from twenty-five pages of an unedited, typewritten manuscript that she wrote in 1936 when she was 92 and living in Port Townsend, Washington. "Journal 1" describes her life in the village of Barnegat. "Journals 2 and 3" describe her life at her father's hotel on Long Beach Island, several miles across the bay from Barnegat at what is now Loveladies. The hotel, popularly known in those years as "Double Jimmie's," for her father, James James, was across the Boulevard and about a hundred yards to the north of the present-day Long Beach Island Foundation of the Arts and Sciences. Another journal tells the story of her trip westward on the new transcontinental railroad to San Francisco and her passage by lumber schooner up the Pacific coast to Port Townsend, Washington. The Jennings family were among the first homesteaders on Whidbey Island in Puget Sound.

## My Recitation:

# Glimpses of Ninety Years

by Margaret James Jennings

## Journal 1

I was born in Manahawkin, Monmouth County, New Jersey in the year 1844 and when I was three, my parents moved to the village of Barnegat on Barnegat Bay. I have always been proud of having been born in Monmouth County because it was the site of the famous Battle of Monmouth in the Revolutionary War.

When I started school, Barnegat was still a part of Monmouth County and would be for six more years. The schools then were called "pay schools." This meant that the county paid a part of the teacher's salary and the parent paid the remainder. Not until later did they become free public schools. I well remember the teacher coming to our home to collect tuition from my parents. The receipts laid in the desk in my home for many years. We children would look at them to see who our teachers had been. I am satisfied that Barnegat was quite a prosperous town then for I recall only one child that was unable to go to school because his parents could not pay for him. A kindly man in the community paid his tuition.

I commenced attending school when very young and I have many pleasant recollections. The first teacher that I remember was a crippled woman. She was a very jolly little lady with a pleasant laugh. Her name was Cornelia Waterberry. She taught a class of small girls the rudiments of an education along with sewing and embroidery

Now I wish to give you a description of our schoolhouse. It reminds me of the barracks used in the World War. It was a long frame building, partitioned off into two or three rooms, not very grand at all but we did enjoy our school, and our teachers. We read a chapter of the Bible every morning and practiced boxing the compass, the marks of which were on the wall of the classroom.

I remember when a new principal took charge. His name was Mr. Ellison. The larger boys told him that they had decided not to study grammar on the grounds that they were all going to sea to be captains and navigators and had no need for it. He listened to them patiently but when it came time for grammar class, they were the first ones called on to recite. They had to admit they were beaten and that they had better learn grammar after all. Later out in the schoolyard we could hear them singing a verse that went like this: "Ellison is a noun. Stinks enough to knock you down. Indicative mood. Present tense. We'll bump him against a fence." Not very elegant but that is the boy for you.

At my age I have caught myself laughing aloud at some of the things that happened so long ago. We were still in the hoop skirt days. One small girl had taken a barrel hoop and ran it through the hem of her petticoat. This incident occurred in the primary department. Another small girl called to our teacher, "Miss Hannen," she said "Ann Busby has put a barrel hoop in the hem of her petticoat and every time it flies up, it shows almost all she's got." Today, I am reminded that girls do not have to put barrel hoops in their skirts to show nigh everything they've got.

I have always been glad that I lived among the

people of Barnegat. Everyone was so pleasant and kind to each other. It was a small town consisting of two general stores, a black smith shop, two hotels or taverns, as they were called in those days, shipyards and a post office. There was one church, which was Methodist, and there was a Quaker Meeting House.

We children were very strictly raised in a neighborhood of old-fashioned Methodists and strict Quakers. We surely had good times too but in a very different way from the youth of today. We earned our parties and really enjoyed them. Some mother would decide to give her little daughter a carpet rag party. We little girls sewed rags together which the mother then would have woven into carpets. Some other mother would give a paring party; we cut up and pared apples to be put away for winter use. There were wool picking parties where we picked wool apart ready to be carded and spun and woven into garments and bedding. Afterwards, we would have a glorious time playing games and singing.

Children enjoyed helping with candle making. Dipping was the most fun. My mother had a candle mold that would make a dozen at a time. We had two whale oil lamps that were kept on the mantle for times when company would come. I imagine it was expensive because they were rarely used. We children would go and pick bayberries and melt them in a brass kettle, which made them green. We had matches as long as I can remember but Mr. Jennings said he could recall times when they used

flint to make fire or borrowed coals from a neighbor. Soap we made from the ashes of hardwood. We soaked it until we had lye and then mixed it with grease. When it hardened we cut it into pieces.

Barnegat was a small seafaring town. In the summer the streets were almost deserted of men as most of them were involved in the coastal trade carrying wood to New York. Others were engaged in building sailing vessels. In the winter the many captains laid up their boats for several weeks and spent time with their families. They put in much time sleighing, skating, dancing and going to what were called oyster suppers. That was the Barnegat of my day.

## Journal 2

In 1855, when I was eleven, my father built a summer resort hotel on Long Beach called the Atlantic House. I dreaded going over there from Barnegat for there had been so many serious wrecks in that vicinity. One evening in late June when we had been at the new place for but a few weeks, we saw rockets going up out over the ocean. A ship had run aground on the outer bar. I was all excited but I was informed that there was no danger on a beautiful night like this. For several days we had been having a west wind, which made the ocean very smooth. In the morning the stranded vessel proved to be the good ship St. Patrick, a sailing ship. As the tide was low and the sea calm, a decision was made to land her 500 passengers, load them aboard local fishing vessels and lumber schooners and send them on to

New York, their destination Only a few persons, however, actually chose to come ashore because in a very short time as many as a hundred fishing smacks and other small sailing vessels had gathered about the stranded ship to take anyone for a fee to New York. It was only sixty miles away; the weather good and they were probably there that very night.

Mr. Jennings, who kept a hotel several miles to the south of us, was the local wreckmaster. He came up the beach by horseback to oversee the salvage of the wreck. The St. Patrick had a ballast load of English coal and a cargo of English crockery, linen and brownstone china. It had to be unloaded, for, as soon as the weather changed, the ship, which was solidly stuck on the bar, would go to pieces. The captain and his officers stayed at our hotel for some time and oh, how brother and my little sister and I enjoyed them.

The day came when they had to leave us. I remember that the captain when bidding mother good-bye remarked, "Mrs. James, the tail of my coat will have to be cut off." Ship's captains at that time all wore long-tailed coats and when they were disgraced they had to cut them off. I guess it meant they were black balled and could not soon get another command. He said he would try to sail out of Boston. Brother and I watched the marine news for years hoping to get some tidings of him, but I guess it was good-bye to Captain Whitney. We never heard of him again.

When the captain left, he presented us children with

a large dictionary. My father remarked that if I read it all the way through he would buy me a silk dress. I studied it quite industriously, and one of the men employed by my father said, "Mr. James, a day will come when we will not be able to talk with this girl."

My father sailed to New York with the captain and the officers so he could go to the underwriter's office to collect for room, board and entertainment. They settled the bill and my father heard them say in the office that Captain Whitney's ship had been a paying boat very popular with Catholic passengers because of the name, St. Patrick. She had a great full sized figurehead of a priest on her bow. It drifted into shore when the ship finally broke up and we children would run and jump on it.

My father kept the hotel open year round for sportsmen and when we were there in the winter months, we saw many wrecks, as we were only three miles south of the Barnegat shoals, which sealed the fate of many good ships. I was greatly affected by these disasters but the one that troubled me the most was the wreck of the British ship, Tasso. It had a very serious side to it. One night while a northeast storm was raging it grounded on the bar not very far from our home. One man was able to swim ashore and make it up the beach to our place. He knocked at our front door in the middle of the night. My father and a man named John Parker, who worked for him and who stayed with us, got dressed and went to the scene of the wreck.

When daylight came they could see the ship out on the bar in a raging storm. Now the problem was to get to her. This was the beginning of the lifesaving stations and the only one near us was an unmanned house of refuge at Harvey Cedars almost three miles to the south, but volunteers with the equipment soon arrived from there and from Barnegat Lighthouse. In those days, there were no regular paid crews. The men were just pushing the lifeboat into the surf and my father was getting ready to board it when the young man John Parker said, "No, Mr. James, you stay. Don't venture. I will go. You have a family."

When the lifeboat was through the breakers and nearing the ship the men found an obstacle in their path. The officers of the ship had cut down the masts thinking to take the strain off the hull. The spars still attached by the rigging had fallen to leeward, the side toward shore. It seems it was a law with British vessels that, in the event of a wreck, the masts must be cut away in order to save the hull, but this made it very difficult now for the lifeboat to approach. They could not go around to the windward side because the swell of the sea would smash them against the ship.

The four men manning the lifeboat tried to approach on the leeward side but the tossing spars struck them and their boat was swamped. Two of the men drowned, one of them being John Parker. The other two climbed onto the fallen mast and got aboard the ship but they had lost the lifeline to shore and their situation was now more perilous than ever.

Meanwhile on the beach, their neighbors had sent for a team of oxen to pull the heavy, new Francis life car up from the house at Harvey Cedars. In order to use this rescue device a line had to be shot out to the ship from shore. A cannon would fire a ball over the ship and the line would catch in the rigging but the Tasso was now without any rigging at all. They fired ball after ball over the hull, missing every time. Just as darkness approached, the last ball hit the bow of the ship, enabling one of the crew to seize the line and now they were connected to shore.

A heavier line was at once attached and the life car, a new feature in lifesaving, was run back and forth and all of the people, as many as five or six on each trip were brought safely ashore. I remember the next morning hearing Mr. Fuller, the head keeper of the Barnegat Lighthouse, telling us that just as they were firing that last ball out to the wreck my father said, "Boys, let's pray that this will reach the boat."

They did, and I knew that these men were not considered to be praying men. They were not churchmen either. The nearest church was seven miles away on the mainland. Did their prayers have an effect? I think it did. They called on God when they were in trouble and He heard them.

## Journal 3

The hotel that my father built on Long Beach in 1855, a few miles below the Barnegat Inlet, was originally a summer resort. People came for sea bathing, fishing and sailing, but then, in the fall and spring, guests started coming from New York and

Philadelphia for the gunning. Although we lived nearly seven miles from town (Barnegat), it never seemed lonely.

From my bedroom window I could look east out over the Atlantic Ocean. Many ships passed carrying firewood to New York. I remember telling my father one morning that I had counted over one hundred sails. He said to me, "You will not count so many some day." And what a change later on! One saw very few sailing vessels; they were all steam vessels. I guess the Civil War killed the coast wood trade. Before the war, the only coal we ever saw came from England as ship's ballast. Then they opened up the coalmines in Pennsylvania, and soon bigger ships were carrying coal into New York.

There were also many ships from the West Indies carrying oranges to New York and Boston. They would sort the fruit off New Jersey and throw the spoiled or imperfect stuff overboard. It would wash up on shore. Oh, they did look so bright and colorful, these red oranges strewn over the white sandy beach. We always had oranges as long as I can remember. They were expensive to buy and this was the only way we got them. They were given to sick people.

When the hotel was open in the spring and fall, I was always there on weekends with my older brother and little sister, but on Monday mornings I had to sail over to Barnegat to go to school. I boarded with a family in town all week, and then on Fridays, after school, my father would, weather permitting, send someone over in a boat to pick

me up. This was why I said I never got lonely. There was never time for that. I was very fond of reading. My people were very bitter against fiction, but we were very much like the children of the day and liked a good story. There was an old man named Uncle Cal who took the men to good points for fishing and gunning, and when the people from New York came down, he would get stories from them and pass them on to us young people.

Many of the boys I went to school with were later drowned at sea. The coastal trade was a rough and dangerous way to make a living. I am reminded of what some of my early friends went through. One girl married a sea captain and went with him to Cuba. On the way back to New York her husband died of small pox. She prevailed on the officers not to bury him at sea. She had them stop at some southern port where they purchased a metal coffin so he could be shipped home and buried on land in Barnegat. Poor Mell Jones. She was some popular girl. Probably that's how she got those men to do her bidding

In the town of Barnegat, there were only two religious denominations, the Methodists and the Quakers. I remember my father telling me that at one of the Quaker meetings, one Elias Hicks got up and said to all, that there was only one devil and he was inside a jug with a corncob stopper in it. As this was not very orthodox thinking, it made a split in the meeting so they built a separate meetinghouse for him and his followers in the same yard. One was called the Orthodox and the other was called the Hicksite meetinghouse. My sister went to a Quaker

school in Moorestown and all the students were expected to attend Quaker meetings when they were home. She told her principal that they had two in Barnegat and asked what was the difference between them. The principal said, "One is going forward and the other is going backward."

I see that both the Quakers and the Methodists are becoming more modern. Our President Hoover is a Quaker, and they are now having singing in the Quaker meetinghouse. I must tell you something that may seem very strange to you in this generation. We had neither engagement rings nor wedding rings. That was not a custom with either the Quakers or the Methodists at that time. I was given one many years later just because so many others were wearing them.

In 1866, I was married to Isaac Jennings of Jennings Mills, a Quaker community near Marlton, Burlington County. A Methodist minister in Waretown performed our wedding and we went to live in Marlton. My mother-in-law informed me that everyone was supposed to speak the Bible language when addressing fellow Quakers and all old people were addressed as uncle or aunt. The women wore gray Quaker bonnets. We lived in Burlington County for five years, and in time I got accustomed to it. My husband still used the plain language after we came west. We left New Jersey early in January of 1871 to take the new transcontinental train to San Francisco.

# Index

John Bailey Lloyd was born in Johnstown, Pennsylvania, and had been on Long Beach Island since 1942, when he was ten years old — in time to see old landmarks like the boardwalk, the Engleside Hotel and the vast emptiness of the Island as it once was. After serving in the Coast Guard, he spent nearly every summer here; in 1977 he and his wife, Jeanette, and their two sons became permanent residents in the family's Beach Haven summer home — a three-story Victorian built in 1879.

A graduate of Mount St. Mary's College in Emmitsburg, Maryland, Mr. Lloyd held a Master's Degree in English from the University of Michigan and a Master's in library science from Rutgers University. He worked as a reference librarian in the Ocean County Library system. Mr. Lloyd was known as "Long Beach Island's historian" for his books, his weekly summer talks at the historical museum in Beach Haven, and for his historical newspaper articles. The Island community was deeply saddened when John Bailey Lloyd died in July 2003; Long Beach Island lost the man who gave it a sense of place.

*Two Centuries of History on Long Beach Island,* the third Long Beach Island pictorial history, is the companion title to Mr. Lloyd's two previous books, *Eighteen Miles of History on Long Beach Island* and *Six Miles at Sea.*
For a John Bailey Lloyd bibliography, visit this web page:
**down-the-shore.com/jblpage.html**

➺➻

Down The Shore Publishing specializes in books, calendars, cards and videos about New Jersey and the shore.
For a free catalog of all our titles or to be included on our mailing list, just send a request:

*Down The Shore Publishing*
*Box 3100, Harvey Cedars, NJ 08008*
or visit our website: **down-the-shore.com**